RACISM IN AMERICA

CULTURAL CODES AND COLOR LINES IN THE 21ST CENTURY

Miami Herald **el Nuevo Herald**

Mango Publishing Group
in collaboration with
the Miami Herald

HERALD BOOKS

Herald Books

Published by Mango Media Inc.
www.mango.bz

Front Cover Image: lassedesignen/Shutterstock.com

Back Cover Image: Miami Herald

RACISM IN AMERICA: *Cultural Codes and Color Lines in the 21st Century*
ISBN: 978-1-63353-447-6

"Race is the stupidest idea in history. It is also, arguably, the most powerful. It determines who goes to jail and who goes to college, who gets loans and who gets rejections, who gets the job and who gets the unemployment check. It determines the life you live and the assumptions that are made about you."

— Leonard Pitts, Jr., December 30, 2012

Table of Contents

INTRODUCTION

Leonard Pitts, Jr.

Sunday, December 30, 2012

RACE

On New Year's Day, it will be 150 years since Abraham Lincoln set black people free from slavery.

And there is no such thing as black people.

The first of those statements is not precisely true; a clarification will be offered momentarily. The second statement is not precisely false. And the clarification begins here:

It is a clarification needed not simply because it helps us to better understand the milestone of history we commemorate this week, but also because it helps us to better understand America right here in the tumultuous now. The Republican Party, to take an example not quite at random, enters the new year still nursing its wounds after an election debacle most observers laid upon its inability to sway Hispanics, young voters and, yes, black people. Then there is the Trayvon Martin shooting, the mass incarceration phenomenon, the birther foolishness.

A century and a half later, in other words, race is still a story. Black people are still a story.

How can that be, if there is no such thing as black people?

Granted, most of us think otherwise. The average 18-year-old American kid, says sociologist Matt Wray, thinks of race "as a set of facts about who people are, which is somehow tied to blood and biology and ancestry."

But that kid is wrong. If you doubt that, try a simple challenge: Define "black people."

Maybe you think of it as African ancestry. But Africa is a place on a map – not a bloodline. And, as the example of Charlize Theron, the fair-skinned, blond actress from South Africa, amply illustrates, it is entirely possible to come from there, yet not be what we think of as "black." Indeed, Theron, who became a naturalized U.S. citizen in 2008, is by definition an African American. Yet, she fits no one's conception of that term, either.

Or, you might define "black people" by physical appearance: i.e., people with dark skin and coarse hair. If so, consider Gregory Howard Williams, a pale-skinned American educator and author of the memoir "Life On The Color Line," who did not learn he was "black" until he was 10. Or consider Walter White, the former executive secretary of the NAACP, whose 1948 autobiography begins: "I am a Negro. My skin is white, my eyes are blue, my hair is blond." Consider the people from India who have dark skin or the ones from Asia, the Middle East or Latin America who have coarse hair.

And perhaps here, you are tempted to throw up your hands and paraphrase Supreme Court Justice Potter Stewart who famously said of pornography that he might not be able to define it, "but I know it when I see it."

The difference is that pornography, at least, exists. But there is no such thing as black people. Or white people. Or Asians. Or Indians.

What is my point? It's simply this: Race is the stupidest idea in history.

Or, as Wray puts it, "race was a big mistake."

To which Nell Irwin Painter adds the observation that a decade of research and writing on the subject taught her "that if you try to consider race as a real thing, it makes no sense."

Wray, a Temple University professor and the author of "Not Quite White: White Trash and the Boundaries of Whiteness," and Painter, a former professor at Princeton and the author of "The History of White People," are leading lights in a burgeoning field of study whose aim is nothing less than the deconstruction of race. It seeks to answer the question of when, how, and why we ever got it into our heads there is such a thing as race; when, how, and why we decided we could divide human beings into subgroups whose members all shared similar traits and that those subgroups could be ranked, superior to inferior.

The "when," as it turns out, is pretty easy to answer, though the answer is surprising, in light of how conditioned we are to think of race as something that always was and always will be. The concept of race, says Painter, dates from about the mid-18th century. It is less than 300 years old.

Though there were always a few people, she says, who attempted to impute character or worth from a stranger's color, it was more likely in that era for people to make those judgments based upon a stranger's religion or wealth. "So if you were a light-skinned person and you met a dark-skinned person in rags, and you weren't [in rags], you'd feel superior," says Painter. "But if you were in rags and that other person was in rags, you'd be trying to figure if that person had something that you could get."

Then came race – that which would allow one person in rags to feel superior to another person in rags. Early on, it was defined not by appearance but as a function of climate. Greek scholars believed people from places where the seasons do not change were placid. Those from places of dramatic seasonal shifts were wild and unsociable. Those from hot places were impulsive and hot-tempered. Those from cooler climes were stiff and intellectual.

Race was also defined geographically. Hippocrates, the great Greek physician, thought people who lived in low-lying areas tended to be dark-skinned, fat, cowardly, ill-spoken and lazy. Those who lived in flat, windy places would be large in stature, "but their minds will be rather unmanly and gentle."

And then, there were those who decided the key to race lay in measuring the size and shape of people's skulls.

"American scientists and anthropologists get ahold of this concept by the early 1800s," says Wray. "For the whole of the 19th century, they're refining and tweaking their models to really give scientific weight and authority to the notion that these racial differences can be empirically verified. In other words, they're out there in the world. We just have to figure out whether it's the distance between the eye sockets and the bridge of the nose, or some combination of measurements from the back of the skull to the chin divided by the circumference of the head that will give us the kind of golden ratio we're looking for – in other words, the one that will enable us to definitively say, this person is African, this person is Caucasian and so forth."

The great Harlem Renaissance author Zora Neale Hurston was fascinated by this thinking. She was known to stand on New York City street corners with a pair of calipers, asking passersby for permission to measure their skulls.

In 1895, D.B. Brinton, an American anthropologist, published a complicated chart purporting to categorize all the races of humankind. He ended up with more than a hundred kinds of Caucasian alone.

Brinton and Hurston were never able to quantify race. No one was. And yet, the nation – indeed, the world – was never able to give it up. Race was, and is, too useful.

Says Wray, "It has enabled in the United States for us to justify and legitimize the conquest of Indian land and the near genocide of Native American tribes. It enabled us for such a long time to justify slavery and when we got done with that justification, when people called B.S. on that, we said, 'Well, this is how we can explain Jim Crow.' When the Civil Rights Movement happens in the 1950s and '60s, when African Americans rise up and say, 'Enough Jim Crow, ' then we use it to justify mass incarceration of black Americans. We find the idea of race and inherent racial differences and the idea that some people are frankly, just better than others, to be indispensable."

Defective whiteness

It is worth remembering that when newcomers from Europe flocked to these shores in search of opportunity, they did not automatically see themselves as white. They were French, English, Scottish, Spanish or German, and far from having some identity in common, they were often in contention for the riches of this land. Whiteness was something that had to be learned and earned, particularly for those – Jews, Poles, southern Italians, Hungarians, the Irish – who were regarded as congenitally inferior. They were seen as white, says Painter, but it was a sort of defective whiteness. They were "off white" for want of a better term, and as such, a threat to American values and traditions. And they were mistreated accordingly until, over the passage of generations of assimilation, they achieved full whiteness.

University of Illinois history professor David R. Roediger recounts a telling episode in his book, "Working Toward Whiteness." It seems David, a Russian Jew, has come to America seeking refuge from anti-Semitic persecution. He arrives in Georgia and begins working with his cousins as a peddler. But soon there is a problem. His cousins complain that he is too friendly with his black customers. "The schvarters here are like we are in Russia," they explain. To treat them too well is to risk his own acceptance.

David replies that he cannot bring himself to treat the blacks as he himself was treated in Russia. "It is easy," he tells his cousin, "for you to forget how to feel and what it is like to be hurt and stepped on when you think of yourself as white today and forget what it was like being a Jew yesterday."

As Jon Stewart noted recently on "The Daily Show," that history is what lends a certain pungent edge to some of the post-election hand wringing among conservatives. Surely, the gods of irony laughed aloud when a television personality named O'Reilly (Bill) and a guest named Goldberg (Bernie) lamented how newcomers were changing "traditional America."

As whiteness was invented, so was blackness. When Africans were gathered on the shores of that continent to be packed into the reeking holds of slave ships for the voyage to this country, they saw themselves as Taureg, Mandinkan, Fulani, Mende or Songhay

– not black. As Noel Ignatiev, author of "How The Irish Became White," has observed, those Africans did not become slaves because they were black. They "became" black because they were enslaved.

But though blackness and whiteness were invented they still, to a remarkable degree, govern perception – and thus, destiny.

Some months ago, my wife Marilyn and I were at dinner with two other couples and somehow, we all got talking about identity. One couple, brown-skinned like Marilyn and me, saw themselves, like Marilyn and me, as black or African American. The other, fair-skinned couple, pointedly declined to define themselves as white. She said she saw herself as Jewish; he defined himself as a first-generation Polish American.

It struck me, not simply because it underlined the ultimate falsity of these identities, white and black, but also because it highlighted what has always struck me as the problematic nature of one of them in particular: white. I've often thought the word "white" had a tendency to discomfit the people to whom it is applied, to carry some hint of accusation that is no less real for being unspoken. In my experience, white people are often ill at ease with being referred to as white people.

There is, I think, a reason for that. "Black" and "white" are equally artificial, but black fairly quickly took on the contours of a real culture. The people to whom it was applied, after all, were required to live in close proximity to one another, sharing the same often-squalid circumstances, the same mistreatment and oppression, conditions that no degree of personal excellence or achievement could mitigate or help them escape. These pressures shaped them, drew them together.

"White," on the other hand, was held together only by the single condition of being not black, being a member of the advantaged class. It has little existence apart from that.

As illustration, try a mind experiment. If someone says to you that she enjoys black literature, what do you interpret her to be saying? Likely that she reads Ernest Gaines, Maya Angelou, Toni Morrison, Alice Walker. But what is "white literature?" What is "white music?" What is "white art?" How often, in media, does one even see "white" used – physical descriptions of crime suspects aside – where it is not positioned as a counterpoint to "black?"

This is the thing that is often misunderstood by people who try to impute some sinister double standard to things like the Miss Black America Pageant. "If there was a Miss White America Pageant," they are fond of saying, "black people would have a fit."

But there is a Miss Italia USA pageant. And a Miss German America pageant. And a Little Miss Irish Princess contest. And a Miss Russian California.

So the problem isn't black people having a fit. It is white people recognizing, if only viscerally and instinctively, that "white" is a problematic word to be avoided when possible.

What to do now?

What, then, do we do with this history? Where does it take us as the future dawns?

Some would say it takes us nowhere. Some would say the best thing we can do with race is leave it alone. If I had a dollar for every person who has ever told me that talking about race causes racism, or even half that much for every person who has ever told me the "hyphenated Americanism" of African Americans causes racism, I'd never have to buy another Powerball ticket in my life.

But such people are looking through the wrong end of the telescope. People embrace hyphenated Americanism because no other Americanism has been available to them. And if we stopped talking about race tomorrow, racism would persist; all we would lose is the language by which we frame and confront it.

You don't end race by silence, nor do you end it by blaming it on the people it has been used against.

Again, race persists because race is useful. If you want to end race, stop allowing race to be useful. Consider some of the political debates of the recent past and note how issues with no obvious racial component soon end up being about race.

"I think you see it with healthcare now," says the historian, Roediger. "Very quickly, something that's kind of a fundamental human right, it'll end up being talked about as if it were a racialized entitlement. The achievement of the right in making the word 'welfare,' which means good, sound like a bad thing, is so connected with the way they can pull on race."

But Roediger does sense that a change is afoot, that perhaps the utility of race has peaked. The election, he says, showed "that this kind of Republican refrain of 'food stamp president' doesn't work quite as well when so many white people are on food stamps and know people who they know are trying to get jobs and can't get jobs."

As a result, he says, the GOP, which has, for generations been able to "take advantage of race," now faces a race problem of its own. "I think there are fewer whites who respond to these kind of dog whistle, coded appeals, partly because they have misery in their own families, partly because anti-racism has made some progress."

There is no such thing as black people.

Except, of course, that there is – even if we have to use what might be dubbed the Justice Potter Stewart standard to define them.

Race is the stupidest idea in history. It is also, arguably, the most powerful. It determines who goes to jail and who goes to college, who gets loans and who gets rejections, who gets the job and who gets the unemployment check. It determines the life you live and the assumptions that are made about you.

For example, Gregory Howard Williams, the man who did not know he was "black" until he was 10, once told the story of how, when he became dean of his law school, a white woman congratulated him on this well-deserved achievement. "Then," said Williams, "she found out that I was black, and her first response – not to me, but to someone else – was, 'Did he get the job because he was black?' When she looked at me and assumed I was white, she assumed that I was qualified for the job. When she discovered I was black, she assumed that I was unqualified for the job."

Then there is Walter White, the "Negro" with blond hair and blue eyes, who was, as a child, cornered in his house with his father, a mail carrier, by a white mob intent on violence. "There's where that nigger mail carrier lives!" they cried. "Let's burn it down! It's too nice for a nigger to live in!"

'No scientific basis'

Back in 2000, a group of scientists announced that, after mapping the genetic codes of five people, self-identified as African American, Caucasian, Asian and Hispanic, they had been unable to tell them apart. As one researcher put it, "The concept of race has no scientific basis."

That same week, I was in New York City where I stood on 44th Street with my hand raised, watching empty cab after empty cab pass me by. The irony was pointed. Science could not define "black," but a New York City cab driver certainly could.

This is the reality to which our history delivers us, one in which these artificial designations – "black," "white," "Asian," etc. – are considered to have all these inborn markers for intelligence, criminality, athleticism, honesty, cleanliness, and we accept it without question, accept it like sunshine and air, as a thing that simply is. And it seems beyond us to look into the face of that other person who sits on the other side of that artificial designation and see reflected in his or her eyes, our own tears, our own laughter, our own self.

A century and a half ago Tuesday, the first Republican president issued the Emancipation Proclamation that freed the slaves. Except that, as most historians will tell you, it didn't actually free anybody; it applied only to slaves in states like Florida and Mississippi, which were then in rebellion and no longer recognized U.S. authority, while ignoring those in states like Maryland and Kentucky, which remained in the Union. As the movie "Lincoln" shows, it actually took the 13th Amendment to abolish slavery.

But the one thing Abraham Lincoln's document did do was challenge a nation's understanding of its fundamental social order, its comprehension of the way things were and were meant to be. At a time when the very humanity of "black" people was in controversy and any suggestion that they might actually be equal to whites was met with scornful laughter, this homely country lawyer put the idea of freedom on the table and forced the nation for the very first time to grapple with that which it had previously accepted without question, like sunshine and air.

Getting the nation to think seriously about the concept of black people, free, was, as much as anything, a triumph of imagination.

One hundred fifty years later, getting the nation to understand that there is no such thing as black people will require a similar jolt to hidebound thinking. If and when it comes, perhaps a nation that once freed itself from slavery will finally free itself from race, as well.

Leonard Pitts, Jr.

Chapter 1

WHAT IS BLACK?

Wednesday, August 9, 1995

EVERYBODY'S GOT A THING

It's a black thing – you wouldn't understand.

I've always wondered how that catch phrase plays among people who aren't black. Do they hear it as exclusion or self-affirmation? Condescension or sly in-joke? Communication is such an inexact science. One can never be sure if what one is saying jibes with what someone else is hearing. Especially when the discussion turns to such prickly topics as race and class, the very mention of which puts most people on guard.

We've talked a lot about the communication gap between cultures, between generations and, famously, between women and men. It occurs to me that there is a similar gulf between blacks and whites. Consider uptight. In the lexicon of black hipsters of the 1950s and '60s, it meant cool, copacetic, under control. "Baby, everything is all right, uptight and out of sight," exulted Stevie Wonder in 1965. But when white hipsters adopted the word in the late '60s, they took it to mean the opposite: a state of anxiety.

Consider this, too: Not long ago, a news story on the return of Alabama's roadside chain gangs quoted a black inmate as saying he'd be ashamed to have any of his "people" see him in such circumstances. Most white readers would doubtless interpret that in racial terms. But in black America – and, for that matter, in the white South – one's "people" is a reference to one's family. I'd bet cash the man was simply expressing the hope that Aunt Tillie didn't happen by.

Back in the '70s, black comic Franklyn Ajaye used to do a routine about a slang term that meant the vagina to blacks but referred to the penis for whites. As Ajaye told it, he was in a gym shower with some white guys when he began loudly discussing his sexual desires, using this particular word. The shower emptied in record time.

So it goes. If such trivial communications are fraught with the potential for misunderstanding, one can only speculate about the larger issues of race and class.

Frank Turner, a news anchor with WXYZ-TV in Southfield, Michigan, recently wrote to say that blacks and whites discussing racism are "like a bear and a rabbit discussing a lion. Each views the lion from such a difference of perspective that it is difficult, if not impossible, for the bear to see the rabbit's point of view.

"The rabbit can certainly see the lion for the threat he is ... the family members he has eaten and ravaged, the pain, fear and anger he has caused ... The bear, however, having never been a victim of the lion, can't understand why the rabbit doesn't just pull himself up by his paw straps and get over it."

Turner, who is black, concluded his letter by saying, "I have given up trying to discuss the ravages of the lion with the bears. Even though this may be closing the doors on making progress through understanding, it's just no longer worth the frustration."

I understand what he's saying. Black and white, a lot of people are saying the same things. But I disagree. Progress and understanding are almost always worth the frustration.

It's when we give up on at least trying to hear that we're in trouble. It becomes that much easier to let rumor stand in for reality and supposition wear the face of fact. Talking through opposing points of view is a leap of faith, an expression of trust that no matter your differences, the party on the other side ultimately wants what you do: resolution and progress.

It's been 10 years since I first saw the "It's a black thing – you wouldn't understand" T-shirt. Since then, the phrase has entered the language and spawned many spinoffs, and I still think what I thought back in 1985: That it was exclusion and self-affirmation, condescension and a sly in-joke.

I thought it was something else, too – another frustrated surrender.

See, "it" may be a black thing, but the fact is, everybody's got a thing. If we never get beyond that point, if we never surmount differences and indifferences, then who'll be left to understand?

RACIAL IDENTITY

Sunday, January 13, 2013

AM I BLACK ENOUGH?

I suddenly find myself concerned about my blackness.

It had never occurred to me to worry about it before. Then came the incident last month on ESPN's "First Take" program that initially got commentator Rob Parker suspended and then, last week, fired outright. It seems Parker, who is African American, analyzed what he saw as the insufficient blackness of Robert Griffin III, rookie quarterback for the Washington, D.C., football team that is named for a racial slur.

Having returned their team to relevance for the first time since the Clinton era, RG3, as he is known, can do no wrong in the eyes of Slurs fans. But Parker, saying that the young man's fiancé is (gasp!) white and that he himself is rumored to be – cover the children's ears – a Republican, found him lacking in the area of authentic blackness. "My question," he said, "which is just a straight, honest question: is he a brother, or is he a cornball brother? He's not really ... OK, he's black, he kind of does the thing, but he's not really down with the cause. He's not one of us. He's kind of black, but he's not really like the guy you really want to hang out with ..."

That explosion you hear is the sound of my mind, blown. I'm left second guessing my own blackness.

I mean, I listen to Bruce Springsteen, for crying out loud! There's even a Dixie Chicks album on my iPod. Should I download more James Brown and Al Green to save my, ahem, soul?

And I read books sometimes, man – even when no one's making me do it. Some of them are thick as bricks. Some aren't even about African-American themes.

It gets worse. I have no natural rhythm, no criminal record and can correctly pronounce the word "ask." I don't curse nearly as much as I ought to. Oh, and I went and married my baby mama.

Obviously, my blackness is on life support.

Many of us have been taught that it is demeaning and delimiting when someone presumes to say who you are, how you will behave, what you think, what you like, and how intelligent you are, from the color of your skin. We have been taught that such behavior abridges the other person's individuality.

But apparently, that's only when white people do it to black people. When black people do it to black people, it's called assessing your blackness, making sure you aren't some "cornball brother."

How enlightening to learn that. It is even more enlightening to discover that we have such easy-peasy rubrics to go by. You can't be black if you are a Republican? That means Colin Powell isn't black. Neither, if published reports are to be believed, are rappers LL Cool J and 50 Cent. Who'd have thought?

And if you can't be black and have a white significant other ... wow. There goes – what? half? 90 percent? – of all the brothers in the NBA.

Poor Frederick Douglass has a double whammy. He was a Republican and had a white wife. Who'd have thought this former slave, one of the towering heroes of African-American history, wasn't black enough?

It is this kind of bold insight and trenchant analysis ESPN loses in sacking Rob Parker. What is the network thinking? Parker, who also contributes commentary to WDIV television in Detroit, defended himself in an interview with the station that aired shortly before ESPN dropped the ax. He pronounced himself shocked by the fallout and suggested his comments were taken out of context.

"You can't be afraid to talk about race," he said. He's exactly right. In discussing race, we must be fearless. We must also be thoughtful. And informed. And exact. And alive to the ramifications of what we say.

Surely, Rob Parker knows this. Or if he didn't before, he does now.

As for being black enough, he is probably a greater expert than he was before. He is, after all, a man out of work. It doesn't get much blacker than that.

Wednesday, June 17, 2015

SO, WHAT IS RACE?

Of the 60 people who co-founded the National Association for the Advancement of Colored People in 1909, only seven were, in fact, "colored." Most of the organization's founders were white liberals like Mary White Ovington. Its highest honor, the Spingarn Medal, is named for Joel Spingarn, who was Jewish and white.

Point being, white people have been intricately involved in the NAACP struggle for racial justice from day one. So Rachel Dolezal did not need to be black to be president of the organization's Spokane chapter. That she chose to present herself as such anyway, adopting a curly "natural" hairstyle and apparently somehow darkening her skin, has put her in the bull's-eye of the most irresistible water-cooler story of the year. This will be on "Black-ish" next season; just wait and see.

As you doubtless know, Dolezal, 37, was outed last week by her estranged parents. In response, they say, to a reporter's inquiry, they told the world her heritage includes Czech, Swedish and German roots, but not a scintilla of black. In the resulting mushroom cloud of controversy, Dolezal was forced to resign her leadership of the Spokane office. Interviewed Tuesday by Matt Lauer on "Today," she made an awkward attempt to explain and/or justify herself. "I identify as black," she said, like she thinks she's the Caitlyn Jenner of race. It was painful to watch.

Given that Dolezal sued historically black Howard University in 2002 for allegedly discriminating against her because she is white, it's hard not to see a certain opportunism in her masquerade. Most people who, ahem, "identify as black" don't have the option of trying on another identity when it's convenient.

That said, it's hard to be too exercised over this. Dolezal doesn't appear to have done any harm, save to her own dignity and reputation. One suspects there are deep emotional issues at play, meaning the kindest thing we can do is give her space and time to work them out.

Besides, this story's most pointed moral has less to do with Dolezal and her delusions than with us and ours. Meaning America's founding myth, the one that tells us race is a fixed and objective fact.

It isn't. Indeed, in 2000, after mapping the genetic codes of five people – African-American, Caucasian, Asian and Hispanic – a researchers announced they could find no difference among them. "The concept of race, " one of them said, "has no scientific basis." The point isn't that race is not real; the jobless rate, the mass incarceration phenomenon and the ghosts of murdered boys from Emmett Till to Tamir Rice argue too persuasively otherwise.

Rather, it's that it's not real in the way we conceive it in America where, as sociologist Matt Wray once put it, the average 19-year-old regards it as a "set of facts about who people are, which is somehow tied to blood and biology and ancestry." In recent years, Wray and scholars like David Roediger and Nell Irvin Painter have done path-breaking work exploding that view. To read their research is to understand that what we call race is actually a set of cultural likenesses, shared experiences and implicit assumptions, i.e., that white men can't jump and black ones can't conjugate.

To try to make it more than that, to posit it as an immutable truth, is to discover that, for all its awesome power to determine quality of life or lack thereof, race is a chimera. There is no there, there. The closer you look, the faster it disappears.

Consider: If race were really what Wray's average 19-year-old thinks it is, there could never have been a Rachel Dolezal; her lie would have been too immediately transparent. So ultimately, her story is the punchline to a joke most of us don't yet have ears to hear. After all, this white lady didn't just try to pass herself off as black.

She got away with it.

Chapter 2

BLACK HISTORY

Saturday, July 15, 1995

I BELIEVE IN US

When we were chained, we believed in freedom.

When we were denied justice, we believed in the courts.

When we had no vote, we believed in the ballot.

What does black America believe in now? It's a question occasioned by recent harsh setbacks from the Supreme Court on the issues of voting rights and affirmative action.

On a deeper level, though, the question is occasioned by a sense that something vital has gone out of us in the last 20 years. Or perhaps more accurately, that something has come into us that is leaden and old.

"Why don't more black people vote?" a friend asked the other day.

And you know, I had to stop and think about that. Approximately 37 percent of eligible blacks voted in the last congressional election, as opposed to 44 percent of all Americans. For people who, 30 years ago, bled and died for the ballot to turn around and leave it unused speaks not only to the laziness and apathy characteristic of American voters in general, but also to something more specific and disturbing.

Many in the black underclass seem to have withdrawn their investment in the greater us.

Even before the Civil Rights movement, black people shared a sense that "we shall overcome someday." In its place now, there is a soul silence as if to say, maybe we won't. And if we won't, then why boycott? Why march? Why vote? Ain't gonna change a damn thing.

It's an attitude that breeds children old before their time, for whom the future is some distant land that may or may not exist and lies, in any case, on the far side of a minefield of violence and drugs, sex and temptation. You do what you've got to do; the future does not matter.

Is this racism's fruit? Well, they keep telling me there is no more racism here in the good old U.S. of A., but of course they are wrong and the answer is yes, it is.

But racism is not the only thief of faith. The black American middle class has not carried out its responsibilities. It has made the right noises and, on an individual level perhaps, even done the right thing. But it has never organized as a group to lift and teach the sisters and brothers who weren't as lucky.

Instead, we moved away.

And save a slice of the blame for the African-American underclass itself. Black folks have been down before, so far down we had to crane our necks to see the butt end of low. But we never let this thing come into us before, this heaviness and despair, where children speak with the coldness of the streets and you don't dare correct them on pain of death. I am told by my elders that once we were a village of clasped hands and consecrated goals, where the children dared not get out of line because if Mama didn't get 'em, Miss Johnson would. More to the point, we always had an idea percolating, a plan laid in expectation of a better day. Get the ballot, go back to Africa, get a good education ... do something.

Now, too many of us do nothing, expecting and accepting defeat. But we are the oldest tribe on Earth. We are tougher than leather, with souls grown deep like rivers, as Langston Hughes once said.

"Up, you mighty race!" roared Marcus Garvey in the early years of this century. It came as a blast of arctic air into a room grown stifling and still. It fired the imagination with dreams of what it must be like to be free.

We need to stir that imagining within us again. Because, underclass or overclass, child of the tenement or lord of the manse, all of us as Africans stand together now in a too-familiar place, surrounded by an indifferent government, unfriendly courts and hostile people, as the horizon roils with dark clouds backlit by lightning.

The conditions of the day demand a gut check and a question: What do we believe in?

And I have to smile, because I already know my answer.

I believe in us.

DIXIE

Sunday, April 10, 2011

A CONSPIRACY OF AMNESIA

"It is not safe ... to trust $800 million worth of negroes in the hands of a power which says that we do not own the property ... So we must get out ..."

- The Daily Constitutionalist, Augusta, Georgia, December 1, 1860

"[Northerners] have denounced as sinful the institution of slavery ... We, therefore, the people of South Carolina ... have solemnly declared that the Union heretofore existing between this State and other States of North America dissolved."

- from "Declaration of the Causes of Secession"

"As long as slavery is looked upon by the North with abhorrence ... there can be no satisfactory political union between the two sections."

- New Orleans Bee, December 14, 1860

"Our new government is founded upon ... the great truth that the negro is not equal to the white man; that slavery, subordination to the superior race, is his natural and moral condition."

- Alexander Stephens, "vice president" of the Confederacy, March 21, 1861

On Tuesday morning, it will be 150 years since the Civil War began.

The bloodiest war in U.S. history commenced with the bombardment of a fort in Charleston Harbor. President Abraham Lincoln was careful to define it as a war to restore 11 rebellious southern states to the Union – and only that.

For those 11 states, it was a war for property rights – property being defined as 4 million human beings. They feared the federal government would not allow the business of trading in human beings to expand to the new territories in the West.

By the time the war ended, four years almost to the day later, Lincoln's view had changed. He had come to see himself and the war he had prosecuted through 48 bitter months of turmoil and tears, as tools of the Almighty's judgment upon the nation for having allowed the evil of slavery.

The South would change its view as well. It would begin to spin grand, romantic fables of a "Lost Cause" that had been fought for "state's rights" or constitutional principle, or any other reason it could invent, so long as it was not slavery. Jefferson Davis, who before the war had flatly declared "the labor of African slaves" the cause of the rebellion, would write after the war that slavery had nothing to do with it.

Thus, the South entered a conspiracy of amnesia that, for many, continues to this day. As in Virginia naming April Confederate History Month last year in a proclamation that did not mention slavery. And recent attempts in Mississippi to honor Confederate hero Nathan Bedford Forrest, who led a massacre of unarmed black people and helped found the Ku Klux Klan. And the "Secession Ball" South Carolina hosted in December to, as one man put it, "honor our ancestors for their bravery and tenacity protecting their homes from invasion."

So this seems an apt moment to speak in memory's defense. As Confederate battle flags flap from truck grills and monuments, as tourists gather around pigeon-stained statues of dead rebels baking under the Dixie sun, as Southern apologists seek glory in acts of treason, and as all of the above studiously avoid coming too close to the heart of the matter, to its cause, it is worth remembering that their forebears were not as circumspect.

To the contrary, they said clearly and without shame that they fought for slavery.

If that makes someone uncomfortable, good. It should.

But you do not deal with that discomfort by telling lies of omission about yesterday. You do not deal with it by pretending treason is glory. No, you deal with it by listening to the hard things the past has to say – and learning from them.

This nation took so much from the men and women it kidnapped. It took dignity, it took labor, it took family, it took home, it took names. In the end, the last thing any of us has is the memory of ourselves we bequeath the future, the reminder that we were here.

And to their everlasting dishonor, some of us want to take that, too.

Sunday, September 24, 1995

STARTING A DIXIE JOURNEY:
THEY SOLD PEOPLE HERE

ST. AUGUSTINE – It seemed right to begin by standing here. In days to come, I will stand on the steps where Jefferson Davis took the oath as president of the Confederacy, on the hill where General Leonidas Polk was ripped in two by a Union shell, at the Shiloh pond that once was red with soldiers' blood. I will stand on the sidewalk where Rosa Parks was arrested, in the park where they turned German shepherds loose on children demanding freedom, at the monument where Martin Luther King Jr. dreamed and at the motel where he died.

But first, I must stand here, in an open-air pavilion in St. Augustine, on a site where human beings reputedly were once bought and sold.

It's barely marked as such. A 65-year-old plaque says: "From 1605 to 1765, there stood on this site a guardhouse and watch tower under British rule that became the market and place of public auction, ever since called the slave market."

As it happens, the slave market sits in the shadow of a grander monument to the Confederate dead of the Civil War. Its inscription waxes poetic about brave soldiers who "died far from the home that gave them birth."

The juxtaposition of the two is blindingly insensitive, glaringly offensive − and not at all surprising to me. It strikes me as emblematic of the denial and contradiction that so often characterize the South on the subject of race.

A friend, white and Southern, has been after me to discuss how I feel about the South as I embark upon this tour of its most hallowed ground. But I have shined her on precisely because she is a friend and white and Southern, and because we don't really need to get into this, do we, can't we all just get along?

But this place, this slave market, won't make room for me to hem and haw. It presses in on me as I walk its uneven bricks in the cool of the morning, watching the eternal sea roll to shore just a few yards away. Presses in with images of them, herded together in this spot by red-faced men who jabbered in a strange language and examined their teeth, testicles and breasts with rough impunity.

Presses in with knowledge of the agony born in the transactions of this place, coursing ahead like rivers to splash pain on the children to the 12th generation and counting. Presses in until there is no escape, nothing to do but stand there and take it, acknowledge the outrage, face the indignity, and choke on the prideful, unmitigated, arrogant, stupid gall that allowed one people to assume they had a right to sell and enslave another.

Somewhere within, the unbidden cry loses itself, an elemental fury ripping free from a restraining wall of decorum, politeness and civility:

God damn you, look what you did to me!

And within the cry, a whisper, an afterthought, an echo that will grow louder in days to come with each step over the grassy plains of Civil War, where boys and men died desperate deaths for an ignoble cause:

Look what you did to yourselves.

The South always seduces me. The rolling greenery of its hills, the fog-clouded mystery of its bayous, the slow motion of its daily life make a powerful impression whenever I travel through.

But I always travel through. I could never live here − at least not outside the big cities. "I wouldn't want to be out here and have one of the good ol' boys have a 1954 flashback," I joke to my traveling companion, Michael Browning, as rural Alabama grinds by under the wheels of our van.

Michael is surprised. I wonder if he's maybe even a little offended. The South falls from the man's mouth like honey that made the bees especially proud. His South, he will inform you with mild, gracious indignation, is not the South of "Hee-Haw," "Gomer Pyle," or truck drivers who fly the Confederate flag from their front grill. Rather, his is the South of gentility, civility, pride and a noble aristocracy much like the one in England, except with mint juleps instead of hot tea.

Problem is, the South that sits in the forefront of my mind is the one where they made a sport out of lynching black people.

Indeed, when Michael tells me he was born in Valdosta, Georgia, before moving to Jacksonville, my immediate frame of reference is the 1918 lynching there, in which a pregnant woman was strung up and set afire, her abdomen slashed, her fetus stomped to death.

My friend is disbelieving. "Is that true?" Michael asks. "Has it been authenticated?"

It's as if he finds it difficult to believe the horror is quite real. His reaction is not hard to understand.

The decades have piled upon one another, and the terror of what happened in the South in those years has become frozen on the pages of historical text like an icebreaker trapped in the floes of Arctic seas. We have become used to describing the raw events of yesterday with words that sanitize them, that draw away the awful heat and lend us the shelter of distance.

We say someone was "lynched," when in truth we mean that in the last awful minutes of his life, a boy chewed up his tongue, clawed for breath and called to Jesus, legs flailing the air. We say he was "maimed," when the fact is, a hot poker was shoved through his eyeball, or his penis was lopped off and pushed, bleeding, into his mouth. And we ascribe his murder to a faceless "mob," when the deed was authored by a crowd of white Christians who watched his death throes, laughing.

I find the same dreadful value in knowing these things that I do in studying the picture of some wasted, walking corpse from Holocaust days – a cautionary reminder of how base and vicious we can be. And so I am consumed, perhaps presumptuously, with a need to make my colleague know it as well. To de-sanitize it, re-heat it, erase the distance, and plant the knowing not just in his mind, but in a place that is deeper, more difficult to reach, and less susceptible to unwelcome truth.

At Jefferson Davis' house in Montgomery, curator Eva New-man is talking about "the great man" and the rebellion he led. Her perspective is educational. Born in Czechoslovakia ("I am a can-celed Czech," she quips), Newman has been in the South 25 years, "so I'm Southern."

She feels, she says, a strong attachment to things Southern – the slowness of daily life, the conservative values, and the Confed-erate battle flag. Anyone who pastes the banner on their truck "should be fined," she says. "That battle flag, I feel strongly about it, represents a part of the history of the United States and nobody has the right to use it to protest something."

I notice she said the United States. "That's what it is," she confirms. "It's all of ours. Because we are the United States. We are not the Divided States."

Upstairs, Lesa David, a white elementary-school teacher from Birmingham, says Civil War and civil rights are sticky subjects in the New South. "I just teach ... about human feelings," she says. "How would you react, whether you're black or white, in the situa-tion they were in?"

At which point Alan Brazzell, a 10-year-old white student, pipes up. "People need to be treated equally," he says. "It's like, no fair you have to do this because you're this color and you have to do that because you're that color and all that stuff."

One's first thought is a paean to the simple wisdom of a child. But there are children and there are children. A child in Selma made me sad and reminded me of the hard work that remains to be done.

His name is Marcus, he's black and he's 16. We sat in his front yard for a few minutes one afternoon and talked.

I asked him what he wants to do when he gets out of school.

"I want to be a doctor," he said, "but, you know ..." Marcus' voice trailed off as if the rest was too obvious to speak, and I guess it was, but I wanted to hear it anyway.

But what? I pressed.

He gave me a resigned shrug. "Ain't no black folks too much 'round here no doctor," he said.

I reminded him he could always get out of the South. But what I should've done is grab him by the shoulders and shake him. Shake him hard and tell him about the progress we have made, how we have come to this place for which our fathers died. Shake him and wake him and make him see that if the South means anything, it means this:

Yesterday is prologue, but tomorrow is unwritten. There is grace to be attained. Redemption to be won. But first you must raise your gaze.

Look up, child. Look up!

Monday, September 25, 1995

WATER STAINED BY BLOOD

VICKSBURG, Mississippi – There is no silence quite so profound as that of the deserted battlefield. Once, awful things happened here. Now there is a hush in which it seems quite natural to listen for the footfall of ghosts.

Only birds serenade the grassy Vicksburg plains that rang with explosions and gunfire and screams. Only beetles disturb the surface of Tennessee's Shiloh pond, where dying men crawled to slake their thirst with water stained by blood. And children play on Maryland's Antietam bridge, where soldiers fell, shot down by snipers on the bluffs above.

It is impossible to be in these places and not feel. And yet ... As my traveling companion, Michael Browning, and I leave the scene of a Southern defeat, he is talking, as is his wont, about some small twist of fate without which "the battle would have been won."

And I tell him, "It was won" by way of reminding him, I guess, that only one of us in this car is white and Southern.

Michael gives me a look, and one might reasonably wonder, is there anything on which a white Southerner and a black American might agree?

Actually, I think we agree on more than we know – are alike in ways we have yet to figure out. It's just hard to get at that, because it is tangled in four centuries of recrimination, denial and outrage.

In the Civil War, the South became The South – a loaded, coded phrase embodying racial violence, lynch law and no excess of intelligence. But of course, history is written by the winners and it's worth noting that the North did not become The North despite the fact it was no hotbed of equality and reason itself.

In the popular mind it was the South – aided in no small part by its own meanness and arrogance – that came to be seen as sole refuge for unsophisticated, semi-literate white buffoons, poorer than dirt and twice as dumb.

This, in turn, helps explain the level and character of the violence those people directed against ostensibly "free" blacks. When one is down, it's a comfort to know that there is someone lower still.

Black people served that purpose for Southerners. We gave them someone to feel superior to.

And in that appalling process, we discovered the same thing they did: Oppression from without creates identity from within. It circles the wagons. It makes you a people.

More than once, I've heard Southerners say they are Southerners first and Americans second. My first thought was how backward and wrong-headed this was. I'm certainly not a Californian first.

But I find myself forced to admit – to myself as much as to anyone – that I am black first and American second.

Do you find that lamentable? Injurious to our sense of nation? I agree.

But if you've never been part of a despised class, you can't know what an emotional lifesaver it is for that class to take you in and confer purpose and identity upon you. You can't know what it means to be told that there is greatness in the thing that makes you despised.

White people never had to reassure themselves that white is beautiful. Northerners never had to say they were Northern by the grace of God. It's easy for them to say tsk; they weren't human chattel. They didn't lose the war.

The ironies are intricate, stark and awful. The givers and receivers of pain are bound in a bloody handclasp across history by the pain itself. By the miserableness of their shared existence, the mutual dependency of master and slave, the circumstance of being lowdown and lower still.

They needed us. And we cannot escape them.

It is a truth too true for shouting, too painful almost to acknowledge with words at all. Maybe it whispers in the silence of the battlefields, but if so, who hears it? White Southerners seem caught up in their fables of glory. And black folks? We don't often come to Civil War battlefields.

Maybe we think they are a white thing. Maybe it taxes our patience to listen to those damned glory tales. Maybe a lot of things.

"Are we running from something?" asks Rogers Lavender, a 49-year-old Californian who, on this morning, is the only black tourist in the Vicksburg gift shop. "Are we keeping ourselves distant from other populations? It's something I can't answer.

"Regardless of how you want to look at it, " he says, "we're still part of this history. We suffered, we gave ... We are part of this."

Tuesday, September 26, 1995

IT'S A BAD DREAM

ATLANTA – Martin Luther King Jr.'s dream didn't come true even in his own neighborhood.

That's the inescapable thought that haunts you as you walk the streets around the two-story frame house where the great man lived as a child. This ain't no dream, Jack. This is nightmare. This is real.

Broken sidewalks. Dirt. Rotting structures that sag like cardboard in the rain. A pervasive smell of garbage and decay.

The sounds of hammers and bulldozers carry through the neighborhood as Atlanta hurries to spruce up for the 1996 Olympics.

But it's a lie, and Atlanta seems not unlike a child rushing to tidy its room before the parents get home.

From a gift shop across the street, King's voice lifts in familiar eloquence. Nearby, Anthony James panhandles.

He is a small man with a reddish brown face scarred by acne. He wears his hat pulled low over his eyes and he smells of old wine.

"This whole perimeter, my brother, is going to be redesigned," he says. Crews seem to be literally rebuilding some of the decrepit structures from the ground up.

And after the games end? "They gonna let it go back to the boys in the 'hood."

It's not hard to buy into his pessimism. It sure doesn't look like anybody cared about this neighborhood before the world decided to come calling.

The problem here, explains James, is crack. "So many people, so distraught. When they smoke that stuff, man, they don't care about nobody."

He pauses, points across a construction site to a modest home with windows barricaded by wood. It looks deserted, but he says people live there – old women. "That's why them elderly ladies boarded their house up like that, so junkies can't break in.

"Let me show you something," he insists. He stoops to pick up a small rock, walks purposefully to a parked car and acts as if he were flinging the rock through the window.

"Pa-YOW!" he says, mimicking the sound of shattering glass. That, he says, is how easy it is for a junkie to steal a car.

"You gonna school me?" I ask, walking along beside him.

"I ain't got no other choice, G."

There is not a lot of optimism in Anthony's neighborhood. Indeed, if this trip is any indication, there is not a lot of optimism in black America.

Things have not changed, except to go undercover, said a store clerk in Birmingham, Alabama

"I think it was better back" before the civil rights movement, said a retiree in St. Augustine.

A couple having lunch in Birmingham's Kelly Ingram Park tells my traveling companion, Michael Browning, that things haven't gotten much better in 30 years. But, Browning points out in confusion, there they are having lunch in Kelly Ingram Park! Surely that would have been impossible three decades ago. The significance of it seems not to register on the couple.

Maybe because the dream that was field-tested here has yet to become real and nobody knows what to do, nobody knows what to believe, nobody knows anything, except that everybody is weary unto the abyss of despair. The new racism demands a new response. A new attitude. And paradoxically, many blacks seem to feel that both might be found in the past.

"We as a black race – it's our own damned fault," snaps Hosie King, 54, who runs a soul-food restaurant near Kelly Ingram Park. "We've got to get back to basics. Blacks have got a better political position now, but they are not doing anything to help one another. When I was growing up, there was no such thing as poor. We all shared everything. If a child got a whipping from his grandfather and his friend was involved, too, the grandfather would whip the friend, and nobody would question him."

And now? "Now we're afraid of each other. It's just like living on work release. You go into your apartment and lock the door and stay locked in there all night. Before, you could leave the door open and enjoy the cool air. We're trying to live white when we need to stay black. "

"I don't need to move into your neighborhood," he tells Browning pointedly. "Just let me fix my own neighborhood up."

It will be easier said than done, if Anthony James' neighborhood is any indication. There, bulldozers grumble and children shout, playing basketball on a patch of dirt with a makeshift hoop.

The dreamer lies in a crypt around the corner, an attraction for tourists. We stand in the midst of the dream deferred.

Thursday, September 28, 1995

WHY DID THEY FIGHT, REALLY?

RICHMOND, Virginia – Somewhere between Atlanta and Vicksburg, Mississippi, Michael Browning and I get into a debate on the cause of the Civil War. "Some historians," he says, "not all of them Southern, have suggested that slavery was not the root cause of the war, though it was certainly a contributing cause. Four out of five Confederate soldiers didn't own slaves."

And I'm sure four out of five American soldiers couldn't find Kuwait on a map before the Gulf War. What does that prove?

In the mind of the antebellum South, says Michael, the war was about states' rights.

But what right were they seeking, I ask, if not the right to hold black people as slaves.

For them, it was an economic issue, he insists. Blacks were their "farm implements." Planters saw economic ruin ahead if the North deprived them of their "tools."

Yes, but these "farm implements," these "tools," were human beings. Slaves.

Somebody let me out of this fun house of logic, I want to scream.

"For Southerners to discuss the war," concedes Browning, "it takes a lot of suspension. That's why they get lost in the minutiae of battle. They don't want to think about the big cause, because as Grant said, no people ever fought harder for a worse cause. The uncontestable bravery of the Southern soldiers could not logically, we think, spring from tainted founts. If we fought that hard, the very sincerity and effort we put into fighting somehow glorifies and ennobles the cause."

But it does not, and after nearly two weeks on the road with Michael, I can't help marveling at how tangled and complex are these issues of race, culture and pride. I long for the clear-eyed simplicity of the 10-year-old white boy in Montgomery who summed up 400 years of racial angst with: "No fair you have to do this because you're this color and you have to do that because you're that color."

But childish conceptions of fair play seem quaint in an era of renewed racial animosity and confusion. One wonders what the boy would make of those blacks who say the civil rights movement failed because covert racism persists, or of Lloyd Smith, a 52-year-old black retiree from St. Augustine who preferred life under Jim Crow because whites "treated you better then."

"Oh, he has to be stupid!" sputters the Rev. C.T. Vivian of Atlanta. "What he's trying to say is, 'I, personally, haven't gotten what I wanted yet.' "

Vivian, a 71-year-old former aide to Martin Luther King Jr., says, "We have seen more change in the 30 years following [the Voting Rights Act of 1965] than in any 30-year period in this country. Before that, you got elected in a good part of this country based on one thing. The term politicians used was, 'I can out-nigger you.' That meant that every election – local, state, national – black people were being used and talked about like animals.

"How can you ever achieve, get support, like yourself, any-thing else, in an atmosphere that destructive?"

The Voting Rights Act, he says, made that behavior impossi-ble – "at least above the table."

Yet, only 37 percent of eligible blacks voted in the November election that swept the Republicans into power. And one could make a credible argument that the spirit of "I can out-nigger you" is alive and well in GOP rhetoric. Might not greater black voter participation have blunted the tide?

Joanne Bland, bloodied 30 years ago during a voting-rights march in Selma, surely wonders. "I think it all goes back to inter-nalized oppression," she says. "After this big war for voting rights, it was sort of anti-climactic because now we got it and we, quote, are 'free.' If you've never been taught to look for the top, you don't miss it. So, once you attain any level better than where you were, you feel like you've made it."

The aftermath of the freedom years seems to be similarly complex for the white South. Martin Luther King once prophesied that "one day the South will recognize its real heroes." And cer-tainly you can argue that that day has arrived. A plaque honoring Rosa Parks has been erected down the street from the Montgom-ery statehouse. Memphis has turned the place where King was killed into a museum and shrine. In Birmingham, Alabama, Kelly Ingram Park, where marchers faced snapping dogs and the fury of high-pressure hoses, has been re-landscaped in tribute to their heroism. Across the street, the Birmingham Civil Rights Institute offers a high-tech tour of the journey toward freedom.

Yet, for all that, the air still changes – I am noticed – whenev-er I venture beyond neon-lit malls and national chain stores into those off-the-track places where blacks are not "supposed" to be. It takes nearly an hour to get a hamburger at a nearly-empty truck stop in rural Alabama. A gas station near Tifton, Georgia, has a large display of mammy dolls.

An old man at a mom-and-pop store just outside Selma talks blithely about his easy relations with "darkies."

At some places in the South, the freedom years seem to have left little mark. Elsewhere, there is simply a palpable need to find a DMZ between black rage and white Southern heritage.

It won't be easy.

"What heritage are they talking about?" demands Vivian. "Their heritage is murder, their heritage is slavery, their heritage is the destruction of human personality. Make them face that and then say, 'And you go to church on Sunday and talk about Jesus and God and decency and love and truth and justice?' Somewhere, you've got to be out of your mind."

Has the South unknotted that conundrum? When I'm in metropolitan Atlanta, I think maybe so. When I walk into the Old Courthouse Museum in Vicksburg, I don't. An old white man stares with cutting eyes as I stand in this temple of the Lost Cause.

He's never seen anything like me in here. And I've never seen anything like this outside of nightmares – a musty shrine to dead ideals where the air does not stir, old lies find new credit, and if you didn't get your mammy dolls down near Tifton, by God, they've got a plentiful supply right here.

Take as an example of the tenor of the place the Ku Klux Klan exhibit, which contends that the notorious hate group was formed to "rid the South of the carpetbag, scalaway (sic) black governments which were often corrupt ... Many people suffered, some no doubt innocently," says the text, "as the Klan tried to restore some semblance of deceny (sic) to the government."

Blanche Terry, who works behind a gift counter selling Confederate flags and Sambo dolls, defends that point of view. "The Klan really didn't get bad until the '20s," she claims, which would doubtless surprise former slaves beaten, bullied and butchered by the night riders during Reconstruction.

And yet ... Terry also says she was "absolutely" for integration in the '60s. Her son, she says, was a Justice Department lawyer in the Civil Rights Division during the '60s. Her husband's business was "completely ruined" because of his pro-integration stance.

I ask her about Southern pride and she says, "To me, it's a sense of being. I'm proud to tell people I'm fourth generation here."

She has given me both rationalization and truth, which I suppose is par for the course. But the rationalizations do not satisfy and the truth has yet to make anyone free.

Traveling with Browning, I notice that he has a tendency to take personal ownership of the events of Civil War – often speaking of how "we" fought this battle or "we" suffered this loss. But never does he say "we" owned slaves or "we" fought to perpetuate an evil system. Then it's "them" and "they."

I push him to take ownership of it all, but that's something he can't – or won't – do.

Not that Michael finds me any bed of roses, either. "That flag really pisses you off, doesn't it?" he says in consternation one afternoon after I've made one too many remarks about the rebel flag. I act, says Michael, like a Jew in the presence of a swastika.

But 10 million to 20 million of my people were fed into the maw of slavery in the New World, half again that many died before ever reaching land, and the people who fought under that flag fought to keep that filthy system in place.

At the sight of the rebel flag, I *am* a Jew in the presence of a swastika.

Would I feel better if Michael took ownership of that as well? Would it make me whole?

Not really.

And so, you might justifiably ask what I expect from the man. Apologies? Reparations? Confession?

I suppose I just want him to know how damaged I am, how angry I feel, by what his fathers did to mine.

But that's the problem, isn't it? Black American or white Southerner, we've not yet learned to stand without our fathers. What if we could, though? God only knows who we might then become.

SLAVERY

Wednesday, March 5, 2014

FACING THIS TERRIBLE HISTORY

A plea for about a dozen people who know who they are:

Will you see "12 Years A Slave" now?

It just won the Oscar for Best Picture. It just came out on DVD. Please see it. I'll even spring for the popcorn.

You see, I keep encountering folks, mostly African American, who have decided that they won't – or can't – see this movie. Some say they don't want to be made angry. Others say they don't want to be traumatized.

I don't blame them for respecting the power of this film. "12 Years," based on the 1853 memoir of a free man kidnapped and sold into slavery, is the most realistic and unsparing depiction of that evil institution ever put on film. This is not "Gone With The Wind." This is not even "Roots." This film will scar you. It will change you. So it is only natural that a person has trepidation about seeing it.

But I remain convinced there is something invaluable to be found in doing so.

As a nation, we have never quite dealt with our African-American history – the unremitting terrorism, the ongoing violations of human rights, the maiming of human spirit. Even when we say we deal with it, we don't. As historian Ray Arsenault once put it, Americans prefer "mythic conceptions of what they think happened."

There is good reason for this. Stripped of "mythic conceptions," presented in its unvarnished, un-Disneyfied, unsugared truth, African-American history tends to make African-American people feel resentment, pain or just humiliation for some poor brother grinning and shuffling his feet and saying "yassuh boss" back in the dreadful long ago. These are unpleasant emotions.

And that same history tends to make white people feel put upon, ashamed or guilty – another set of unpleasant emotions. A few years ago, I watched a documentary on the lynching of Emmett Till in the company of a white college student. This young man, born almost 40 years after Till's murder, said he felt so personally "embarrassed" he wanted to peel off his skin.

I felt for him. I feel for all of us who struggle with facing this history.

But I can't see where not facing it has helped us surmount it. To the contrary, it is lodged like a bone in the throat, sits astride virtually every aspect of our American lives, ever present even if unspoken. Ignoring it has not made it go away.

Indeed, ignoring it has only emboldened mythmakers to reshape it for their own purposes, rewrite our story for political advantage.

Did you know the Founding Fathers "worked tirelessly" to end slavery?

Did you know the Civil War was fought over tariffs?

Did you know conservatives freed the slaves?

Did you know they passed the Civil Rights Act?

These and other imbecilic lies circulate freely now while those of us – black and white – who should be the most ardent custodians of this story stand passively by and watch it happen.

I, for one, have had enough of that. It is disrespectful – a sin against our forebears. African-American people have given this country some of its finest literature, its liveliest music, its most noteworthy scientific achievements, its most heroic soldiers, its

most luminous business successes, its most celebrated athletes –
all midwifed by that trauma we find so difficult to speak about, the
one we eagerly avoid.

But I persist in the belief that if reconciliation is truly what
black and white Americans seek in this great chimera called
"race," then the pathway to that lies not in going around, but together, through that which brings us heartache and sorrow and
makes us weep. If we could ever get to the other side of anger and
humiliation, reach the far shore of embarrassment and guilt, what
might we then find? Who might we then become?

This country has never truly committed to finding an answer
to that question. "12 Years A Slave" provides an excellent place to
start.

FREEDOM RIDERS

Sunday, January 12, 2003

A GRUESOME TRUTH THAT HAD TO BE TOLD

If you ever saw that picture of Emmett Till, you never forgot it.

Not the one that shows a handsome brown teenager, hat tipped up slightly off his forehead. Not, in other words, the before picture.

No, I'm talking about the picture that was taken after. After he went down from Chicago to visit family in Mississippi in the late summer of 1955. After he accepted a schoolboy dare to flirt with a white woman working behind the counter of the general store. After he called her "baby," and allegedly gave a wolf whistle. After her husband and his half brother came for him in the dead of night. After his body was fished from the Tallahatchie River.

The picture of him that was taken then, published in Jet magazine and flashed around the world, was stomach-turning. A lively and prankish boy had become a bloated grotesquerie, an ear missing, an eye gouged out, a bullet hole in his head. You looked at that picture and you felt that here was the reason coffins have lids.

But his mother refused onlookers that mercy, refused to give him a closed-casket funeral. She delayed the burial for four days, keeping her son's mutilated body on display as thousands came to pay their respects.

"I wanted the world to see what I had seen," she later explained. "I wanted the world to see what had happened in Mississippi. I wanted the world to see what had happened in America."

The world saw and was electrified.

Mamie Till Mobley died in Chicago last Monday, apparently of a heart attack. And if one were seeking to sum up her life, it might be enough to say that she spent 47 years keeping the casket open, speaking, writing and agitating in the name of her murdered son. Indeed, her book "The Death of Innocence" is due for release later this year.

I met her once, maybe 30 years after her son's death, by which point she must have told his story a million times. And she still welled up as she spoke, her voice stammering and turning gray.

At the time, I was writing and producing a radio documentary tracing over 500 years of black history. I'll never forget my narrator's response when he reviewed a script that recounted Emmett's ordeal and the ordeals of other black men and women who were hanged, burned and hacked to pieces for the crime of being. He jokingly dubbed me "the Stephen King of black history" for my insistence on including the grisly details.

But I happen to believe Mamie Till Mobley was right to keep the casket open.

We're always so eager to hide the horror. Close the casket, turn your eyes, use euphemism to obscure truths too obscene.

Consider Trent Lott's first attempt at apology, when he blithely described segregation as "the discarded policies of the past." If you didn't know any better, you might have thought he was talking about farm subsidies or tax code, so bloodless and opaque was the language.

But segregation wasn't opaque and it surely wasn't bloodless.

It was a Mississippi courtroom where the sheriff sauntered in everyday and greeted spectators in the colored section with a cheery, "Hello, niggers." It was two white men freely admitting that they had kidnapped a black Chicago boy. It was witnesses who placed the men at a barn inside which they heard a child being tortured. And it was a jury of white men who heard this evidence, then deliberated for less than an hour before returning an acquittal.

As one of them told a reporter, "If we hadn't stopped to drink pop, it wouldn't have took that long."

This is the fetid truth behind the flowery words, the stinking fact much of the nation would prefer not to know.

But by her very presence, a murdered boy's mother demanded that we be better than that, demanded that we be, at least and at last, brave enough to face the horrors we have made and that have, in turn, made us.

Mamie Till Mobley was 81 years old at the time of her death. Her only child was 14 at the time of his.

Saturday, May 14, 2011

50 YEARS LATER

NASHVILLE – John Seigenthaler should write a book.

Actually, Seigenthaler, former aide to Attorney General Robert F. Kennedy, has authored several books, including one on Watergate. But as near as can be gleaned, from a search of Amazon.com, he has yet to write the book he ought to write. Meaning, a book that struggles with a question that seems, in some ways, to have haunted him most of his life.

What does it mean to be a white person of conscience in a racist nation?

It is a question that is applicable to millions, of course, yet one that has seldom even been posed, much less grappled with in any meaningful way. Seigenthaler is uniquely qualified to do both.

This becomes clear in a poignant meeting with the 2011 student Freedom Riders at the First Amendment Center that bears his name. He is a decent man. You get that sense. He's the one the attorney general dispatched to the South to rescue the Freedom Riders after a bus was burned and a mob set loose on the defenseless college students who committed the "crime" of riding interracially on interstate buses.

He is the one who took a pipe blow to the back of the head while trying to rescue two young black women from that self-same mob.

So a decent man, yes. But he is a decent man who, not unreasonably, still wonders, 50 years later, at 83 years of age, how the tragedy of American racism could have been so invisible to him and his contemporaries until movements like the Freedom Rides forced them to see. How could something that seems so obvious now have been imperceptible then?

"I think back to my childhood, " he tells the students. "Those two [African American] women, Lela Gray and Birdie Mai Liddle, at times were surrogate mothers to my siblings and me. And they were treated with great respect in my home. Once they were on the street and in a crowd ... I don't mean I wouldn't have recognized them if I had seen them or been courteous to them or caring for them.

"But I will tell you, like Ellison said, they were invisible. I don't know how many times I was on a bus or trolley car when I was a child or young adult, not paying any attention to the signs. Lela Gray or Birdie Mai Liddle, Rosa Park's counterparts here, paid their fare, and went where the signs told them. Some were carrying (burdens) maybe taking laundry home from some white woman's kitchen to press it during the night and get it back in the morning. They struggled to the back, where they had to go. My parents had told me, if a lady needs a seat, stand up and give her your seat. It never occurred to me they meant a black lady. And indeed, my parents never meant a black lady."

He is perched on a stool in the front of the small room, arms folded over his chest, eyes turned inward, reflecting. "Until you read Ralph Ellison," he says, "you don't' understand what the invisible man or the invisible women really were. We who are white, maybe went out of our way not to see them, but we didn't see them. That's not entitled to absolution. It's a condemnation of our ignorance."

There is wonder in his voice. "I look back at that time," he says, "and that's when I say, 'Where was my head, where was my heart, where were my parents' heads and hearts?' Never heard from my teachers about the indignity, the indecency. Not one time did I ever hear a sermon in my childhood or young adulthood, directed in any way at the injustice of a society that separated people by race. It was part blind ignorance and part blatant arrogance. And I confess that with great and deep regret and if I could change it, I would. But you know, I'm 50 years too late from the time I first really started intensely thinking about it."

You sense the soul struggles of a good man who will probably go to his grave wondering how the society, the very soil from which he sprang, could have gotten so much so tragically wrong.

In 1899, Rudyard Kipling wrote a poem "The White Man's Burden," in which said burden was described as a colonizer's obligation to the welfare of the colonized nation, "your new-caught, sullen peoples." If Seigenthaler is any example, though, it might be argued that the white man's true burden – at least, the burden of the white man who regards himself as decent, enlightened, moral, good – is to figure out what to do with the legacy of injustice that attaches like glue to the very concept of whiteness in America.

Many years ago, the late Michael Browning, a white Miami Herald reporter, wrote of his encounter with Reverend C.T. Vivian, an aide to Martin Luther King Jr., who spoke of how he asked his white seminary students if they had ever prayed for forgiveness for the sin of racism. Browning felt indicted by the question.

"Southern irresolution," he wrote. "How, if I am as benevolent as I think I am, can black people see me as such a monster? Am I an inert part of some vast weighty boulder of oppression? Do I injure blacks by breathing and just being white?"

And the answer is probably less important than the asking.

"You know," says Seigenthaler, "it was a cliché, maybe, when Jack Kennedy said each of us can make a difference. But it's no cliché to say each of us should try."

He grieves of things that were invisible to him a lifetime ago.

Perhaps the only sensible and moral response, then, is to wonder: What things are invisible to us now?

Sunday, May 15, 2011

DON'T LOOK BACK

We are on the 2011 Student Freedom Riders bus rolling toward Augusta, Georgia, watching "The Murder of Emmett Till," a PBS documentary on the savage 1955 lynching of a black boy in the nothing town of Money, Mississippi. On the old newsreel footage, white person after white person spews the grotesque bigotry that was common to white people in that time and place and somebody asks Ryan Price a question:

How do you feel as a white guy, watching a film like this?

"It was a good question, " he tells me that evening at the hotel. He pauses a long time, thinking.

"Watching 'The Murder of Emmett Till' as a white person, " he says, "it's hard not to ..."

Another pause. He gathers himself. "It's hard not to be embarrassed," he says finally. "While I was watching that movie, you get to the point where you almost want to change your skin color so you can show how much you care about issues of race, how much you care about the overt hatred and vitriolic discrimination of the past and today. Of course, you can't change your skin color, but you can be an ally to those who are marginalized in society and that's something it really spurs me to do."

It is a good – and brave – answer. Sadly, such bravery often eludes people two and three times the age of Price, a 20-year-old student from Drake University in Des Moines. Their preferred answer, proffered reflexively whenever discussion turns to the African-American sojourn in this country, can be summed up in three words: don't look back.

As the bus full of college students rolls across the South celebrating the young people who famously defied segregation ordinances 50 years ago, and promoting "Freedom Riders," a new PBS documentary, that preferred answer is being heard yet again. Indeed, a story on the freedom rides by your humble correspondent, who is traveling across the South with the student riders, drew the following odd, but entirely predictable, rebuke on a Miami Herald message board.

"Cars' windshields are so large and the rearview mirrors are so small because our past is not as important as our future. So, look ahead and move on."

One never encounters this wholesale dismissal of the past when one commemorates, say, the Kennedy inauguration or the Holocaust. That's because those things make us feel sorrow, nostalgia, resolve. As Ryan Price would testify, African-American history makes us feel ... other things.

And if we find those things difficult to process, that's understandable. But to respond to that difficulty by declaring this one strain of history off limits is to commit an act of plain moral cowardice.

That cowardice is unfortunately common. Ray Arsenault, who wrote "Freedom Riders," the book upon which the PBS documentary is based, says that instead of doing the difficult work of seeking to understand the forces that made us, Americans too often choose to create "mythic conceptions of what they think happened" in the past. Those myths, he says, are "based on half-truths and a kind of civic indoctrination which makes them feel perhaps more comfortable, but that trains them to be followers and not leaders, not to ask the difficult questions." Without posing those questions, he says, we will never find the answers.

Which is, I suppose, just fine by some of us because it is those answers we fear. I mean, "windshields?" Really?

The funny thing is, every car I've ever driven had one in the back nearly as big as the one in the front – along with three mirrors reflecting the road behind. It suggests that automakers, at least, recognize what some of us do not.

To navigate the road ahead, it helps to have some sense of the road behind.

VOTING RIGHTS

Sunday, January 8, 2012

LIFE IN THE MARGINS

So here's how it is:

You have no driver's license because you have nothing to drive. You have no passport because you've never been out of the country. You have no other photo I.D. because you have no bank account. You work and get paid under the table, a wad of cash sliding from hand to hand.

It is a life lived in the margins. And if South Carolina and a number of other GOP-controlled states have their way, it will be a life to which a significant new impediment will be added: you will not be able to vote.

Over the holiday, the Justice Department rejected a South Carolina law requiring a photo ID – as opposed to just a voter registration card – for would-be voters. The department called the law discriminatory against African Americans. Under the Voting Rights Act of 1965, South Carolina and other states and localities with histories of infringing the voting rights of African Americans are required to get federal approval before changing their voting laws. This is the first time the feds have rejected such a change since 1994.

South Carolina Governor Nikki Haley has blasted the decision as political. She probably has a point. The law would have disproportionately affected the poor, who are disproportionately likely, for the reasons outlined above, to lack photo IDs. The poor are disproportionately black, and black people are disproportionately likely to vote Democratic. It would be naïve to believe that did not enter into the thinking of the Obama Justice Department.

But the inverse is also true. As similar voter ID laws are passed in other Republican-controlled states – including those that not covered by the Voting Rights Act – it would be naïve to believe politics does not also enter the GOP's thinking. Though lawmakers swear their only interest is to combat voting fraud (which is not known to be a rampant problem), it is difficult not to feel their true intent is to suppress the black vote.

Granted, race is nowhere mentioned in the voter ID bills. It was not mentioned in bills imposing grandfather clauses, poll taxes and literacy tests, either. All were officially race-neutral, yet the intention and effect was to bar blacks from voting.

As Richard Nixon once said of his War on Drugs, another "race-neutral" policy that somehow victimizes mostly blacks, the idea is to target African Americans while appearing not to.

The Justice Department was right to block this law, but it is nonetheless hard not to feel a certain pox-on-all-their-houses cynicism as people who live on the margins are both targeted – and defended – for political reasons, but otherwise go unremarked and unrecalled.

Democrats depend upon the votes of black and/or poor people, but do little to earn them – no jobs training, no criminal justice system reform, no attention whatsoever to the things that delimit their lives. Meantime, Republicans write off the votes of black and/or poor people and do all they can to suppress them.

They are made mute and forgotten even as the public square rings like a cash register and monied interests ka-ching! their way into positions of power and influence with politicians on both sides of the aisle who are ostensibly elected to represent us all – even if we lack a photo ID.

Corporations are people, we have been told. Poor people, evidently, are not.

Tuesday, July 10, 2012

STILL FIGHTING JIM CROW

Kemba Smith Pradia went to Tallahassee last week to demand the right to vote.

Back in the '90s, when she was just Kemba Smith, she became a poster child for the excesses and inanities of the so-called War on Drugs. Pradia, then a college student in Virginia, became involved with, and terrorized by, a man who choked and punched her regularly and viciously. By the impenetrable logic of battered women, she thought it was her fault. The boyfriend was a drug dealer. Pradia never handled drugs, never used drugs, never sold drugs. But she sometimes carried his gun in her purse. She flew to New York with drug money strapped to her body.

Eventually, she was busted. And this good girl from a good home, who had never been in trouble before, was sentenced to over 24 years.

In the 12 years since President Bill Clinton commuted her sentence, Pradia has theoretically been a free woman. Except that she cannot vote. Having returned home to Virginia after living awhile in Indiana, she had to apply for the restoration of her voting rights. She is still waiting.

So last week, Pradia, along with actor Charles S. Dutton, joined NAACP President Benjamin Todd Jealous at Florida's old state capitol building to launch a campaign demanding restoration of voting rights to former felons.

CNN reports that Florida, Virginia and nine other states embrace what might be called policies of "eternal damnation," i.e., laws that continue to punish former felons and deny them the vote long after they have done their time, finished their parole, rejoined society.

The state's former governor, Charlie Crist, had streamlined the process, making voting rights restoration automatic for non-violent felons. His successor, Rick Scott, reversed that. In Florida, an ex-felon is now required to wait up to seven years before even applying to have his or her voting rights returned.

"Welcome back, Jim Crow" said the headline on a Miami Herald editorial. Ain't that the truth? Between policies like these, new restrictions on Sunday and early voting and, of course, Voter ID laws, the NAACP estimates that 23 million Americans stand to be disenfranchised – a disproportionate number of them African American.

We have seen these shenanigans before: grandfather clauses, poll taxes, literacy tests. Yet African Americans – heck, Americans in general – seem remarkably quiescent about seeing it all come around again, same old garbage in a different can.

"If you want to vote, show it," trilled a TV commercial in support of Pennsylvania's Voter ID law before a judge blocked its implementation. The tenor of the ad was telling, though, implicitly suggesting that voting is a privilege for which one should be happy to jump through arbitrary hoops.

But voting is emphatically not a privilege. It is a right. By definition, then, it must be broadly accessible. These laws ensure that it is not.

We are indebted to the NAACP for bringing attention and leadership to this. Five years ago, a newspaper columnist – a guy named Pitts, actually – raked the organization for being "stagnant, static and marginal to today's struggle." But that was then. In fighting to restore the voting rights of ex-felons, in calling last year for an end to the failed "War on Drugs," the NAACP has done more than energize itself.

It has also challenged us to recognize that the brutish goals of Jim Crow America never died, but simply reshaped themselves to the sensibilities of the 21st century, learned to hide themselves in the bloodless and opaque language of officially race-neutral policy. It would be a critical mistake not to understand this.

Indeed, the advice of the late Teddy Pendergrass seems freshly apropos: Wake up, everybody. And realize:

Garbage is garbage, no matter how pristine the can.

Sunday, July 15, 2012

THE SOUNDS OF SILENCE

An open letter to African America:

In the late '90s, the Internet belched forth a rumor that the Voting Rights Act was soon to expire and that black folks would lose the vote as a result. Though stupid and untrue, the rumor spread like a dust cloud till it was inescapable. You couldn't get away from it in a confession booth. You couldn't get away from it in a phone booth. Everybody was up in arms.

Flash forward to 2012. Now the threat is real. There is a sustained effort to suppress the black vote as we approach this pivotal election. And what is our response?

Silence.

"I don't sense that African Americans are truly aware of what is in the process of happening or could happen to them," says Rep. John Lewis, Democrat from Georgia. "People should be angry. There should be a sense of righteous indignation. African Americans and people of good will, Latinos and young people, should be saying, 'How dare you? The gall of you!'"

Lewis, of course, is the man whose skull was cracked in 1965 on a bridge in Alabama in the fight for black voting rights. Fifteen years ago, he couldn't walk down a street without being assailed by a false rumor that those rights were imperiled. Now, when the threat is real, he is appalled by the silence he hears.

Here is what is going on in that silence. In Washington, conservative Republicans are seeking to gut the Voting Rights Act. In Florida, they are, in effect, purging Democrats from the voting rolls. In Kansas, there is a law requiring a voter show proof of citizenship. And in 30 states, according to the National Conference of State Legislatures, there are Voter ID laws, either passed or under contemplation.

Conservatives argue that such laws are needed to prevent voter fraud. This argument might hold more water if there actually were any significant voter fraud in our elections. There is not.

In a speech last week before the NAACP, Attorney General Eric Holder likened Voter ID laws to the poll taxes of yesteryear. He is right. Like the poll taxes, like the grandfather clauses, and literacy tests of decades past, Voter ID laws are officially race-neutral. And like those discarded laws, these new ones have the intention and effect of preventing African Americans from voting. Poor people, you see, are less likely to have photo IDs – and black people are disproportionately poor.

Keep in mind that blacks are already disenfranchised by laws denying the ballot to former felons. Given the phenomenon of mass incarceration – i.e., a criminal injustice system that will bypass 10 white cocaine dealers to jail one black guy dealing crack – disenfranchising former felons largely means disenfranchising us.

Voter ID laws add fresh insult to standing injury. And let no one be fooled by GOP claims that this is not political. Mike Turzai, who sits in the Pennsylvania state legislature, inadvertently set fire to that lie last month. In a speech to a Republican State Committee meeting, he praised, "Voter ID, which is gonna allow Governor Romney to win the state of Pennsylvania ..."

So where are we in all this? Silent, that's where.

It is easy to rally in the face of a tragedy like Trayvon Martin. That was a visceral, emotional thing. Still, what happened to that child is only representative of systemic injustice. This is systemic injustice, and we should be just as exercised about it, if not more so.

And yet ...

Silence.

From the barber shops, silence.

From the beauty parlors, silence.

From the pulpits, silence.

In the face of a naked attempt to steal not just an election, but a right that was purchased for us at a cost of bones and blood, silence. It's happening now, right under our noses.

"And we're too quiet," says Lewis. "We're just too quiet."

Sunday, March 3, 2013

HISTORY REPEATS

One day, many years ago, I was working in my college bookstore when this guy walks in wearing a T-shirt. "White Power," it said.

I was chatting with a friend, Cathy Duncan, and what happened next was as smooth as if we had rehearsed it. All at once, she's sitting on my lap or I'm sitting on hers – I can't remember which – and that white girl gives this black guy a peck on the lips. In a loud voice she asks, "So, what time should I expect you home for dinner, honey?"

Mr. White Power glares malice and retreats. Cathy and I fall over laughing.

Which tells you something about how those of us who came of age in the first post-civil rights generation tended to view racism. We saw it as something we could dissipate with a laugh, a tired old thing that had bedeviled our parents, yes, but which we were beyond. We thought racism was over.

I've spent much of my life since then being disabused of that naiveté. Watching media empires built upon appeals to racial resentment, seeing the injustice system wield mass incarceration as a weapon against black men, bearing witness as the first African-American president produced his long form birth certificate, all helped me understand just how silly we were to believe bigotry was done.

So a chill crawled my spine last week as the Supreme Court heard arguments in a case that could result in gutting the Voting Rights Act. That landmark 1965 legislation gave the ballot to black voters who had previously been denied it by discriminatory laws, economic threats, violence and by registrars who challenged them with nonsense questions like, "How many bubbles are in a bar of soap."

One of the act's key provisions covers nine mostly Southern states and scores of municipalities with histories of such behavior. They must get federal approval before changing their voting procedures. The requirement may be stigmatizing; but it is hardly onerous.

Yet Shelby County, Alabama, seeks the provision's repeal, pronouncing itself cured of the attitudes that made it necessary. "The children of today's Alabama are not racist and neither is their government," wrote Alabama Attorney General Luther Strange in USA Today last week.

It was rather like hearing a wife beater say he has seen the error of his ways and will no longer smack the missus around. Though you're glad and all, you still hope the wife's testimony will carry a little more weight in deciding whether the restraining order should be lifted.

But the court's conservatives seemed eager to believe, peppering the law's defenders with skeptical questions. Indeed, Justice Antonin Scalia branded the law a "racial entitlement."

Sit with that a moment. A law protecting the voting rights of a historically disenfranchised minority is a "racial entitlement?" Equality is a government program?

Lord, have mercy.

There is historical resonance here. In the 1870s, the South assured the federal government it could behave itself without oversight. The feds agreed to leave the region alone where race was concerned. The result: nearly a century of Jim Crow. Now here comes Shelby County, saying in effect: We've changed. Trust us.

It is an appeal that might have seemed persuasive back when I was young and naïve, sitting on Cathy's lap (or she on mine) and thinking race was over.

But that was a long time ago.

Yes, the South has changed – largely because of the law Shelby County seeks to gut. Even so, attempts to dilute the black vote have hardly abated. We've just traded poll taxes and literacy tests for gerrymandering and Voter ID laws.

So we can ill afford to be as naïve as a top court conservative at the prospect of softening federal protection of African-American voting rights. "Trust us," says the South. And the whole weight of history demands a simple question in response.

Why?

Wednesday, March 4, 2015

WHAT WAS WON THEN BEING LOST TODAY

First, they sang "God Will Take Care of You."

Then they walked out of Brown Chapel to a playground where they organized themselves into 24 groups of 25 each and set out marching. Their route out of Selma took them onto Highway 80, which is carried over the Alabama River by a bridge named in honor of Confederate general and Alabama Ku Klux Klan leader Edmund W. Pettus.

It was about 2:30 on the afternoon of Sunday, March 7, 1965.

At the foot of the bridge, the marchers were met by Alabama state troopers. Some were on horseback. Major John Cloud spoke to the marchers through a bullhorn. "It would be detrimental to your safety to continue this march," he said. "And I'm saying that this is an unlawful assembly. You are to disperse. You are ordered to disperse. Go home or go to your church. This march will not continue. Is that clear to you?"

He gave them two minutes to comply. Just over one minute later, he ordered troopers to advance.

They moved toward the marchers, truncheons held waist high, parallel to the ground. But something seemed to overtake them as they pushed into the demonstrators. The troopers began to stampede, sweeping over unarmed women, children and men as a wave does a shore.

Tear gas filled the air. Lawmen on horseback swept down on fleeing marchers, wielding batons, cattle prods, rubber hoses studded with spikes. Skin was split. Bones were broken. The marchers were beaten all the way back into town. A teenager was hurled through a church window. On the bridge, the cheers and rebel yells of onlookers mingled with the shrieks of the sufferers and became indistinguishable.

Thus was the pavement of the freest country on Earth stained with the blood of citizens seeking their right to vote.

By rights, this 50th anniversary of those events should be an unalloyed celebration. After all, the marchers, fortified by men and women of good will from all over the country, eventually crossed that bridge under federal protection, marched for four days up Highway 80 and made it to, as the song says, glory. They stood at the state capitol in Montgomery and heard Martin Luther King exhort them to hold on and be strong. "Truth crushed to Earth," he thundered, "will rise again!"

The Voting Rights Act was signed into law. And African Americans, who had been excluded from the ballot box for generations, went on to help elevate scores of citizens who looked like them to the mayor's office, the governor's mansion, the White House.

So yes, this should be a time of celebration. But the celebration is shadowed by a sobering reality.

In 2013, the Voting Rights Act was castrated by the Supreme Court under the dubious reasoning that its success proved it was no longer needed. And states, responding to a nonexistent surge of election fraud, have rushed to impose onerous new photo ID laws for voters. When it is observed that the laws will have their heaviest impact on young people, poor people and African Americans –

those least likely to have photo ID – defenders of the laws point to that imaginary surge of fraud and assure us voter suppression is the furthest thing from their minds. How can it be about race, they cluck piously, when the laws apply to everyone?

Of course, so did grandfather clauses, poll taxes, literacy tests and other means by which African-American voting rights were systematically stolen for decades and a Whites Only sign slapped onto the ballot box. It is disheartening that we find ourselves forced to fight again a battle already won. But the events of half a century past whisper to us a demand for our toughness and faith in the face of that hard truth. They remind us that, yes, injustice is resilient.

But truth crushed to Earth is, too.

MLK

Monday, January 15, 2007

SUMMONS TO ACT

And so Dream season rolls round again.

That's Dream, of course, as in "I Have A ..." We celebrate Martin Luther King Day today, which means schoolchildren dutifully reciting the great 1963 oration, television news dutifully replaying the grainy black-and-white footage – and many people dutifully missing the point.

At least, that's how it often seems to me.

In some ways, King is a victim of his own success. The controversial ideals he championed and for which he was killed – voting rights for all, access for all, liberty and justice for all – have become accepted to a degree he would have found difficult to believe.

The march he led, the one that troubled the president and riled the conservatives, has become revered as one of the signature moments of the American experience. And as a result, that speech he gave, that tough-minded recitation of American wrongs, that preacherly prophecy of American redemption, has become a Hallmark card, elevator Muzak, bland cliché.

I have a dream, the schoolchildren say. I have a dream, the newscast says. I have a dream, the people say. I have a dream. A dream. A dream.

They wax eloquent about the dreamer and the dream and, listening, you find yourself wondering if they realize that it was much more than a dream. That it was not, in other words, some airy-fairy castle in the sky to be reached by dint of hoping and wishing, but a noble place to which the nation might lift itself if people were willing to sacrifice and work. Nor did King counsel endless patience in expectation of that goal.

"We have also come to this hallowed spot," he said, standing at Lincoln's doorstep, "to remind America of the fierce urgency of now."

Over and over, he said it: "Now is the time. Now is the time."

None of which is to demean "I Have A Dream." To my mind, King's speech trails only Lincoln's address at Gettysburg on the list of the greatest public utterances in American history. But it seems to me that this most revered of speeches is also one of the least understood.

You see, King spoke to an audience that had been working for civil rights – not just dreaming. They were an audience of marchers and sit-in organizers, of boycotters and committers of civil disobedience. "I am not unmindful," he said, "that some of you have come here out of great trials and tribulations. Some of you have come fresh from narrow jail cells." Because these were people who had laid their bodies, their freedom, their time, their treasure, their very lives on the line for a cause they believed in.

I think of them when I am asked by young people, as I often am, "What can I do?" about the war in Iraq or the encroachment of civil rights, or the genocide in Darfur, or the continuing intransigence of racism. They hate these things, they say, but feel helpless to respond. "What can I do?"

It always amazes me that people who command technology their forebears could not have imagined can feel so powerless after those forebears, armed with little more than telephones and mimeograph machines, went out and changed the world.

"What can I do?"

I tell them to start by realizing that they can do. When did we become so narcotized, so benumbed and bereft, as to forget that? As Margaret Mead once said, "Never doubt that a small group of thoughtful, committed citizens can change the world. Indeed, it is the only thing that ever has."

That is one of the most enduring lessons of Martin Luther King's life and career. One hopes that lesson is not lost on all the people quoting his most famous speech today.

It is a fine and noble thing to have a dream. But having a dream is no excuse for accepting an onerous status quo and waiting passively on "someday" to make things right. A dream is not an excuse. It's a responsibility.

And now is still the time.

Sunday, March 30, 2008

MARTIN LUTHER KING'S FINAL CAMPAIGN

MEMPHIS – Forty years later, they are old men, many with bent backs and gingerly steps. And they are taciturn, strangers to an era of confession, getting in touch with your feelings.

So if you ask them what it was like, being a black man and a sanitation worker in this city in the 1950s and '60s, they will say simply that it was "tough" or it was "bad." And it will take some pushing for them to tell how you had to root through people's backyards, collecting their tree limbs and dead cats and chicken bones, because there was no such thing as a garbage can placed out by the curb. Or about white bosses who carried guns and called you "boy" and worked you 10, 12, 14 hours a day but only paid you for eight, at as little as $1.27 an hour. Or about how it was when the metal tubs you toted on your head rusted through and the garbage leaked.

"I have got maggots out of my head, what done fell in there. Sometimes, you find 'em in your collar," says Ozell Ueal, 68.

"I come home on the bus," says Elmore Nickelberry, 76, who, like Ueal, is still working, "[People] couldn't sit next to me. They say, 'You stink.' Most of the time, I'd get way in the back. Most of the time, I'd walk home."

This is a story about the Memphis sanitation workers' strike of 1968, how black men who were, in their words, treated like "beasts," like "animals," like the garbage they collected, decided enough, no more. It is a story about how a demand for higher wages and better working conditions soon turned into a demand for something more.

And it is a story about Martin Luther King's last campaign – the one that took his life, 40 years ago this Friday.

The great civil rights leader was besieged from all directions that season. Estranged from the White House for his stand against the war in Vietnam. Ridiculed by young blacks who thought him out of touch with the new militancy of guns and separatism. Tormented from within by depression, fatigue and a haunting presentiment of his own death.

That presentiment entered a sermon, "The Drum Major Instinct," he preached that February.

"Every now and then," King said quietly, "I think about my own death and I think about my own funeral." And then he told them how he wanted it to go. The person who delivered his eulogy was not to talk too long, was not to mention where King went to school, was not to bring up his Nobel Peace Prize.

"I'd like for somebody to mention that day that Martin Luther King Jr. tried to give his life serving others!" His voice was like a clap of summer thunder.

Because he saw death coming. In Memphis, it had already come.

Sanitation workers Echol Cole and Robert Walker had climbed into the back of one of the old garbage trucks to get out of the rain. But as the vehicle rumbled along, the hydraulic ram that compacted the trash started up on its own. Cole and Walker were crushed. Just like garbage.

The men had complained for years about that truck in particular, about raggedy, malfunctioning old trucks in general. The city never listened. Now it gave each man's widow one month's salary – likely less than $300 – added another $500 apiece, and called it square. Burial expenses alone were $900 a man.

"They felt a garbage man wasn't nothing," says Nickelberry. "And they figured they could treat us any way they wanted to treat us. ... Make you feel bad, 'cause you know you wasn't no garbage. You supposed to been a man."

It was, finally, one indignity too many.

At a mass meeting 10 days later, years of accumulated anger exploded. Hundreds of men, represented by no union and taking no formal vote, decided, Enough. The next day, 930 of 1,100 sanitation workers, 214 of 230 sewer and drainage workers, did not show up for work. The final act of the Civil Rights Movement had begun.

No one knew it at the time. At the time, it was just a strike, just the workers against the city, the latter represented by its new-ly elected mayor, a stubbornly intransigent cuss named Henry Loeb who drew a line in the sand early on and refused to budge, even when his advisers advised him to, even when budging seemed a matter of plain common sense. In his book, "Going Down Jericho Road: The Memphis Strike, Martin Luther King's Last Campaign," historian Michael K. Honey paints a striking pic-ture of the mayor: racist, virulently anti-union, stridently anti-communist.

"Anti-communism was just a huge layer over the white popu-lation at that time in Memphis. In the first negotiation that [union organizer] Bill Lucy had with them, Mayor Loeb brings up the communist issue and the war in Vietnam. [Lucy] was dumbfound-ed and he said, 'What did that have to do with anything?' "

The men were talking about raises. About a place to shower the filth off before they went home. About getting paid for time worked. About having a place to urinate. The mayor was talking communism.

In the minds of white conservatives, says Honey, "If you stood up for civil rights, you were automatically a communist."

So instead of moving toward settlement, the strike only grew. It drew in national union leaders trying to help the men win recognition. Then came preachers, local activists, high school kids, college students. It also attracted a militant youth group, the In-vaders. They were disciples of revolution and Black Power who scorned daily marches, sit-ins, boycotts, negotiations and other tools of working through the system. They demanded confronta-tion. They demanded disruption.

It was an unwieldy coalition of egos and agendas, answerable to no one authority. Worse, from the city's point of view, were ru-mors that the workers would call in "outside agitators." Maybe the fiery black power advocate Stokely Carmichael. Maybe Martin Luther King himself.

On February 23, the strike exploded into violence. Sanitation workers were holding one of their daily marches when police ap-peared, riding five and six to a car, brandishing rifles and using their vehicles to force the marchers, who were walking several abreast and commandeering much of the street, back toward the sidewalk. Cars brushed dangerously close. March leader the Reverend James Lawson told the marchers, "They're trying to provoke us. Keep going."

Then, say the workers (the point is still disputed, 40 years later), a police car ran over the foot of a woman marcher. And parked there. And the men had had enough. "They picked that car up," says Joe Warren, an 86-year-old retired sanitation worker, "and turned it over on its side. That's when all hell broke a loose."

Out came the nightsticks. The violence was indiscriminate: women, old men, ministers, not resisting, just standing there, didn't matter. Some policemen took off their badges as they whaled away.

"Them white police was mean with those sticks," says Warren. "They hit you with those sticks; they juke you with those sticks." Some men fought back with their protest signs.

And then, out came the Mace, sprayed into eyes and nostrils at close range. Lawson got three shots full in the face. He fell, eyes burning, throat raw, disoriented, unable to breathe. His offense: He asked the police to stop.

"When you hit Main Street," says Nickelberry, "that was just like a war zone. People marchin', people hollerin', people gettin' tear gas throwed all over them."

"I had on a long coat," says Ueal. "I was trying to cover my head up. [A police officer] went under my coat and sprayed Mace in my face, told me, 'Nigger, go jump in the river.' "

Soon after, a new slogan appeared on the signs the black men carried. Four words, but they were provocative. Four words, but in that time and place, they were incendiary. Four words, but they managed to encapsulate at long last something black men had never quite been able to get America to understand.

Four words.

I AM A MAN.

"When you been overseas fighting," says Nickelberry, who served in Korea,"... look like you should be treated as a man. But they always call you a boy. 'Come here, boy. Do this here, boy. Do that there, boy. Come in the office, boy.' You just come from a war zone and be treated, not as a soldier, not as a man, just a boy. It's real hard."

What had been a strike was now fully something more.

Standing in front of the former Lorraine Motel, the site of the Martin Luther King, Jr. assassination, a Memphis sanitation worker holds a replica of the placard used by strikers, April 4, 1968.

Martin Luther King came to town in March, invited by Lawson. He was supposed to give one speech, rally the workers, and then leave. Memphis would be just a quick diversion from planning for the Poor People's Campaign, through which he intended to lay the concerns of the American underclass – black, white, brown – before its government. But the diversion became a priority.

Because as he stood before that crowd in Mason Temple, it lifted him, brought him up from the valley of the shadow, buoyed him every time they talked back to him, shouting "Amen!" And "Yes!" King was in his glory. He told them it was a crime for the citizens of a wealthy nation to subsist on starvation wages. He told them America would go to hell for failing its humblest citizens. He told them to stand together.

And then he told them what he had not meant to tell them, what came to him unplanned in that moment of inspiration and heat. They should "escalate the struggle." They should mobilize a work stoppage. Not only the sanitation men, but the teachers, the students, the clerks, the clerics, the maids, the mechanics.

They should shut Memphis down.

A march was set. And King, having floated the idea, had little choice but to lead it.

"King," says historian Honey, "was always a strong supporter of the unions, from his teenager years when he had summer jobs and saw how the workers were treated when they didn't have unions – including the white workers." He had spent years trying to get the AFL-CIO to "get off this Cold War bandwagon" and join organized labor in common cause with the civil rights movement. So Memphis seemed tailor-made for him.

But Memphis had become poisonous and chaotic. There was garbage in the streets, sit-ins at City Hall, mass arrests. High school students picketed downtown. Rocks were thrown through the windows of businesses owned by Mayor Loeb. There were trash fires. Gunfire.

Sanitation worker Ben Jones, 71, says, "I would tell my wife, when I leave home, 'I might be back and I might not.' Just lettin' her know, don't keep your hopes up."

You had to accept the reality of your own death, they say. Make your peace with it. "I didn't care," says Warren. "And don't care now." His voice breaks and tears fall. "We worked hard," he gasps. "Some hard times."

The march was a disaster. Unlike demonstrators in the early days of the struggle, these had not been drilled in the discipline and tactics of nonviolent protest. They were excited and unruly and when King arrived, they pushed and shoved, trying to get near him. "The people were trampling over my feet," recalled King's friend and confidant the late Reverend Ralph Abernathy, "crowding over me. The atmosphere was just wrong."

The march stepped off with King and his ministerial allies in the lead, flanked by sanitation workers. But young people soon elbowed their way to the front, shoving the sanitation workers aside. And then, from behind, came the sound of shattering glass. Members of the Invaders had taken bricks and pipes to storefront windows, screaming "Black Power!"

The nation's premiere pacifist found himself at the head of a mob. He would not, he said, lead a violent march. Fearful for his safety, his men swept him away.

Behind them, police gassed and clubbed looters and bystanders alike. A black boy was seen stomping a white department store mannequin. "I wish this was a real live one," he cried. A lone police officer surrounded by a menacing black mob was rescued by two black women in a car. An apparently unarmed black boy was shot to death at close range by police. Finally, National Guardsmen sealed off the black neighborhoods.

The media response was scathing. King, they said, had stirred up trouble and then run away. Even those sympathetic to King said the violence had damaged his credibility.

And so he had to return, to lead a new march, to prove nonviolence was still a viable tool of social change. "Either the movement lives or dies in Memphis," he said.

On April 3, he returned to a city under storm watch. The skies were menacing, the winds, punishing. Exhausted, King begged off speaking at the rally planned for that night and sent Abernathy in his place. He settled down to bed.

But Abernathy called. The hall was packed. The people wanted him, would accept no one else. So King dressed and went out into the storm.

He spoke to them without notes as the wind howled and the rain drummed down. There was a valedictory quality to it as King recounted the triumphs and tragedies of the 13-year civil rights movement. He linked the sanitation workers' plight to that of the beaten and robbed man in the Bible who is rescued by the Good Samaritan.

Then, the presentiment touched him and he spoke, one last time, of his own death. "Like anybody, I would like to live a long life," he said. "Longevity has its place. But I'm not concerned about that now. I just want to do God's will. And He's allowed me to go up to the mountain. And I've looked over and I've seen" – singing the word – "the Promised Land. I may not get there with you, but I want you to know tonight that we as a people will get to the Promised Land."

A spirit of defiance seemed to seize him now and he roared in the face of his own demise. "So I'm happy tonight," he cried. "I'm not worried about anything! I'm not fearing any man! Mine eyes have seen the glory of the coming of the Lord!"

It came the very next evening. Standing on the balcony of the Lorraine Motel, bantering with his men in the parking lot below, Martin Luther King was shot to death by a sniper.

And we lost, says Honey, the one man who was able to speak to rabbis and working men and preachers and militants alike, "to communicate across almost all the barriers and boundaries of the 1960s."

"I was shocked," says Nickelberry. "I was mad. It hurt me. Even hurt me now, just to think about it and talk about it."

The strike was settled on April 16. The city recognized the union. The workers got a raise of 10 cents an hour, with another nickel an hour hike to take effect in September. The city agreed to make promotions on the basis of seniority and competence – not race. The men also won – this had been a key sticking point – the right to have union dues automatically deducted from their paychecks.

And 40 years later, you arrive in an era where a black man is running for president and, for all the myriad issues of race and identity with which he is forced to grapple, he is not required to prove himself a man. His manhood is a given. The men who helped make that possible are aged and dying and largely forgotten. And feeling, some of them say, cheated.

They say the union they won is not strong and receives little support from younger workers. The job benefits aren't great, either. Ben Jones says he's still working at 71 because he needs to pay off his house; when he retires, his only income will be from Social Security. Sanitation workers have no pension.

Nor did racism disappear. "Some of 'em still call you boy," says Nickelberry. "In some of 'ems eyes, you ain't nothin' but a boy. Still a boy."

But there is, he says, a difference: You don't have to take it anymore. "I tell 'em, 'I'm 76 years old. I'm old enough for your daddy. I ain't no boy. I am a man.' "

Sunday, January 16, 2011

DOING BETTER BY OUR MOST VULNERABLE

Monday we celebrate Martin Luther King Day for the 25th time. And for the 25th time we will seek to answer the question that has bedeviled this observation from the beginning: How shall we observe this day?

We know what to do with other holidays. On Christmas, we unwrap gifts and go to grandma's house. On Thanksgiving we eat and watch football. On Independence Day we barbecue and wait for the fireworks.

King Day, thus far, lacks a defining tradition. This is not to say people have not evolved ways of celebrating it. There are interfaith breakfasts, speeches, parades and recitals. But there is not, as of yet, that one or two things we do that emblematize this day.

A good deal of that failing likely owes to the relative newness of the holiday. It has not yet had time to find its traditions.

But it can also be argued that at least some of the failing owes to a certain vagueness of comprehension. Ask the average high school student to explain the significance of King's life and ideals, and brace for disappointment.

Marc de Lacoste, who teaches U.S. and world history at Hialeah High, says that while his advanced kids would probably know a little more about King, most students would be in the dark. "They know generally about Martin Luther King, but beyond that, if you ask them any specific questions, even years of civil rights bills or what the civil rights years were even about, they would be totally lost."

He says some kids are surprised at how relatively recent those years are. Some think it happened at the turn of the last century.

Julie Biancardi, assistant principal at Cooper City High, sees much the same thing. "The kids today can't believe that this happened," she says. "They cannot believe people ever had to go through this. 'Why, why, how come, how come?' "

Not to pick on the kids. One suspects their elders would do but marginally better if asked to assess the significance of King. They might be aware that he used non-violent civil disobedience to effect social change, but the fullness of that change and the driving vision behind it would be another story.

Consider Glenn Beck last year, fulminating against those who criticized him for attempting to claim King's movement in the name of the conservatives who tormented King till the last day of his life. When Al Sharpton observed that issues of economic injustice loomed large in King's vision, Beck pitched a fit, accusing him of perverting and distorting King's dream.

He thereby proved that Sharpton had read what King had to say while he, Glenn Beck, had not.

It frustrates Lerone Bennett, Jr. The venerable historian, author of "Before the Mayflower: A History of Black America," says King lives on the top tier of American heroes with Washington, Jefferson and Lincoln. But the King holiday gets "bogged down" in soundbites of I Have A Dream, "and gives no sense of the greatness of the man and the majesty of the man and the fundamental changes he demanded."

For Bennett, King's last crusade, which he died trying to fulfill, is symbolic of his broader vision: The Poor People's Campaign was designed to move the struggle for equality beyond race to the common ground of class.

"He believed, and he said as much almost, that one demonstration after another will not solve this problem. You must have a consistent structural approach to deal with the structural problems. One of the major structural problems is the continued inequality ... between poor Americans and other Americans. His message to us – and I hope somebody this January will hear it now, especially – is that we need a Poor People's March. We need poor people to stop begging and start organizing. Black people, white people, Hispanic Americans, we need poor people to go to Washington" he says, and demand "a level playing field."

Michael K. Honey, editor of "All Labor Has Dignity," a collection of King's speeches on labor issues, notes that while he deplored communism for its totalitarian bent, King longed for some modified form of socialism. "King was really impacted when he went to get the Nobel Prize," says Honey, "and he talked about how Norway and Sweden and Scandinavian countries didn't have homeless people or poor people on the streets. They were capitalist countries, but they also had this socialist democratic framework. He was that kind of socialist."

Doubtless, that will come as a jarring surprise to some people (paging Glenn Beck) who have grown comfortable with an image of King that is static and safe, unthreatening of the status quo, frozen forever at the Lincoln Memorial saying, "I have a dream."

But the same King who said that once said this: "I am now convinced that ... the solution to poverty is to abolish it directly by a now widely-discussed measure: the guaranteed income."

And the same King who spoke of color of skin and content of character also said this:

"It is a cruel jest to say to a bootless man that he should lift himself up by his own bootstraps. It is even worse to tell a man to lift himself up by his own bootstraps when somebody is standing on the boot."

And the same King who declared he had been to the mountaintop also declared:

"If we assume that life is worth living and that man has a right to survive, then we must find an alternative to war. In a day when vehicles hurtle through outer space and guided ballistic missiles carve highways of death through the stratosphere, no nation can claim victory in a war."

The point being that King did not just fight for racial equality. He fought for labor rights. He fought against economic exploitation. He fought for fair housing. He fought for better schools. He fought against war.

The common denominator in all that he fought for was simply a demand that America do better by its most vulnerable: the poor, the racial minorities, the unhoused, the uneducated, the left out, left behind and forgotten, the ones the Bible calls "the least of these."

King, says Bennett, "talked about a dream that has never existed in this country. George Washington didn't believe in that dream. Thomas Jefferson didn't believe in that dream. Abraham Lincoln didn't believe in that dream."

But King did. So for those who share that belief, perhaps it is not all that hard to find a way to mark his day. Maybe it ought to be a day for committing acts of faith, seeking some small way, some big way, to make a difference for the least of these. Why not do that on Martin Luther King Day?

And then, the next day, do it again.

Chapter 3

RACE RELATIONS

Sunday, September 23, 2012

HATE IS STILL WITH US

This is for Vanessa in South Florida.

She emailed me a few days ago after spotting a bumper sticker that read: 2012 Don't Re-Nig. "Honestly," she wrote, "I don't know how to process my outrage, so I'm handing it off to you. I know that President Obama's race has always been an issue to many people, and perhaps I live a relatively sheltered life in Democratic-leaning Broward County, but I'm still stunned by the sentiment. I'm even more stunned, naive though that may be, by the fact that some people believe it's appropriate to flaunt that sentiment – and that it's not a source of shame."

Vanessa, I'm afraid I'm not nearly as shocked as you. After all, the sentiment that bumper sticker expresses has been part of the Obama narrative since before he took office.

Some of us grapple with a sense of racial and cultural dislocation, the jolting sensation in a changing nation, that their prerogatives as white people, assumptions so ingrained as to have never previously required the slightest thought, are now in question. They want "their" country back. As the great satirist Randy Newman sings in a new ballad:

"I'm dreaming of a white president

Just like the ones we've always had

A real live white man who knows the score

How to handle money or start a war."

But for others of us, it's not anything so nuanced as a sense of dislocation – just the same old hate as always.

Either way, the world has changed enough that one cannot openly express such things. So instead, it gets hidden in oblique language, false controversies and putative "jokes."

But Vanessa – when one in four Americans thinks there's some mystery over the president's birthplace, while Mitt Romney (son of a man born in Mexico) and John McCain (born in the Panama Canal Zone) face no such scrutiny; when tea partiers denounce health care reform as "reparations;" when Representative Lynn Westmoreland calls Obama "uppity," then-Representative Geoff Davis calls him "boy" and Representative Joe Wilson yells out, "You lie!" during a presidential speech; when Rush Limbaugh says Obama's election means it's open season on white kids; when Obama is called a terrorist, a "food stamp president" and a "Chicago thug" – why should "Don't Re-Nig" come as a surprise? It's just the next logical step.

One cannot openly express one's hate – right up till the day one can. Though even then, one may have to delude oneself.

When he was asked about that bumper sticker, Billy Smith of Ludowici, Georgia, who manufactured it with his wife Paula told a reporter: "We didn't mean it in a racist way." The driver of that car would likely have said the same.

But they do not lie for our benefit. They lie to conscience – and to self.

So this is the paradigm of our age – self-delusion on the one hand, a guy trying to govern on the other, while hemmed in by race, defined in crude, stereotypical imagery, yet unable to fight it, talk about it, or even admit he sees it, for fear of compromising his effectiveness, being dismissed as, God forbid – "an angry black man."

Yet we hope our way forward anyhow.

There hangs in the White House this photo of the president bowing to allow a little black boy to touch his head. The 5-year-old, his brother and his parents were in the Oval Office with Obama and the boy had a question. "I want to know if my hair is just like yours," he said, so softly Obama had to ask him to repeat himself. He did, and Obama invited him to see for himself. The boy hesitated.

"Touch it, dude!" the president said.

The boy did. "So, what do you think?" asked Obama.

"Yes," said the boy, "it does feel the same.

That child's name is Jacob.

And Vanessa, while some of us are dreaming of a white president, well ... it's likely Jacob has some new dreams of his own.

STEREOTYPING

Saturday, January 20, 1996

DEFINITION DISTORTED

This is a true story.

Man calls my house, says he's doing a public opinion survey. He asks me some questions, I give him some answers. At the end, he needs some personal information.

Age? he asks. I give him my age.

Education? Yes, I have some of that.

Race? I say, "Black."

He laughs. Actually laughs and says, "Good one. So I put you down as white, right?"

"No," I say, "I'm black."

"Wow," he says, surprised, "you don't sound black."

Today, we will discuss What Black Is, a discussion that will be complicated by the fact that many people already think they know. They'll say black is ... that urban dysfunction thing, that certain bad-itude, a walk, a talk, a coolness, a coldness.

Call it ghetto chic. It's all the rage, animating everything from movies to TV commercials to high fashion. And now it's even being lampooned with devastating effectiveness in a rude, crude new movie called – deep breath, everybody – "Don't Be a Menace to South Central While Drinking Your Juice in the Hood." Menace is primo cinema silliness in the tradition of "Naked Gun," except with beepers, bad language, 40-ounce malt liquor bottles and guns.

The movie is the proverbial laugh riot. But on some level, it also made me sad knowing that for some people this is What Black Is.

Now, "some people" could easily refer to bigots, mass media, pop culture or telephone pollsters. Troublingly, "some people" also means some blacks.

For example: Once upon a time, some blacks – OK, virtually all blacks – rejoiced in the educational achievement and communicative skills of their own. But in recent years, those things have become despised by some blacks. More to the point, they have "become white."

Now, speaking mainstream English is derided by some as "talking white;" displaying any affinity for learning is slammed as "acting white." Hearing this, you might note the obvious: Anyone who thinks linguistic or intellectual excellence are provincially "white" has never heard of Maya Angelou and Malcolm X. Or, for that matter, Pauly Shore and Roseanne.

But there is a deeper dynamic at work here: Somehow, some blacks have come to accept ghetto chic – or, less glibly, urban dysfunction – as the definitive black experience. People say "black" all the time when what they really mean is "poor," "ignorant," "ill-spoken" or "crime-prone." That those terms are not interchangeable with black is an elemental truth and yet, one that somehow slips by some of us. Especially some blacks, who wear those unnatural afflictions like a badge of backward honor as if they somehow make one's blackness more "authentic."

I like to think the point "Menace" makes, albeit subversively, is that we have lost sight of What Black Is. And if here you expect me to recall proud history or quote the triumphs of Joe Louis, Sojourner Truth and Kunta Kinte ... sorry, no.

The point is that black is not any one of them, but the sum of them: an extraordinarily ferocious will, blessedly, cussedly stubborn in its refusal to stop or settle ... or die.

That's how the slave faced another awful dawn. That's how the sharecropper stood up when a nation sought to beat him down. That's what the gospel song means when it says, "My soul looked back and wondered how I got over." And that's What Black Is. Holding on. Getting over.

As the old ones disconnect from the young ones, these are truths we stand to lose. Those who know don't tell and those who don't know won't listen, anyway. Instead, they make it up as they go along, filling the blanks with guns and ignorance and other articles of failure. And calling it black.

Watching "Menace," I laughed out loud, but laughter could not drown a loud whisper that rattled up from the silence of the subtext. A whisper of sorrow that, collectively, we have failed to hold, cherish and teach What Black Is.

And, What Black Is Not.

Monday, September 13, 2004

IS THAT STRANGE RUMOR WE HEARD TRUE?

So why is it that so many gay men seem to speak with a lisp?

While you pick up your jaw, let me appease the gods of full disclosure.

I'm writing about a new book by Phillip J. Milano. Though I have no connection with this one, I did write the foreword for Milano's last book. For this, I was paid zip dollars and zero cents. Frankly, I'd have written it for half as much.

So you may draw your own conclusions about my objectivity or lack of same when I say that, from a garage office in his home near Jacksonville, Milano, a newspaper editor, is quietly revolutionizing cross-cultural communication.

Or, to put it another way: Does having thicker lips make black people better kissers?

You'll find lots of questions such as that in the aforementioned book, "I Can't Believe You Asked That!" It's a compilation of the best postings from Y? The National Forum on People's Differences, a website (www.yforum.com) that Milano founded seven years ago.

The site was built on the idea that we are all curious about those people over there who are not like us – because of race, religion, gender, class, sexuality or culture. And it's not necessarily the hot-button issues such as gay marriage and affirmative action we want to ask about.

No, we tend to wonder about smaller things such as why do they dress that way, how do they get their hair like that, and is that strange rumor we heard about them really true. But how to ask such questions without being rude, crude or even sued?

Enter yforum, an ongoing, online exchange that offers a safe place to ask unaskable, even hurtful, questions about communities other than your own. And to get candid answers from members of those self-same communities. In other words, a place to talk.

Seven years, more than 10 million hits and 50,000 postings later, yforum has been recommended and praised by everyone from The New York Times to The Guardian of London to The Helsinki News.

Milano says that the early reviews were less auspicious. "Pathetic liberal," somebody called him. "Dumb-ass" white guy, said somebody else.

Actually, Milano was just a man who had twigged to an inherent flaw of political correctness – meaning its tendency to stifle the communication it purports to enhance, making people so nervous about saying the wrong thing that they end up saying nothing.

Indeed, shutting up must sometimes seem like a smart move in a nation where the victim hat is always being passed around and people seldom miss an excuse to declare themselves mortally affronted. You learn to keep questions to yourself; cultural difference becomes something that polite people do not discuss or even acknowledge – which leads to a chain of events as predictable as a chemical reaction: silence to ignorance to prejudice to hate to heaven knows.

Milano believes that people are beginning to understand that. When he talks about yforum in public, he says, people seem more engaged than they once did. He thinks that a terrorist atrocity rooted in a culture that many of us find alien may have been a catalyst to encourage us to look beyond labels. As he sees it, we may be ready to break down "the last barrier to improved race and cultural relations: actually talking to one another."

And who knows? If we manage to demystify all the differences, real and perceived, we might be left with fewer things to argue about. Maybe we would just keep talking.

As dreams go, it's a noble one.

By the way, and not to keep you hanging: The thing about gay men lisping was called both an unfounded stereotype and a campy act of self-parody by gay men who answered the question. And there seemed to be a narrow consensus that full lips are best for kissing.

Next question: Do white people have a natural inclination toward sexual perversion?

I'll let you look that one up for yourself.

HATE

Saturday, June 3, 1995

TIME TO PUT ASIDE THE BLOODIED N-WORD

This is an open letter to young black America.

People are asking me about you again. They're writing and calling, challenging me to explain why you sometimes call each other "nigger," then profess anger and hurt when a white person uses the same word.

They think you're hypocritical. They think you're hypersensitive. They think you should be more like the Italian guy who'll let a friend get away with the word "wop" or the Irish person who, in the spirit of good fun, now and then tolerates being called a "mick."

They think you should emulate those people in other ways, too: Stop whining about the names you are called and the mistreatment you have received. Life here has been no picnic for them, either. They worked, they educated themselves, they moved ahead and assimilated. Why can't you?

But you aren't Irish or Italian, are you? You're African. Skin the color of creamless coffee. Or pecan shell. Or sandy shore. Skin that makes you stand out in a crowd of Europeans like "a fly in the buttermilk," as the old folks used to say.

That's why your forebears and mine were chosen to bear the burden of slavery – the fact that it was beyond their ability to run off and blend in. And there you have the defining difference, the thing that makes our experience unique. With the possible exception of the original tenants of this land, no group of Americans – not Irish, Italian, Chinese, woman nor gay – ever suffered on these shores as we did.

Ten million to 20 million kidnapped from the bosom of home. Half again that many left dead by the horrors of the Middle Passage. Centuries of enslavement, rape, torture, disenfranchisement, theft, poverty, ignorance, murder and hate. And then someone asks in well-meaning innocence why we can't be more like the Irish.

Makes we want to holler.

That's why you call yourself "nigger" sometimes, I know.

Oppression long ago taught us how to build a mansion from a stack of debris, weave a symphony from a moan of pain. Look at the record. Given hog entrails, we made chit'lins. Given agony, we invented the blues. Given the bruising hardness of city streets, we created cool.

And given "nigger," a word white men meant as an emblem of our stupidity, meanness and filth, we made a multipurpose word useful in the expression of everything from anger and humor to sarcasm and fraternity. We made it our word. And the whole weight of history bars white people from using it the way we do – or even understanding it the way we do.

But here's my problem: unlike chit'lins, unlike cool and unlike the blues, this gift of oppression always took from us more than it gave. Meaning that if there's a certain sense of in-group smugness in greeting your brother as a "nigger," there is also, unspoken between the consonants, an admission that the white man was right when he said we were lower and lesser.

That word is drenched with four centuries of blood and tears. It hates us, even when it issues from our own lips.

And it is time we got beyond self-loathing.

I know what "Action News" says about you. I know how police act like you're a crime waiting to happen. I know the advice the

crack man gives, know the terrible things family and friends sometimes say because they don't know better and they don't know you.

Love yourself anyway. Love yourself past the hateful words
and the hurtful lies. Love yourself over the empty pockets of poverty and the bare walls of spirit. Love yourself through the
narrowness of days and the meanness of nights.

Love yourself with a fierceness and an urgency, and I promise
that it will lead you up to this truth: You are the flower of 400
years. You are the dream a slave once had.

And there is no such thing as a nigger.

There never was.

Monday, December 4, 2006

BY ANY SPELLING IT'S STILL HATEFUL

The N-word has had few friends better than comedian Paul
Mooney.

Put aside that the word was long a staple of his act. Put aside
the promotional pamphlet he once sent out that screamed the
word in big, fat type. Consider instead what he told anyone who
argued that blacks should stop using the word. He replied that he
said it a hundred times every morning. "It keeps my teeth white."

Last week, the selfsame Paul Mooney joined the Reverend
Jesse Jackson and California Representative Maxine Waters in a
news conference asking black folks to stop using the N-word. In
other news, there are unconfirmed reports of pigs flying above
Times Square.

Mooney says he was "cured" of his N-word addiction by Michael Richards' infamous meltdown last month at the Laugh
Factory. I tend to think he's not the only one. From strangers
online to my neighbor down the street, everywhere I turn lately, I
find black folk debating the stubborn insistence some of us have
on using this word.

Which leaves me as much vexed as pleased. More power to
them for belatedly getting religion. Still, are you telling me that
nearly 20 years after hip-hop made that word unavoidable, it takes
some white TV actor losing his mind to make black folks see what
should have been obvious all along?

I mean, what do we learn from Richards' rant that we should not have known already from Snoop Dogg or Ice Cube? That the word is ugly? That it is hateful? That it demeans, denigrates, diminishes and denies? Anyone with the barest historical memory already knew these things. So where was black outrage when black rappers began putting that word into the minds and mouths of black children? When we – African Americans – began hating ourselves to a beat?

And if I hear one more Negro offer a pseudo-intellectual justification for that self-loathing, I will not be responsible for my actions afterward. Don't give me the "it means something different because we spell it with an 'a' on the end" speech. Spare me the "it doesn't mean black, it means a bad person of any race" load of bull.

And for mercy sake, don't subject me to the addled argument proffered by John Ridley in December's Esquire. He says that, as whites feel no particular solidarity with their impoverished racial brethren in Appalachia, it is time for "ascended blacks" to bid farewell to, as he puts it, "niggers."

Don't tell me any of that, because it quails in the face of historical fact. We are talking about the word that was used as Gus Clarke's back was split open with a whip and salt was rubbed into the wounds. The word that was used when Mary Turner's baby was cut from her womb with a knife and stomped to death in its birth cries. The word that was used when James Byrd was tied to the back of a pickup truck and dragged until his body was torn to pieces.

To the people who did these things, it did not matter how it was spelled. They knew precisely what race they were referring to. And they saw no difference between "ascended blacks" and any other kind. Nor should that last surprise us. In the calculus of race, I am not my brother's keeper. I am my brother. Individuality is the first casualty of bigotry.

Black people, like other Americans, tend to flee from the burdens and demands of history. History, ours especially, hurts too much.

But what Michael Richards taught, and what blacks may be learning belatedly, is that history doesn't care. Not about your feelings, not about your rationalizations, not about your subtleties of spelling.

Because they don't realize that, some blacks, Paul Mooney prominent among them, seem surprised to learn that this word still hates us. That it always has and always will.

And if Richards is the catalyst that finally forces them to understand this, there's only one thing I can say to him:

Thank you.

Wednesday, March 25, 2009

IS THERE NO 'CURE' FOR A NATION'S HATE?

There are now 926 hate groups in this country.

Take a second and consider that number. It represents an increase of more than 50 percent since 2000. And by "hate groups," I don't mean guys in their bathrobes who go online and pretend their followers are legion. No, I mean actual Klan cells, Neo-Nazi sects, gay-bashing "churches," cliques of black separatists, white nationalists, nativists, racist skinheads and other merchants of venom who meet, plot and recruit in all 48 contiguous states (Alaska and Hawaii have no known hate groups). Nine hundred twenty-six of them. The number is a record.

We learn all this from the Southern Poverty Law Center (splcenter.org) in Montgomery, Alabama, which has, since its founding in 1971, become a leading authority on the business of hate. According to the latest issue of Intelligence Report, the SPLC's quarterly magazine, that business is booming.

And maybe you wonder how this can be. How can hate enjoy such phenomenal growth in a nation where a Jew serves as senator from Connecticut, a Muslim serves as representative from Minnesota, a Hispanic is governor of New Mexico and a black man is president?

The answer is that we are a nation where a Jew serves as senator from Connecticut, a Muslim serves as representative from Minnesota, a Hispanic is governor of New Mexico and a black man is president. Because if those things strike you as signs of progress, well, they are signs of apocalypse to those who believe only white, male Christians are fit to lead.

But that's not the only reason for the increase. SPLC also cites the debate over illegal immigration that has dominated much of this decade. Though former President George W. Bush offered thoughtful, moderate leadership on the issue, he was drowned out by demagogic extremists competing to see which could most effectively scapegoat undocumented workers. They, too, bear responsibility here.

Finally, there is the economy. When things get tough, people become more receptive to the idea that their miseries are all the fault of some alien other. So the stock market, too, is implicated. Hate rises when the Dow falls.

I imagine the SPLC findings land like cold water in the faces of those who took Barack Obama's ascension to the presidency as proof that the nation was finally cured of the sickness of hate. The truth, I'm afraid, is more nuanced than that.

Maybe it helps to think in terms of alcoholism, a disease that can, with treatment, be contained, controlled, put into remission – but never cured. Even when you've got years of sobriety under your belt, the germ of it lurks in your bloodstream. Which is why alcoholics do not call themselves cured. Rather, they say they are recovering.

Hate is something like that, a fact some of us have never quite understood. Such folks are convinced there is a goal line out there somewhere which, once crossed, will allow the nation to declare itself cured. And once cured, we'll never have to grapple with hatred again.

But it doesn't work that way.

In a nation so deeply riven by culture, race and religion, there is always a temptation to hate somebody, to blame some group of others for the job you lost, the crime committed against you, the fear and uncertainty you feel. There is a simplicity and a seductiveness to it that are all too easily mistaken for righteousness.

So there is no "cure" for a nation's hate. There is only an ongoing process of getting better, not unlike the alcoholic who must daily earn his sobriety anew. This explosion of hate is a reminder of what happens when we forget that, when we are undeservedly sanguine about how enlightened we've become.

It is said that eternal vigilance is the price of freedom. Well, that's the going rate for tolerance, too.

FACTS CAN GET IN THE WAY OF YOUR WORLD VIEW

I got an email the other day that depressed me.

It concerned a piece I recently did that mentioned Henry Johnson, who was awarded the French Croix de Guerre in World War I for singlehandedly fighting off a company of Germans (some accounts say there were 14, some say almost 30, the ones I find most authoritative say there were about two dozen) who threatened to overrun his post. Johnson managed this despite the fact that he was only 5-4 and 130 pounds, despite the fact that his gun had jammed, despite the fact that he was wounded 21 times.

My mention of Johnson's heroics drew a rebuke from a fellow named Ken Thompson, which I quote verbatim and in its entirety:

"Hate to tell you that blacks were not allowed into combat in-tell 1947, that fact. World War II ended in 1945. So all that feel good, one black man killing two dozen Nazi, is just that, PC bull."

In response, my assistant, Judi Smith, sent Mr. Thompson proof of Johnson's heroics: a link to his page on the website of Arlington National Cemetery. She thought this settled the matter.

Thompson's reply? "There is no race on headstones and they didn't come up with the story in tell 2002."

Judi: "I guess you can choose to believe Arlington National Cemetery or not."

Thompson: "It is what it is, you don't believe either ..."

At this point, Judi forwarded me their correspondence, along with a despairing note. She is probably somewhere drinking right now.

You see, like me, she can remember a time when facts settled arguments. This is back before everything became a partisan shouting match, back before it was permissible to ignore or deride as "biased" anything that didn't support your worldview.

If you and I had an argument and I produced facts from an authoritative source to back me up, you couldn't just blow that off. You might try to undermine my facts, might counter with facts of your own, but you couldn't just pretend my facts had no weight or meaning.

But that's the intellectual state of the union these days, as evidenced by all the people who still don't believe the president was born in Hawaii or that the planet is warming. And by Mr. Thompson, who doesn't believe Henry Johnson did what he did.

I could send him more proof, I suppose. Johnson is lauded in history books ("Before The Mayflower" by Lerone Bennett, Jr., "The Dictionary of American Negro Biography" by Rayford Logan and Michael Winston) and in contemporaneous accounts (The Saturday Evening Post, the New York Times). I could also point out that blacks have fought in every war in American history, though before Harry Truman desegregated the military in 1948, they did so in Jim Crow units. Also, there were no Nazis in World War I.

But those are facts, and the whole point here is that facts no longer mean what they once did. I suppose I could also ignore him. But you see, Ken Thompson is not just some isolated eccentric. No, he is the Zeitgeist personified.

To listen to talk radio, to watch TV pundits, to read a newspaper's online message board, is to realize that increasingly, we are a people estranged from critical thinking, divorced from logic, alienated from even objective truth. We admit no ideas that do not confirm us, hear no voices that do not echo us, sift out all information that does not validate what we wish to believe.

I submit that any people thus handicapped sow the seeds of their own decline; they respond to the world as they wish it were rather to the world as it is.

That's the story of the Iraq War.

But objective reality does not change because you refuse to accept it. The fact that you refuse to acknowledge a wall does not change the fact that it's a wall.

And you shouldn't have to hit it to find that out.

Sunday, December 1, 2013

BURY THE 'N-WORD'

The N-word again. Of course.

Six years after the NAACP staged its symbolic burial, that word has proven rumors of its demise greatly exaggerated.

In just the last few weeks we've had the following: Richie Incognito, a white player for the Miami Dolphins, tags a black teammate, Jonathan Martin, with that epithet and black players defend the white guy because he's an "honorary" brother; Matt Barnes of the Los Angeles Clippers tweets the word in criticizing his teammates and says people who have a problem with that should "get used to it;" Trent Williams, a black player for Washington, D.C.'s professional football team (speaking of racial slurs) is accused of using the word against Roy Ellison, a black referee, a charge Williams denies.

Then it gets worse. The mushrooming controversies prompt two African-American NBA analysts, Charles Barkley and Michael Wilbon, to defend their usage of the N-word. And it's not just the jockocracy, either. Last week in The New York Times, celebrated social critic Ta-Nehisi Coates, who is African American, made the old "context" argument; i.e., it's OK if we say it, but it's not OK if you say it. In defending the N-word as an "in-word" Coates noted how some women will jokingly call other women by a misogynistic term or some gay people will laughingly use a homophobic slur in talking with or about one another.

Some of us would say that's not such a good look, either. Some of us think there is cause for dismay when women, gay people or any put-upon people adopt the terminology of their oppressors as self-definition.

But the larger point is this: so what? Like it or not, the N-word is not like the words used to denigrate women and gay people or, for that matter, Italian, Irish or Jewish people, simply because the experiences those peoples endured in this country do not compare with those of African Americans.

The N-word is unique. It was present at the act of mass kidnap that created "black America," it drove the ship to get here, signed the contracts at flesh auctions on Southern ports as mother was torn from child, love from love and self from self. It had a front row center seat for the acts of blood, rape, castration, exclusion and psychological destruction by which the created people was kept down and in its place. The whole weight of our history dictates that word cannot be used except as an expression of contempt for African Americans. The only difference when a Matt Barnes or Ta-Nehisi Coates uses it is that the contempt is black on black.

"Context?" That argument grows more threadbare every time it's made. It may also be growing less effective in cowing white people of good will. As reporter Richard Prince recently noted in his online "Journalisms" column, a number of white journalists have refused to be silenced on this. That includes Mike Wise of the Washington Post who wrote a brave piece confronting those who would deny him the right to be concerned because of his race.

"That doesn't work for me," he said. "I deserve a seat at this table. This is about the world my 3-year-old is going to live in." Indeed, it is about the world all our children will inherit. African Americans are not walled off from that world, cannot commit this sin of self-denigration in our little corner of existence and command everyone else to ignore it or pretend it doesn't matter.

Our stubborn insistence otherwise speaks volumes. As does the fact that some so determinedly defend the indefensible. How can we require others to respect us when this word suggests we don't respect ourselves?

So burying the N-word, well-intentioned, as it was, turns out to have been fruitless. Something in some of us seems to need this word. And to agree with it.

Let us find a way to bury that instead.

Wednesday, June 24, 2015

CHARLESTON MASSACRE

This is for Elisabeth Hasselbeck of "Fox & Friends," who described last Thursday's act of white extremist terrorism at Emanuel AME church in Charleston as an "attack on faith."

It's for Rick Perry, who said maybe the shooting happened because of prescription drugs. It's for Jeb Bush, who said, "I don't know what was on the mind" of the killer. It's for Governor Nikki Haley, who said, "We'll never understand what motivates" a crime like this. It's for Glenn Beck, who said, "I don't know why this shooter shot people. He might shoot people because he's a racist. He might have shot people because he's an anarchist. He might have shot people because he hates Christians."

This is also for the reader who called the tragedy a "hoax" perpetrated by the White House to promote racial hatred and gun control, and for the one who said, "Charleston was not a hate crime." Finally, it's for any and everyone who responded to the massacre by chanting, tweeting or saying, "All lives matter."

For all of you, a simple question: What the hell is wrong with you people? Why is it so hard for you to call racism racism?

It is not news that some people go to extraordinary lengths to avoid conceding that America remains a nation stained by racial discrimination. Bring them a hundred testimonies illustrating it and they are unmoved. Bring them a thousand studies quantifying it and they say that numbers lie. They deny self-evident truth because otherwise, they must concede racism did not, in fact, end 50 years ago, and they are heavily invested in that fiction.

Still, it is breathtaking and heartbreaking to learn that this recalcitrance holds firm even in the face of so blatant a crime. Nine people dead following an attack upon a storied African-American church. The alleged killer: Dylann Roof, a 21-year old dropout with a Moe Howard haircut whose racist motivations were pretty clear to authorities from the beginning and have only become clearer since.

He said he wanted to shoot black people. You don't get plainer than that.

Yet, even in the face of this utter lack of mystery, some of us professed confusion about the killer's motives.

An "attack on faith?" Only the "War on Christmas" delusions and anti-gay fixations of Fox could make this about that.

"All lives matter?" Of course they do. But what is it about the specificity of declaring "Black Lives Matter" that some people object to? What is it they find problematic about acknowledging that black lives in particular are under siege in this country? It certainly wasn't "all lives" Roof sought to snuff out when he entered that church.

And Glenn Beck's professed confusion about the shooter's motive? It is simply bizarre that a man who once famously dubbed President Obama "a racist" based on no evidence beyond the voices in his head has such difficulty being that definitive about a white man who drove 100 miles to shoot up a black church.

A few days ago, a Toronto Star reporter tweeted video of a mostly-white crowd that marched through Charleston chanting "Black Lives Matter." God, but that was a welcome sight – ice cold lemonade on the hottest day in August. It was a stirring, needed reminder that compassion has no color.

All this obfuscation and pretend confusion, on the other hand, is a less welcome reminder that, for all the undeniable progress we have made in matters of race, there remain among us not simply moral cowards, but far too many moral cripples hobbling about on stumps of decency and crutches of denialism.

Last week, nine people were slaughtered in a house of God for no other reason than that they were there, and they were black. It is a sad and simple truth that some of us, for some reason, have not the guts to say.

For that, they should be profoundly ashamed.

RACIAL PROFILING

Friday, April 7, 2006

RACE ENTERS AND STUPID IS SELDOM FAR BEHIND

Race makes people stupid.

You wouldn't think we'd need a fresh illustration of that truism, but here it is, anyway, needed or not. For which we can thank the Democratic representative from the 4th District of Georgia.

If you haven't heard, well, I'm sorry your TV blew up and your hard drive crashed. And that your telephone is on the fritz and you don't get out much. And that your paperboy was eaten by wolves.

Those of us who are still connected to the outside world know all about Cynthia McKinney's confrontation last week with a Capitol Hill police officer. According to police, she was attempting to enter a Capitol office building when she was stopped by an officer who didn't recognize her.

McKinney, who was not wearing the lapel pin given to all 535 members of Congress, reportedly failed to heed requests that she stop and identify herself, whereupon the officer grabbed her and she allegedly jabbed him with her cellphone. CNN reports that prosecutors have decided to seek charges against her.

You would, under other circumstances, consider this a rather minor contretemps. But McKinney is black, which brings race into the picture. And where race enters, stupid is seldom far behind.

The first injection of which comes from McKinney herself. She has said she was a victim of racial profiling. It seems the pin she failed to wear, which allows legislators to circumvent the metal detectors, frequently goes unworn by Congresspersons because they are known to Capitol police on sight. She questions why the cops find it so hard to remember her and why she is frequently assumed not to belong in hallways of power.

Those are good questions. But you know what? You still don't hit a cop. That's Black 101, something we instill in our boys for when they get pulled over for the crime of being. Heck, it's Common Sense 101. Even if the cop is rude, wrong or racist, stay cool and complain through channels.

But hitting? After you've ignored commands to stop? That's stupid. And stupid is like kudzu. Once it gets a foothold, it just grows wild.

So you had Tom DeLay, the ethics-challenged representative from Texas, popping up on Fox News to call McKinney a "racist." And we have to take that seriously because as everyone knows, DeLay has worked tirelessly for the cause of racial justice and even got his nickname "The Hammer" from his fondness for the old folk song which promises to "hammer out love between my brothers and my sisters all over this land."

And you had white guys e-mailing black columnists – i.e., me – taunting them about what McKinney did because, you know, we're just as much to blame as she is because all us colored folk think alike.

And you had Harry Belafonte and Danny Glover backing McKinney at a press conference – not, said Glover, to judge the facts of the case, but "to support our sister."

Because you know, even if she were found smoking crack with Osama bin Laden, you still have to support a sister.

And you had the GOP pushing a resolution commending the police because, you know, everybody else despises cops with a passion.

And you had Democrats maintaining a studied silence because, you know, even stupid has its limits.

Which may explain why McKinney issued a belated apology Thursday.

But a better woman would have nothing to apologize for.

A better woman would never have trivialized racism to gratify her ego.

And a better nation would be less susceptible to such spasms of stupid.

Last week, somebody was beaten because he was black. Went hungry because he was black. Died because he was black.

Yet the face of racial injustice was Cynthia McKinney being asked for ID. You think there's something wrong with that picture?

Well, duh.

REVERSE DISCRIMINATION

Sunday, June 22, 2008

GRABBING THE VICTIM HAT

Someone is going to think this column is racist.

That person – he or she will be white – will be unable to point to so much as a semicolon that suggests I believe in the native superiority of my, or any other, race. Rather, the accusation will be based in the fact that the column discusses race, period. It's a phenomenon I've seen many times, most recently when a friend of mine told me that a friend of hers regards me as racist because I write about race. To which I gave my standard answer: If that's how it works, I'll start writing about money. Then I'll be a billionaire.

I offer the foregoing as a gesture of solidarity with an elementary school teacher in California who wrote to ask my opinion of two incidents that happened in her class.

In the first, a white boy – we'll call him Bobby – disagreed with a black boy. The black boy, who had been explaining something about his family to the teacher, told Bobby he would not understand because he was white. Bobby said this was racist.

In the second, Bobby complained that a classmate had called him a white boy. The classmate was a white girl. Bobby said she was racist.

For those of you playing along at home, here are two salient facts: 1) according to his teacher, Bobby frequently complains about racism against white kids; 2) 85 percent of the students at the school are white kids.

So, what do I think?

I think Bobby is troublingly eager to wear what I call the "victim hat," i.e., to be the one who gets to declare himself morally affronted, the one whose hurt feelings we are obligated to assuage, the one whose complaints we are required to listen to. In this, he is an accurate reflection of the nation in which he is coming of age. He is learning what we have taught.

The need, the abject eagerness, of some white people to wear the victim hat is something I have noted with alarm in recent years. They are motivated, I think, by the fact that some black people make wearing the victim hat look like so much fun. Meaning that African America has too often been caught crying "racism" reflexively, crying "wolf!" repeatedly, refusing, where perceived racial insult is concerned, to differentiate between the profound and the petty. We cry racism when the justice system is unjust or a Don Imus spews vitriol. Unfortunately, we also cry it when a Michael Jackson gets hauled up on charges of child molestation or a white bureaucrat uses the unfortunate, but inoffensive, word "niggardly."

If you are white, I suspect, you get tired of being on the receiving end, especially when much of what is called racism plainly is not. You figure two can play at this game and besides, you wouldn't mind being the one catered to for a while. So you grab the victim hat and, like Bobby, present yourself as mortally wounded by "racism" against you.

The problem with that is, if you represent 85 percent of the playground, no other group can organize to deny you access to the swings. Granted, they might call you names and I don't condone or minimize that. But there is a qualitative difference between suffering only that and suffering that, plus exclusion from the swings. There is racism and there is racism, if you catch my drift.

If you are white, I suspect, you get tired of being on the receiving end, especially when what is called racism is not.

And Bobby? I wish his black classmate had phrased his observation more tactfully, although since we're talking about kids, I understand why he did not. Still, Bobby is ultimately a "victim" only of his desire to be a victim.

I don't blame him for that. I blame us, his elders, for lacking the ability, the willingness, the vocabulary and the guts to talk about race frankly and intelligently. Some of us think that talking about race equals racism, others cry "racism!" with spasmodic frequency, and yet others fight for their turn to wear the victim hat.

In short, we act like children.

Bobby, at least, has an excuse for that.

TALKING ABOUT RACE

Sunday, February 22, 2009

WE NEED THE DISCUSSION BUT WE'RE BAD AT IT

It is not precisely true that Americans don't talk about race.

Race informs our discussions of everything from crime to education to who got picked for "American Idol." We talk race in the lunchroom with people who look like us, yell race at the television when irked by people who don't. We read race in our newspapers and magazines, then write race in letters and e-mails to editors. January rolls around and we celebrate Martin Luther King, Jr. February sweeps in and we observe Black History Month.

We talk about race, all right. We are just really bad at it.

As you may have guessed, the foregoing is occasioned by a speech Eric Holder, the nation's first African-American attorney general, gave last week. In it, he characterized the United States as "a nation of cowards" when it comes to discussing our tortured racial history. There is, however, more to it than that.

A large component of my work for nearly 20 years has involved talking about, and persuading my fellow Americans to talk about, race. After hundreds of columns, dozens of speeches and thousands of face-to-face and e-mail exchanges with Americans of all stripes, I consider myself something of an expert on the subject. And I'm here to tell you that race is like a four-car pileup on the freeway: it simultaneously attracts us and repels.

Because of this, we can't not talk about it. Yet at the same time, we can't talk about it, either. At least not in any sort of honest, intelligent or sustained way, because doing so requires cross-cultural trust we do not have and takes us places we prefer not to go.

So we talk about race, but we don't. More often, we yell about race. Or talk around race. Or deliver self-righteous monologues on race. All of it tainted by a gaping ignorance of, and stubborn refusal to grapple with, the hateful, hurtful history that makes talking about race necessary in the first place.

We play games instead. Many African Americans lie in wait to cry "Got'cha!" when some hapless white person inadvertently says some questionable thing, as though innocent ignorance were indistinguishable from actual malice.

As when a white analyst on TV's Golf Channel said something dumb about Tiger Woods, and the Reverend Al Sharpton demanded her head, telling a reporter, "What she said is racist. Whether she's a racist ... is immaterial."

We play games. Many white Americans go about with fingers in ears singing "la la la la" at the top of their lungs rather than hear inconvenient truths that challenge their fantasies of how we have overcome. You can bring them a thousand anecdotes, you can bury them in studies from universities, think tanks and the federal government itself, documenting ongoing racial bias in housing, employment, education, criminal justice, and they will still tell you all that stuff ended yesterday.

This is what I have repeatedly seen. And small wonder, if you are black, you stop trying to have substantive discussions about race with white people: They refuse to listen. Small wonder, if you are white, you stop speaking freely about race with black people: Every little thing is racism with them.

And small wonder, in recent years, the discussion on race has come to be dominated by loud, intolerant voices using the reach they are afforded by the Internet and the intellectual cover they are provided by conservative extremism to promulgate a neo-racism more raw than anything the mainstream has seen in years. Small wonder the Southern Poverty Law Center reports the number of hate groups in this country has risen over 40 percent since 2000.

We live in an era where the bad people among us are feeling emboldened by the silence and compassion fatigue of the good ones. But after all we've been through, after all we have done and suffered to bring about change, we cannot afford silence or fatigue, cannot afford to turn the conversation over to the voices of loud intolerance.

So thank Eric Holder for the reminder. If good people do not lead this discussion, the bad ones happily will.

Wednesday, August 17, 2011

WE LIE ABOUT RACE

Mother used to tell this story.

She was working as a domestic – this was the late '40s or early '50s – for a Memphis doctor when one day his daughter came up and inexplicably began rubbing her skin. It turned out the child had asked her grandmother why mom's skin was dark, and the woman, a daughter of the unreconstructed white South, had said the darkness was dirt. The poor little girl was trying to rub the "dirt" off and was surprised it wouldn't come. Years later, Mom's voice still mixed anger and humiliation when she told that tale.

But such incidental cruelties were to be expected. Mom was "The Help," as in the Kathryn Stockett novel that was released last week as a motion picture. I find myself with irresolute feelings toward both. In this, I am hardly alone. Indeed, "The Help" has met with a certain amount of scorn from some African Americans unseduced by its story of black maids and their white employers in Jackson, Mississippi, in that pregnant year, 1963.

An organization called the Association of Black Women Historians has slammed the movie for "stereotyping." Author Valerie Boyd's review, which appeared on an Atlanta arts blog, was headlined "A Feel Good Movie for White People." Some black literati have noted it as yet another example of a white writer reaping great rewards from chronicling African-American passages while black writers who traffic in those same passages cannot get the time of day from publishers and movie makers.

Though the literati have a valid point, the criticism of "The Help" strikes me otherwise as more reflexive than felt. Stockett told the story of a white misfit bonding with a black maid and helping her find her voice in a society that had rendered her mute. If it is not exactly a black-power manifesto, well, neither is it "Birth of a Nation II."

So what, then explains my own irresolution? I suspect it traces to nothing more mysterious than the pain of revisiting a time and place of black subservience. And, perhaps, the sting of an inherited memory. That episode cost my mom something to tell – and even more to live.

As Americans, we lie about race. We lie profligately, obstinately and repeatedly. The first lie is of its existence as an immutable reality delivered unto us from the very hand of God.

That lie undergirds all the other lies, lies of Negro criminality, mendacity, ineducability. Lies of sexless mammies and oversexed wenches. Lies of docile child-men and brutal bucks. Lies that exonerate conscience and cover sin with sanctimony. Lies that pinched off avenues of aspiration till "the help" was all a Negro woman was left to be.

I think of those lies sometimes when aging white southerners contact me to share sepia-toned reminiscences about some beloved old nanny who raised them, taught them, loved them, and who was almost a member of the family. Almost.

Reading their emails, I wonder if those folks understand even now, a lifetime later, that that woman did not exist simply as a walk-on character in a white person's life drama, that she was a fully formed human being with a life, and dreams and dreads of her own.

It is Kathryn Stockett's imperfect triumph to have understood this and seek to make others understand it, too.

STARBUCKS HAD GOOD INTENTIONS

Am I the only person in America not making fun of Howard Schultz?

The Starbucks CEO bought himself a ton of ridicule recently when he attempted to jumpstart a national dialogue on race by having baristas write the words "Race Together" on customers' cups of Cinnamon Dolce Light Frappuccino Grande or Caffe Misto Venti with extra coconut.

On Twitter, the campaign was dubbed "patronizing," "absurd" and "a load of crap." On "The Nightly Show with Larry Wilmore," Rosie Perez said, "I don't want to be forced to have a conversation. Especially early in the f--- morning." Some folks questioned the wisdom of calling for racial dialogue when your executive team has all the rich cultural diversity of a GOP convention in Idaho.

Starbucks says there will eventually be more to the campaign, but what we've seen so far has been epically bad – naive at best, dumber than a sack of coffee beans at worst. Give it this much credit, though: It came out of an earnest conviction that the future health of our country requires us to solve race. In other words, Starbucks had good intentions.

You may say that's not much. You may note that good intentions are the macadam on the road to hell.

Me, I think we dismiss good intentions at our own peril.

Besides, Schultz's biggest mistake was not in having baristas write a trite slogan, but in his failure to realize that much of the country is simply not equipped for the conversation he is inviting them to have. Last week, even as "Race Together" was being lampooned, I spent 41 minutes I'll never get back on the phone with a white, Jewish reader who had insisted she wanted to have the "conversation on race" I have often said this country needs. It was not a productive encounter.

She starts on a spiel about blacks and drugs. I point out that only about 15 percent of drug use in this country is by blacks and that the vast majority of dealers are white. There is a silence. She says this is something she had not known.

We move on to the fact that Jews were foot soldiers and financiers of the Civil Rights Movement, so she is offended that black people never attend Holocaust remembrance services. She has no statistics to prove this, but insists her observation is valid based on her lived experience. I point out that her lived experience is in Tucson, which has a black population of maybe 17.

And so it goes.

What it illustrated for me, and not for the first time, is that often, when people think they're talking about race, they really aren't. They are talking instead about the myths, resentments, projections and suppositions by which they justify half-baked notions about who those "other" people are.

You can't wholly blame them. Who can speak sensibly on a subject he doesn't understand? And we've been foiled in our quest to understand by an institutional conspiracy of ignorance. Race is the rawest wound of the American psyche, but somehow, you can graduate high school without knowing who Emmett Till was or that Martin Luther King ever said any words other than "I have a dream." Race has done more than arguably any other social force to shape this country, yet somehow news media do not cover it, unless forced to do so by crisis or controversy.

So here is what I've come to realize: Before we can have a fruitful "conversation on race," we need to first have education on race. We will not be a well nation or a whole one until we cease to fear and begin to understand this force that has made us who and what we are.

And how dare we reject from that cause any good person who earnestly seeks the same end, even if his solution is as dumb as a slogan on a coffee cup? Yes, I recognize the limitations of good intentions.

But they sure beat heck out of the other kind.

RACIAL PROGRESS

Friday, April 8, 2005

PROGRESS AND PERVERSITY

Call it proof that progress is sometimes perverse.

Meaning Eddie Jordan, district attorney for Orleans Parish in Louisiana. First black district attorney in New Orleans' history. That's the progress.

Here's the perverse: Soon after he took office in January 2003, Jordan fired 53 white employees en masse and replaced them all with blacks.

Last week, a federal court ruled that he committed racial discrimination against 43 of those workers. A jury of eight whites and two blacks ordered the district attorney to pay $1.9 million in back pay and damages.

Though he denies firing people on the basis of race – he claims he doesn't know what color the axed employees were – Jordan does allow that he sought to make his office more racially representative of its community.

The explanation taxes credulity, requiring us to believe all the people he fired just happened to be white while all the ones hired to replace them were only coincidentally black.

Making the district attorney's office representative is a worthy goal. But you simply do not come into a place and start clearing people away like brush on the basis of race. There are better ways of achieving the objective – casting a wider net when jobs come open, for instance.

Still, with all that said, this episode is instructive.

In recent years some white people have attempted to co-opt the language of the Civil Rights Movement and turn it against itself:

Consider those conservatives who piously quote Martin Luther King Jr. to buttress their opposition to affirmative action.

To listen to them, you'd think he never said anything except that famous line about color of skin and content of character. You'd never know that when challenged to say why the nation should do something special for "the Negro," he pointedly observed that the nation had done something special against "the Negro" for centuries.

And then there's the whole "reverse racism" thing. It works like this: an African-American bigot mistreats an unoffending white person. White observers tout it as proof the discrimination shoe is now on the other foot.

When you refuse to agree that white Americans are grievously wounded victims of black bias, they start mewling about double standards.

So you try to explain. You say that if racism meant only occasional mistreatment by the occasional unenlightened moron, there'd never have been a need for affirmative action. Or the Civil Rights Act. Or the Voting Rights Act. Or all that shooting in the 1860s.

Not to minimize mistreatment, but that, per se, was never the problem. Rather, the problem was the ability of one group to codify that mistreatment in law and custom, wielding the levers of power to make life difficult for another group. Not simply to mistreat them, but to deny them work, lodging, education, housing, justice, life. And to do so with impunity. Systemic racism, you say.

And they look at you and tell you they have no idea what you mean.

Eddie Jordan is what I mean.

I called this perverse progress because the very fact that he is in a position to hurt 43 white people suggests that black people enjoy unparalleled new access to the levers of power. It's sad – but predictably consistent with human nature – that he used those levers as he did.

However, in doing so, maybe he offers some of my white countrymen a chance to see what they say they cannot.

Maybe, in employing his office to injure strangers whose only sin was melanin deficiency, he helps my countrymen understand what they find incomprehensible. And maybe they should ponder what might have happened, what options would have been left the plaintiffs, had the lawyers, the bailiffs, the clerks, the judges, the system, all been lined up against them.

Consider that scenario, and understanding might become clearer still.

Friday, May 20, 2005

JUST TRYING TO GET THROUGH THE DAY

"This world is full of people, all kinds of people. And everybody wanna live on." – The Masqueraders, 1975

Chances are, you've never heard of the song or the singing group referenced above. Both are pretty obscure.

But I dig up the refrain from "Everybody Wanna Live On" because I've always thought it an especially insightful summation of the conundrums of race, culture and creed. Indeed, the Masqueraders tell more truth in 15 words than some people do in 15,000. Because when you get right down to it, when you strip away the guilt, indignation and recrimination that invariably attend any discussion of cross-cultural enmity, aren't you left with the simple fact that most of us – black and white, gay and straight, Muslim and Jew – are just trying to get through the day?

The new movie "Crash" understands this. I guess that's why I found it compelling.

For those who don't know, "Crash" is an ensemble film starring a handful of Hollywood's more recognizable stars: Don Cheadle, Sandra Bullock, Brendan Fraser, Larenz Tate, Matt Dillon and the rapper Chris "Ludacris" Bridges among them. It tells a series of interlocking stories, all proceeding from conflicts carrying a subtext of culture and/or race.

Two young black men carjack a white couple. A Persian shopkeeper who speaks little English clashes with a Hispanic locksmith. A hateful white cop assaults a black woman while her husband can only watch.

Criminal black men, English-deficient foreigners, racist cops ... you've seen those types before, haven't you? Of course. That's the point. Seldom has any film subverted stereotype so intelligently. "Crash" knows what you expect – what you have been conditioned to expect from other movies and just from living life itself – and it uses that expectation against you. It shows you nobility burning inside the meanest soul. Penury hiding within the most generous heart. Saintliness and sin sharing a single skin.

In "Crash," nothing is as it seems on first glance. Its people surprise you in ways large and small. You find that you never know who you're dealing with until you've spent some time with them.

It's a valuable lesson. One hopes people take it with them when they leave the multiplex.

Because in a real sense, that's what racism, religious bigotry and homophobia are: expectation. People thinking they know before they actually do. People responding to the you they have prejudged instead of to the you that presents itself before them. Responding, in other words, to what they believe brown skin signifies instead of responding to the human being with brown skin who stands before them asking for a job or a home loan or justice.

And if you're the person with brown skin, or pink skin, or an Arab name, or a same-sex lover, the frustration is that you can never get some people to see beyond what they expect, never get them to see you as you are. Indeed, never quite get them to see you at all.

The point is not simply, as some critics have said, that we're all capable of bigotry. It is, rather, that we are, all of us, so absorbed by our own pain that we often fail to comprehend the pain of our fellow travelers, even when we are the ones who have inflicted it.

You watch the movie and you wonder how much of the acrimony it depicts could have been avoided if the people had simply found a way to talk to one another, found a way to make themselves seen and heard. You wonder if the whole torturous history of how human beings hate one another's tribes could really devolve to something as simple, as stupid, as a failure to understand that everybody feels, everybody hurts.

That's a foolishly optimistic question, but I don't know if that makes it a bad one.

Yes, the hows and whys of human prejudice are thorny and byzantine. Yet, at heart of that complexity lives a truth as simple as a song.

There are all kinds of people in the world. And everybody wanna live on.

Wednesday, April 2, 2008

HALF EMPTY, HALF FULL

"I may not get there with you." – *Martin Luther King Jr., April 3, 1968*

A few words about the Mountaintop and the Promised Land.

On the last night of his life, Martin Luther King Jr. famously told an audience in Memphis that he had stood on the one and seen the other. He did not define the Promised Land, but he did not need to. That audience of striking sanitation workers and their supporters, those long-suffering women and men who erupted in cries and shouts, already knew.

The Promised Land was where you did not have to march for your dignity. It was where you did not have to sing for your freedom. It was where there was no need for speeches to verify your humanity. The Promised Land was that sacred place where all of God's children would stand as equals on level, fertile ground.

Friday marks 40 years since King was killed. And the search for that promised land has shrunken until it fits inside an old riddle, the one that asks whether the glass is half empty or half full.

I'm moved to this conclusion by a column published last week in The Washington Post by Shankar Vedantam, who writes on issues of human behavior. Vedantam's piece recounted two studies. The first, by Philip Mazzocco of Ohio State University and Mahzarin Banaji of Harvard, asked white volunteers a question: If they were to be reborn black in America, how much money would they ask for to cover the lifetime disadvantages? Most gave amounts less than $10,000. Mind you, to go a lifetime without television, they wanted $1 million.

When it was explained to them that being black meant that they would earn a fraction of what whites earn, suffer higher rates of infant mortality, be unemployed at a rate nearly twice the national average, be more likely to be poor and live at dramatically greater risk of being jailed or killed, whites raised their asking prices a hundredfold.

That blacks and whites live different realities is hardly news. What's intriguing is the reason, as suggested by the second study. Yale University researcher Richard Eibach found that whites and blacks employ different measures in assessing racial progress. Whites judge it by looking at how far we have come ("How can you say there's still racism when we have an Oprah Winfrey and a Barack Obama?"). Blacks judge it by how far we have yet to go ("How can you say there's no racism when police keep stopping me for no reason?").

So each side of America's most intractable debate chooses the path of least resistance, the path that shoves the onus for change off to the other side. Thus, whites can feel justified in noting the incredible progress we have made, and blacks can feel equally justified in feeling still victimized, and it never seems to occur to any of us that both views are true, that they do not contradict one another. We never seem to realize that we are having an argument over how much water is in the glass.

I guess you can't see that from the narrow valley of cynicism and self-interest. But in his last public exhortation, King called us up from there, called us up to the grand view, the big picture, the mountaintop. From there, he said, you could see the Promised Land.

Whites, Eibach told The Post, see that promised land – racial equality – as an ideal, something it would be nice to achieve someday. Blacks see it as a necessity, something you work to make manifest here and now. The urgency embodied in the one view, and the luxuriant indolence in the other, speak volumes about the cognitive distance between blacks and whites.

And explain why, rather than being inspired by the possibilities glimpsed from a mountain peak, we trudge through a valley arguing how much water is in the glass. Is it half empty? Half full?

I guess that would depend on how thirsty you are.

Wednesday, February 11, 2009

100ᵀᴴ BIRTHDAY

It began before it began.

This was in 1905 when the great black scholar W.E.B. DuBois called a meeting of prominent black men. They met on the Canadian side of Niagara Falls because hotels in their own country would not accommodate them and formed what became known as the Niagara Movement.

The Movement, which held a subsequent meeting at Harper's Ferry, West Virginia, issued a statement that said in part, "We claim for ourselves every single right that belongs to a freeborn American, political, civil and social; and until we get these rights we will never cease to protest and assail the ears of America." But the movement, hampered by various difficulties, soon sputtered and became inactive.

Then the riot came.

For six days in August 1908, a mob of white people surged through the streets of Springfield, Illinois, lynching and maiming black people at will and at whim. The irony of this happening in the hometown of Abraham Lincoln, earnestly if somewhat simplistically revered as the Great Emancipator, was lost on no one, the rioters least of all. "Lincoln freed you, we'll show you your place," they cried as they flogged black people through the streets.

The appalling spectacle energized white liberals like Mary White Ovington and Oswald Garrison Villard. On Lincoln's 100th birthday, February 12, 1909, they joined with DuBois and other remnants of the Niagara Movement to issue a call for a conference on race.

That call – a century ago Thursday – was the birth certificate of the National Association for the Advancement of Colored People.

The milestone simultaneously demands and defies commemoration.

It is, after all, hard to hug an institution. And if it's true that history is biography, it's not hard to understand why the NAACP has often seemed overshadowed by larger-than-life personalities like Malcolm X, Marcus Garvey, Martin Luther King Jr., Jesse Jackson. Even its most celebrated members – DuBois, Ida B.

Wells-Barnett, Thurgood Marshall, Medgar Evers, Rosa Parks –
are better known for what they did than for the organization to
which they belonged.

Who regards the NAACP with the reverence those men and
women inspire? DuBois notwithstanding, there is in the NAACP
story no central charismatic figure. Instead, there is The Work.
There is fighting voter suppression and protesting lynch law and
writing legal briefs. There is issuing press releases and filing complaints and lobbying lawmakers. There is awarding scholarships
and publishing reports and sponsoring workshops and holding
accountable. There is advancement made in increments.

Until one day you look up and see that because of those increments, the world has changed as if in a bolt of lightning. The
1954 Brown v. Board of Education decision is the most obvious
illustration, but really, the proof is the whole country since 1909. It
is Sidney Poitier and Condoleezza Rice and Guion Bluford and
Barack Obama. And me. Maybe even you.

For all that, one often senses in African America a certain ambivalence toward the NAACP. Too middle class, says one school of
criticism. Not relevant, says another. Still others are offput by
scandals of leadership over the last 15 years or so. And for some,
perhaps the organization's greatest sin is simply this: It is not ex-
citing.

Organizations seldom are.

But they do The Work, don't they? The Work that is bigger
than one person and longer than one life. Because the NAACP has
done The Work, we can pause upon a milestone in a world trans-
formed, a world in which Obama is president and Oprah is queen.
If the difference looks like a lightning bolt, we know better.

And we celebrate the increments by which we advance.

STARS AND BARS

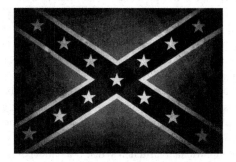

Sunday, May 3, 2009

IT'S JUST HERITAGE

A few days ago, a high school student in Sarasota failed history and another failed civics. As a result, the one wound up shot in the chest and the other jailed on a charge of aggravated battery with a deadly weapon.

Here's the story, as reported by The Sarasota Herald-Tribune: On the last Friday in April, an 18-year-old white kid named Daniel Azeff and a friend went riding downtown in a pickup truck, yelling racially disparaging remarks and waving a Confederate battle flag. Azeff's grandfather, Joseph Fischer, told the paper he has cautioned his grandson repeatedly about his fascination with that dirty banner. Azeff, he said, does not really understand what the flag means.

If so, he's hardly alone in his ignorance. A generation of apologists for the wannabe nation symbolized by that flag has done an effective job of convincing the gullible and the willfully ignorant that neither the nation, the flag, nor the Civil War in which both were bloodily repudiated, has anything to do with slavery. It's just "heritage," they say, as though heritage were a synonym for "good." As though Nazis, white South Africans and Rwandans did not have heritage, too.

For the record: In explaining its decision to secede, South Carolina cited "an increasing hostility on the part of the nonslaveholding States to the institution of slavery." Georgia noted its grievances against the North "with reference to the subject of African slavery." Mississippi said, "Our position is thoroughly identified with the institution of slavery." To which Confederate "vice president" Alexander Stephens added: "Our new government is founded upon ... the great truth that the Negro is not equal to the white man, that slavery, subordination to the superior race, is his natural and moral condition."

So the notion that the Confederacy and its symbols have nothing to with slavery is tiresome, silly and delusional. In choosing to adopt one of those symbols that night, David Azeff took a history test of sorts – and failed.

As noted, Michael Mitchell's test was in civics. Police say Mitchell, who is 18, black and a student at Sarasota Military Academy, saw Azeff's flag, took offense and, when the white kid parked and walked down the street, confronted him. Azeff denied being a racist; he was, he said, just exercising his First Amendment rights. Police say the argument escalated, until Mitchell pulled a gun and shot Azeff in the chest.

Thus did Mitchell fail his own test. This is America. Daniel Azeff has a perfect right to express virtually any opinion he chooses, no matter how asinine or provocative, without being shot for it.

Thankfully, Azeff is expected to make a full recovery. Meantime, Mitchell, said to be a good kid who has never been in trouble before, remains jailed in lieu of $50,000 bail. It is difficult not to see a certain symmetry.

That's not an argument of moral equivalence: Mitchell allegedly pulled a gun, so the moral weight for what happened rests squarely upon his shoulders.

And yet it's also true that each teenager had what the other lacked. One knew his rights, the other, his history. But neither realized that you cannot fully appreciate the one without understanding the other. So each young man fell into the other's blind spot.

If we were a people with the courage to teach our racial history fearlessly, and the foresight to inculcate in our children a reverence for civil liberties, this tragedy might never have happened. We are not those people. And because we aren't, these two boys hurtled toward collision, hopped up on grievances and rage they were ill-equipped to speak – or hear. They took a test that night in Sarasota, and let no one be surprised they failed.

They never had a chance.

BLACK LIVES MATTER

Black
Lives
Matter

Wednesday, July 20, 2016

GETTING TO POINT WHERE NO LIVES MATTER

How can anyone ever explain this to Mason?

He's only 4 months old, so that moment still lies years in the future. Still, at some point, too soon, he will ask the inevitable questions, and someone will have to tell him how his dad was shot to death for being a police officer in Baton Rouge.

Montrell Jackson was not the only cop killed Sunday, nor the only one who left a child behind. Officer Matthew Gerald and Sheriff's Deputy Brad Garafolo also had kids. And it's likely that in killing five police officers earlier this month, a sniper in Dallas robbed multiple children of their fathers, too.

So there are a lot of people having painful discussions with a lot of kids just now. But Mason's father was the only one of these eight dead cops with the maddening and paradoxical distinction of being an African-American man killed in protest of police violence against African-American people. He left a Facebook post that gave a glimpse into how frustrating it was, living on both sides of that line – being both black and a cop and therefore, doubly distrusted.

"I swear to God," he wrote, "I love this city but I wonder if this city loves me. In uniform I get nasty hateful looks and out of uniform some consider me a threat."

"Please," he pleaded, "don't let hate infect your heart."

Nine days later, he was dead.

Counting two New York City policemen murdered in 2014, this makes at least 10 cops randomly killed in the last two years by people ostensibly fighting police brutality. But those madmen could hardly be bigger traitors to that cause.

One is reminded of something Martin Luther King said the night before his assassination, when he explained "the problem with a little violence." Namely, it changes the discussion, makes itself the focus. King had been protesting on behalf of striking sanitation workers in Memphis when unruly young people turned his march into a riot. "Now ... we've got to march again," he said, "in order to put the issue where it is supposed to be."

These cop killers leave us a similar dilemma. Instead of discussing the violence of police, we are now required to discuss violence against police and to say the obvious: These killers serve no cause, nor does any cause justify what they did. They are just punk cowards with guns who have changed the subject, thereby giving aid and comfort to those who'd rather not confront the issue in the first place.

But if we don't, then what? One often hears men like Rudy Giuliani and Bill O'Reilly express contempt for the Black Lives Matter movement of protest and civil disobedience; one is less likely to hear either of them specify what other means of protest they would suggest for people whose concerns about racially biased and extralegal policing have been otherwise ignored for decades by government and media. If not Black Lives Matter, then what? Patient silence? Acceptance of the status quo?

That isn't going to happen, and the sooner the nation understands this, the sooner it moves forward. Sadly, that move, whenever it comes, will be too late for Mason and dozens of others left newly fatherless, sonless, brotherless, husbandless and bereft. Still, we have to move. The alternative is to remain stuck in this place of incoherence, fear, racial resentment ... and rage. Always rage.

But rage doesn't think, rage doesn't love, rage doesn't build, rage doesn't care. Rage only rends and destroys.

We have to be better than that. We have no choice but to be better than that. We owe it to Mason to be better than that. He deserves a country better than this mad one in which his father died, and life is poured out like water.

Jocelyn Jackson, Montrell's sister, put it best in an interview with the Washington Post. "It's getting to the point where no lives matter," she said.

Chapter 4

THE MEDIA

Sunday, July 28, 2013

ABYSMAL JOB OF COVERING RACE

Book editor's note: *The following is part of an address Leonard Pitts gave to the Florida Press Association and the Florida Society of News Editors.*

Eight years ago, a storm came barreling through the Gulf of Mexico and smashed the Gulf Coast of the United States. Hurricane Katrina leveled the city of Waveland. It buckled roads in the city of Biloxi. It ripped the city of Bogalusa. And it absolutely smashed the city of New Orleans.

Eight years later, the images from that time feel as if they happened in someone else's nightmare. But they were real. The bodies floating in the canals were real. The dead woman in the wheelchair covered by a sheet was real. The people trapped in the heat and stench of the Superdome were real. The people sweltering in their attics as the floodwaters rose were real. The people making camp on the highways and bridges were real. The people looting, the people wading through chest-high waters in search of bread and diapers, were real.

Real, too, was the sense of surprise, of abject shock, with which the nation and their news media realized an astonishing thing. There are poor people in America. Indeed, it turns out there are people in America so desperately poor that they lack the means even to run to higher ground in the face of a killer storm.

They don't have cars. They don't have credit cards. They don't have the things that the rest of us are able to take for granted.

As an Illinois senator named Barack Obama put it, "I hope we realize that the people of New Orleans weren't just abandoned during the hurricane. They were abandoned long ago – to murder and mayhem in the streets, to substandard schools, to dilapidated housing, to inadequate health care, to a pervasive sense of hopelessness."

For a brief moment, the astonishing news that there is poverty in America seemed to galvanize the news media. We wondered how in the heck we could have missed this. Newsweek responded with a cover story: "The Other America." The public editor of the Atlanta Journal-Constitution chastised the paper for dedicating a reporter to coverage of the zoo and the aquarium but none to cover welfare and public housing. A reader wrote the New York Times to express disappointment in that paper's failure to bring attention to poverty. "As a close reader of The Times and of poverty trends,'" he said, "I was surprised to learn of the poverty conditions that prevailed in New Orleans. Why didn't the economic-social-racial conditions in New Orleans get some attention in the paper?"

"The Times," he added, "let us down."

The Times, or at least its public editor, agreed, writing: "Poverty so pervasive that it hampered evacuation would seem to have been worthy of The Times' attention before it emerged as a pivotal challenge two weeks ago." The paper's coverage, he added, "falls far short of what its readers have a right to expect of a national newspaper."

In the wake of Hurricane Katrina, there arose a consensus in American journalism that we had done a terrible job of covering poverty. I am here to tell you that we have done an equally abysmal job of covering race.

Many of us, I suspect, will resist that characterization. They will point to the attention given the furor over Paula Deen, the Henry Louis Gates affair and the subsequent "beer summit," the headlines out of Jena, Louisiana, the gutting of the Voting Rights Act, the opening of the Martin Luther King monument on the Washington Mall, the sliming of Shirley Sherrod. And, yes, they will point to the wall-to-wall coverage given the shooting of Trayvon Martin – especially this week, as Martin's assailant was acquitted and the nation grappled with the aftermath.

But that is not covering race. That is covering the tragedies, dramas and sideshows that periodically arise from race. We are always there when the circus comes to town.

So what do I mean, then, by race?

If you read the first of the two columns I wrote in the aftermath of the Trayvon Martin verdict, you may remember that I made reference to a social experiment I once saw on television. "What Would You Do?" is one of those hidden camera shows in which they set up a situation and watch to see how average people respond. In the segment I wrote about, a young white actor sets to work trying to steal a chained up bicycle in a park. He uses a hacksaw, a bolt cutter and even an electric saw. The cameras watch for an hour. A hundred people pass by. A few mildly question what he's doing, but most don't even bother. Out of that 100 people, only one couple calls authorities.

It was when they did the experiment with a black kid that things got interesting. Within the first minutes, there's a crowd of people around him. They challenge him. They lecture him. They whip out cellphone cameras and take video of him for use in court. They call the police. And afterward, when they are asked if the color of the young man stealing the bike had any bearing on their actions, they swear it did not.

As one man put it, "Not at all. He could've been any color, it wouldn't have mattered to me."

So when you ask yourself what I mean by "race," I mean that. That is race.

And can we pause and just deal with that for a moment? Ask yourself what it means that, after an experiment that demonstrates with stark clarity the dimensions of racial bias, that man can assure us all race had nothing to do with his decision to harass the black kid and that he absolutely would have given the same treatment to the white one. We know from watching the video that he very likely would not.

The point is not that that man is lying. Far from it. The point is that he is telling the truth as he understands it. How can he be guilty of racial discrimination? He doesn't burn crosses on people's lawns. He doesn't post Whites Only signs in his place of business. Black people are welcome at his house, as Archie Bunker once put it, through the front door as well as the back. So there is no way he looked at that black kid in the park and committed racial profiling. This is his truth. Race had nothing to do with it.

It is a statement of self-delusion that finds its echo all throughout the Trayvon Martin case. Race had nothing to do with my shooting him, said George Zimmerman. Race had nothing to do with our letting Zimmerman go, said the police department. Race had nothing to do with our acquittal said the jury.

This, friends and colleagues, is the story we are not telling. Because this influence that color still has over our perceptions half a century after the Civil Rights Movement – and our denial of that influence – has implications far beyond the killing of Trayvon Martin, tragic as that was. No, it bears directly upon the decisions we make, the policies we embrace, in the fields of criminal justice, education, the environment, healthcare, the economy, politics, foreign policy, terrorism, you name it. It bears upon how we all perceive the world. So where are our enterprise stories documenting these effects? Why are we as an industry – with a few noteworthy exceptions – silent on these issues?

As I said a moment ago, race is not an easy topic. If you are white, race can be difficult because you have to grapple with the sense of feeling guilty or that someone is trying to make you feel guilty for an ugly past. I remember watching a documentary on the murder of Emmett Till with a young white kid who told me afterward that it made him want to pull his skin off. This is a child born three and a half decades after Emmett Till died and yet, watching those white people on screen in the middle 1950s saying all those vile, hateful, stupid things, made him, personally, feel bad. Feel indicted. We have to recognize that and be sensitive to that. We have to evolve some way of talking about race that allows white people of good intention to feel as if they can be part of the solution and not just a new iteration of the problem.

It is easier for black folk to discuss race, but even with us, there can be some hesitation. It you are black, race can be a difficult subject because like sediment at the bottom of the pond, it stirs up so many feelings of anger, shame and boiling frustration. It can be easier just to not deal with it, easier just to leave it alone. We have to find some way of pushing to the other side of anger, of using it not as a fuel for bitterness, but as a fuel for determined, focused action.

Those are hard things to do. And instead of helping the nation find ways to do them, our industry has instead entered, I think, into a kind of conspiracy of silence where race is concerned. In this, we are not unlike many of the readers we serve.

I had a reader tell me once that I must stop writing about race because the subject is "impolite."

I get told all the time that if I didn't talk about race – me, personally – race would not be a problem in this country.

I am frequently instructed that I create racism – and become a racist myself – by writing about race.

I think what these people mean to say is that they wish I would not violate the conspiracy of silence. By mutual, unspoken consent, we have decided that we will speak of these things only when doing so becomes unavoidable, only when we are pushed to by drama, tragedy or sideshow, only when the circus comes to town. The problem is, that is precisely when emotions are apt to be most high and voices most shrill. That is precisely when people are most likely to retreat into their bunkers of fixed opinion and yell across at each other and no one ever hears a thing that is said. No understanding is ever broached, no reconciliation even remotely possible.

By acceding to this conspiracy of silence, we as journalists - and I would also indict the school system in this - have helped create a generation of socio-historical idiots where race is concerned. You may think that description is a little harsh. I would ask you to spend some quality time talking to some of my many earnest readers who insist with a straight face that conservatives fought for civil rights in the 1960s and died to stop slavery in the 1860s. You may just change your mind.

So it is not enough to cover the Trayvon Martin trial. We should have already been writing about the forces that made that trial a sensation, meaning this abiding perception that black equals criminal. We should have been asking local police chiefs and district attorneys how it is that African Americans commit, say, 15 percent of drug crimes in a given jurisdiction, yet account for upwards of 70 percent of those doing time for drug crime.

It is not enough to cover the "beer summit" that ensued when a black professor was arrested on his own front porch. We should have been writing more about the disparities in educational achievement that make an African American man on a college campus such a rarity in the first place.

It is not enough to write about the sliming of Shirley Sherrod. We should have been writing about what seems to some of us an organized attempt by elements on the political right to stir racial resentment, to give those resentments moral and intellectual cover, and to use them as a lever of political power.

It is not enough to write about the opening of the Martin Luther King monument on the Washington Mall. We should have been writing about the erosion of progress toward the Dream he famously articulated there.

I will tell you the truth: there are days when I come uncomfortably close to despairing of my country's ability to ever come to terms with itself, heal itself, on the subject of race. My assistant Judi, who handles my email and is thus on the front lines of the socio-historical idiocy I mentioned, periodically blows her top at some of the ignorant things people say. She sent me an email once that said, "I don't understand why you don't just hate white people."

Judi's white. She's about my age. And I suspect she feels what I feel: that sense of betrayal unique to those of us who came of age in the post civil rights era thinking that all this stuff was fixed, all this stuff was over, all this stuff was past, that it was finished for us by Martin Luther King and the generation of marchers who followed him toward the Promised Land. I went to college in the '70s, roomed with a white guy, discovered Simon and Garfunkel, watched "All In The Family" on television, thankful all that idiocy was now distant enough and safe enough to laugh at.

The ensuing 40 years – the bulk of my life – have been a bitter process of watching the backlash take form and discovering just how naïve and mistaken I was.

The Civil Rights Movement would not have been won without Martin Luther King's incandescent leadership. It would not have been won without that army of marchers and boycotters and non-violent protesters. But it also would not have been won without the pens and typewriters and cameras of reporters who turned the nation's eyes to the injustices flourishing in places like Little Rock, Selma, Montgomery, Nashville, Greensboro and St. Augustine.

This is what our words and pictures can do. In the civil rights years, they shattered stereotypes, they shredded preconceptions and they destroyed self-deluding fantasies. Sometimes, I don't think we really appreciate just how dramatic a change that was. We are talking about wrongs that had endured for generations, yet they were rendered inert in just 13 years, in part because our professional forebears saw a story that appalled them and told the world about it.

That is the power we wield.

So what appalls us now? Government spying, government lying, rapacious banks and terror threats are likely somewhere on your list, and with good cause. But I would ask that you also spare a little bit of moral indignation for the fact that, not 50 miles from here, a black child, walking through a gated community wearing a hooded sweatshirt and khaki skinny jeans carrying nothing more dangerous than iced tea and candy can somehow be inflated into a thug and a threat. Or for the fact that you could stalk and kill that child and be acquitted of any wrongdoing in the same state where Marissa Alexander is doing 20 years for shooting a wall. Or for the fact that some of us can look at this and assure themselves, assure us all, that race has nothing to do with it.

I ask that you see this as a story and a priority and a moral imperative. I ask that we use our great power to batter down self-delusion and socio-historical idiocy. I ask that you reconsider the price we've paid for our conspiracy of silence – and that you do it before the next circus comes to town.

NEWS

"*Police and deputy sheriffs hunted Wednesday night for a negro 'beast man'…*"

- The Billings Gazette,
Sept. 19, 1929

"*An original Guinea negro whose blood has not been crossed is as docile as a shepherd dog…*

- The Atlanta Constitution,
June 4, 1899

"*Miss Mary Henderson The Victim of a Negro Beast*"

- The Moberly Weekly Monitor,
Aug. 29, 1901

"*For two minutes [Joe Louis] was a throwback to a wild jungle creature…*"

- The Associated Press,
Jan 14, 1940

"*Towering above them all, his black apelike face, distorted with rage…*"

- The Oelwein Daily Register,
April 24, 1919

"*Northerners cannot realize how low in intelligence, how irresponsible the pure negro is. He is an animal…*"

- The New York Times,
June 9, 1901

Wednesday, February 25, 2009

SHUT UP AND LISTEN

Just so we're all clear on why black folk tend to get annoyed when newspapers compare them to animals.

For all that, though, it was not the New York Post's now-notorious chimp cartoon that offended me. Rather, it was everything that came after.

Last week's cartoon, referencing a recent incident in which police killed a chimpanzee that mauled a woman in Stamford, Connecticut, depicts two officers standing over the bullet-riddled body of a dead ape. One says to the other: "They'll have to find someone else to write the next stimulus bill."

Some observers were outraged, believing that cartoonist Sean Delonas had likened President Barack Obama to a chimp. I thought it equally likely he meant to taunt congressional Democrats (the president, after all, did not "write" the stimulus bill) and had inadvertently blundered into an awful racial stereotype. Given that ambiguity, my instinct was to give Delonas the benefit of the doubt.

Then he opened his mouth.

He and his bosses, actually. First, there was the strident defense: "absolutely friggin' ridiculous" said the cartoonist in a statement to CNN. Later, with protesters ringing its building and finding itself questioned and criticized by everyone from the National Association of Black Journalists to New York Governor David Paterson to the NAACP, the paper issued a grudging, churlish apology in which, even while expressing regret, it tried to blame the controversy on "opportunists" to whom "no apology is due."

It took nearly a week before it dawned on the paper's braintrust that maybe people had good reason for their vexation. Tuesday, media baron Rupert Murdoch, who owns the Post, issued a new apology, no strings attached.

That it took so long to do the obvious speaks volumes.

Let's be clear on one thing: The Post has a right to provoke and even offend. That is absolute and sacrosanct. But it is difficult not to be troubled by a suffocating cluelessness that allows it to provoke and offend without knowing it or meaning it or even, apparently, caring about it – and then, to dismiss provocation and offense as the work of "opportunists" instead of seeking to understand why people were so upset.

The paper's attitude, its evident ignorance of historical context, are not unique. Rather, they have their echo in too many white Americans whose default defense is the proverbial good offense whenever they feel cornered on the subject of race.

And yes, that attitude is fed by the fact that in recent years too many African Americans have found it convenient to cry wolf where race is concerned. But if arrogance on the one end and disingenuousness on the other are our only alternatives, we're in trouble.

Fittingly, this all unfolds in the wake of Attorney General Eric Holder's contention that we need to become better and braver in talking about race. Take the Post's self-satisfied ignorance as Exhibit A.

The paper didn't know that it didn't know. One hopes the next time controversy comes calling it will, before deploying its defenses, do what it should have done here.

Shut up and listen.

SPORTS

Monday, November 22, 2004

WARPING OUR WORLD VIEW

I wish I was offended.

So many other people are that it feels lonely not to be. So I've tried to channel the anger I've seen in Internet postings. Tried to agree with Tony Dungy, a black football coach who says he was racially insulted.

But all I see is a naked chick and a football player.

Meaning, of course, actress Nicollette Sheridan, Philadelphia Eagles receiver Terrell Owens and a Monday Night Football promotional skit that had folks gathering three deep at the water cooler last week. In it, Sheridan, a star of ABC's "Desperate Housewives," shows up in the locker room wearing only a towel. The actress, who is white, seduces Owens, who is black, into skipping the game in order to, ahem, spend some time with her. She ends up dropping the towel and jumping into his arms.

The spot has produced a torrent of criticism, most of it coming from one of three directions.

Number one, some people say they were offended by the raciness of the skit – which seems a stretch, given the raciness of your average football game beer commercial.

Number two, some African Americans say race – not raciness – is the reason many whites took offense. They think many good ol' boys simply could not deal with seeing a desirable blonde in a black man's arms. That's probably true, but it just makes me wish Owens and Sheridan had also lip-locked for a minute or two. Nothing's more fun than making bigots stroke out.

It's complaint number three, though, that moves me to offer a few words. You see, some African Americans say the promo promotes an ugly old stereotype: black men as sexual predators lusting after white women. That's a ghost that has long haunted the national consciousness, as a source of beatings during slavery, murder during Jim Crow, hysteria during the O.J. Simpson trial, and imprisonment for Marcus Dixon, a black kid in Georgia who drew a 15-year term – since overturned – after a sexual encounter with a white girl.

It's a torturous history one is morally bound to honor.

But the question is: does that history – should that history – automatically come into play every time there is a sexual encounter between black and white? Is there ever a point where you are not a racial symbol but just a human being?

I have to admit that I didn't see the skit in question, though I have seen numerous excerpts. As near as I can tell, Owens did not bug his eyes out like Jimmie Walker at the sight of Sheridan's naked body. As far as I know, she did not say, "Come plow these fields, stud." There was, in other words, nothing overtly racial about the encounter beyond the fact that her skin is light and his is dark.

So I have trouble seeing it as an example of racial insensitivity. It seems instead an example of the ability race has to warp our worldview, to make us see what isn't there.

Thing is, it can also make us fail to see what is there.

Consider black folks' continued support for singer R. Kelly as he fights charges growing out of a videotape that allegedly shows him having sex with and urinating on an underage black girl. Many of us are content to accord him the benefit of the doubt.

And I wonder: Would we be as calm if it were Tom Cruise who was alleged to have done those things to a black child? Would we be this quiet if white people continued to go see Cruise's movies and give him prizes? I don't think so.

Why, then, is it "OK" as long as Kelly and his alleged victim are both black?

The answer is that race is and always has been a producer of dichotomy and double standard. It changes what we see and how we see it.

That's what this latest contretemps proves yet again, and it would almost be funny if it didn't speak so tellingly to the hurt and irresolution that still attach to African-American life – especially where the subject is black men and white women.

I wish it didn't matter, but I guess that's still too much to ask.

Friday, November 26, 2004

ERA OF ATTITUDE

Fine, suspend Ron Artest. Anyone who follows pro basketball knows his reputation as an emotionally unstable nitwit is no accident. And yeah, while you're at it, suspend his Indiana Pacers teammates Jermaine O'Neal and Stephen Jackson for their part in last Friday's fracas in the suburbs of Detroit. Suspend Ben Wallace, the Detroit Pistons center who triggered the initial altercation with a two-handed shove to Artest's face.

But after you've done all that, can we talk about the fans? Because if there was any single factor that turned a routine confrontation between athletes into an indoor riot, they were it. And to my mind, that speaks volumes about issues much larger than sports.

For the record: The conflict between Wallace and Artest was over pretty quickly. After Wallace expressed his rather emphatic objection to being fouled by Artest, the latter uncharacteristically walked away from conflict and reclined on a scorer's table. The matter was well on the way to being settled.

Then some "fan" threw a cup of liquid that hit Artest in the face. Next thing you know he's charging into the stands, and the throwdown in Motown is under way. Somebody slings a chair, fans are spilling onto the floor, people are hanging off O'Neal like Christmas tree ornaments, beer cups and popcorn and Lord knows what else are flying through the air.

And I'm sorry, but I'm having trouble blaming it all on an excess of beer. Alcohol, by and large, does not create emotion so much as it magnifies and distorts it.

Alternately, some observers say race contributed to the melee – specifically the jealousy and anger of white sports fans alienated by black basketball players they perceive as too rich, too showy, too cornrowed and tattooed. And insufficiently humble.

That's a good point, but I'm hesitant to place all the weight there, either.

Something broke loose Friday.

I don't know what to call it. Civility, maybe? Decorum, perhaps? Or maybe what broke is simply that old-school belief that there are some lines you don't cross.

As such, this modern Detroit riot offers irresistible symbolism: players going into the stands where they are forbidden; fans going onto the floor from which they are restricted. People crossing lines that were once considered inviolable.

You cannot convince me that's only a sports phenomenon, just a beer and race thing. Listen to the blowhards of talk radio and crossfire politics. Check the empty vulgarism of rap music and fear factor television. Listen to the cynicism and entitlement of our children. And tell me that mentality played no role in some fool's decision to fling his cup.

This coward – a prosecutor identified him as a self-employed contractor with a record of felony assault and drunken driving – tipped the balance with a single act of abject stupidity.

And once that happened, wasn't the rest preordained? Artest charging in for retribution? The entire stadium erupting in a furor? If your behavior is unchecked, doesn't that give me license, too? And the whole house of cards, the whole veneer of civil society, comes tumbling down.

Some would argue it's not that solid to begin with. We have become a chest-thump nation. An I-don't-take-no-stuff nation. A nation that crosses lines – not because lines need crossing, but because lines are there.

It's a lame and misguided echo of the '60s, when attitude was a political statement and people broke barriers because breaking barriers was necessary to force closed places open. But in the Ohs, attitude is its own reward and we break barriers because.

Friday night was a postcard from across the line. Friday night, something broke loose in Detroit.

But the truth is, it's been tearing for a very long time.

Wednesday, October 24, 2005

CLOTHES MAKE THE MAN

I am trying to feel Marcus Camby's pain. I am also trying to keep a straight face. I cannot do both.

Camby, for those who never read the sports page, is a very tall man who is paid $8 million per annum to play basketball for the Denver Nuggets. You'd think life would be good, but Camby is feeling put upon.

This is because last week the National Basketball Association instituted a dress code for its players. No more sunglasses worn indoors, no more sleeveless shirts, no more headphones during news conferences, no more caps cocked to the side, no more do-rags, no more rumpled sweats, no more chains bearing gaudy pendants the approximate size and weight of a small child. Business casual dress is now required of every player while on team business.

Camby feels this is an unfair burden. He told a reporter that if the NBA wants to impose a dress code, it should give each player a clothing allowance.

Did I mention that Camby is paid $8 million a year?

Of course, not every NBA player who opposes the dress code has cited financial hardship as his reason. At least two – Stephen Jackson of the Indiana Pacers, Paul Pierce of the Boston Celtics – have cited race. They think the code is aimed at ridding the league of the hip-hop "gangsta" look that is so popular among young black men.

"I think that's part of our culture," said Pierce. "The NBA is young black males."

Does he have a point? Is race a factor here? Having given the matter considerable consideration, I have an answer. In fact, I have three:

1) No. The new dress code will also require a wardrobe upgrade for such noteworthy white slobs as Dirk Nowitzki and Steve Nash.

2) Maybe. Given that over 75 percent of its players are black, the NBA can hardly avoid being a microcosm of racial issues.

3) Who cares?

Actually, No. 3 is my favorite. Let us assume that NBA Commissioner David Stern is indeed motivated by a perception that basketball fans find it increasingly difficult to relate to a league of Scary-Looking Young Black Men – especially after last year's brawl between players and fans.

So what? This is business. Stern is entitled – obligated – to use any moral means to protect his multi-billion-dollar corporation. If you earn a lavish living from that corporation you should also be concerned.

As for race: Let's grant that for some, all young black men, indeed, all black men, are scary-looking. Still, to believe the dress code is racist, you must ignore that the gangsta look is not popular among middle-aged blacks, but is often embraced by young whites. Point being, this is less racial than generational.

Meaning a generation of young black people choosing a style of dress that connotes criminality and street values. And it's childish to say, as Camby did, that "You shouldn't judge a person from what they wear." Unlike skin tone, unlike nationality, unlike sexual orientation, clothing reflects a conscious choice.

So, judging people by what they wear is fair. One has an absolute right to dress in a lime green suit with red shoes and an orange tie. But one has no reasonable expectation of being treated seriously as a candidate for the executive position while so attired. Because the company also has rights, including the right to ensure you represent it well.

Clothes, we used to say, make the man. The man, if he has a lick of sense, realizes this. The African-American man – so often scorned simply for being – should understand that better than anyone, particularly if he is fortunate enough to be lavishly compensated for playing a game.

So it's hard to muster sympathy for Marcus Camby. Poor baby thinks he's being mistreated? I can think of eight million reasons he's wrong.

Monday, March 20, 2006

IT'S ABOUT CHEATING, NOT RACE

Last week, I received an e-mail from a man named Keith in Atlanta.

He wrote: "I keep hearing and seeing all these allegations and books about Barry Bonds using steroids, but I've yet to hear one person, other than some clown trying to make a dollar by slandering his name, say they have ever seen him use them. He has not admitted to using steroids, nor has he ever tested positive, so why is the media feeding this nonsense?! As far as I'm concerned, it's all a bunch of hearsay ...

"I wonder if Barry were a white baseball player trying to break the home-run record if the media would entertain these unfounded allegations? ... Once again racist America has reared its ugly head. ..."

It goes on, but you get the point. I wish Keith didn't feel that way, but I'm not surprised he does.

I've spent 11 years writing about race – among other things – in this space. In that time, two frustrating truths have become clear to me. The first is that many white Americans labor under the self-justifying fantasy that racism just up and disappeared 40 years ago. The second is that many black Americans labor under the equally vexing belief that racism explains everything, that it is the all-purpose excuse any time one of "us" gets in trouble, gets criticized or just gets rude service in the checkout line.

I'm assuming here that Keith is black, something he doesn't say in his e-mail. If I'm mistaken, I apologize, but he certainly fits the pattern.

Meaning the O.J. Simpson pattern, the Michael Jackson pattern, the Mike Tyson pattern, the tiresome pattern of reflexively treating as a racial martyr any one of us who gets in dutch. Even if, as was the case with Simpson and Jackson, that person had largely severed ties with our community before trouble arose.

The aforementioned Barry Bonds, for the uninitiated, is a powerhouse slugger for the San Francisco Giants who has issued credibility-straining denials that his Incredible Hulk physique has anything to do with steroids.

But in their new book, "Game of Shadows" (recently excerpted in Sports Illustrated), reporters Mark Fainaru-Wada and Lance Williams allege that Bonds undertook a furious doping regimen in 1998 in hopes of claiming the record for most home runs in a single season, which he did. And Hank Aaron's record for most all-time home runs is within his reach.

The "hearsay" Keith refers to includes, according to the authors, over a thousand pages of documents, grand jury testimony and over 200 interviews, including talks with Bonds' former girlfriend, who turned over legal transcripts and audiotapes of voice mails Bonds left her. Perhaps most damning is Bonds' silence since the story broke. If you were falsely accused of being a liar and a drug user, wouldn't you – or your attorney – be screaming bloody murder?

To the degree this story is about anything, it is about the new American predilection for cheating one's way to the top. I hope Keith's e-mail does not presage any effort by the African-American community en masse to make it a story about race. In the first place, because there are enough real stories, horror stories, about race that we don't need to make any up.

And in the second place, because it diminishes our credibility and moral authority. It puts us on a par with the fabled boy who cried wolf.

This will come as a news flash to some of us, but black people, being human, are capable of doing bad things. Not every story that is unflattering to an African American is evidence of racial animus. Nor is every sin committed by a black person traceable to racial discrimination.

To say otherwise is lazy reasoning at best, an insult to our ancestors' suffering at worst. They understood, I think, better than we, what racism does to you and demands of you.

Sometimes, yes, it is a ball and chain. But it should never be a crutch.

Wednesday, January 16, 2008

POLITICALLY CORRECT TO THE EXTREME

Me, I've lost no sleep over what Kelly Tilghman said.

She's the Golf Channel broadcaster who is sitting out a two-week suspension for a throwaway comment on the air about Tiger Woods. It seems Tilghman and analyst Nick Faldo were discussing how little chance young golfers have of stopping Woods. "To take Tiger on, maybe they should just gang up for a while, " Faldo said.

To which Tilghman replied with a laugh, "Lynch him in a back alley."

Ha ha ha.

Oh, yeah, right.

Given that thousands of young black men actually have been lynched in back alleys – and town squares – in our history, there wasn't anything remotely funny about this "joke." Tilghman evidently realized this soon enough. She apologized off camera to Woods, whom she considers a friend. She also apologized on camera to viewers.

Woods has called the incident a "non-issue." The Reverend Al Sharpton issued a statement calling for Tilghman to be fired.

From where I sit, they're both wrong.

Woods, for one, has long struck me as distressingly obtuse on issues of race in particular and human rights in general. This is, after all, the same Tiger Woods who was once quoted in a national magazine telling off-color jokes about blacks and lesbians, who shrugged off controversy that arose over his playing at an all-male club where female employees were not allowed to even be seen by members, who concluded "no personal animosity ... was intended" when Fuzzy Zoeller, a white golfer, called him a "boy" and suggested that Woods might choose, as the menu for his Masters tournament champions dinner, fried chicken and collard greens.

One has to wonder what it would take to get a rise out of this guy: burning crosses on his front lawn?

Of course, one never has to wonder what it takes to get a rise out of Sharpton. He's playing to his own caricature in demanding Tilghman's head for his trophy wall. The demand seems reflexive and shrill, designed more to attract publicity than to generate justice.

As near as I have been able to determine, Tilghman has no pattern of saying racially obnoxious things, nor did she speak from malicious intent. This was not Don Imus with his long history of giving intentional offense, nor was it Jimmy "The Greek" Snyder spewing odious stereotypes, nor was it Rush Limbaugh grinding his political axe. This was ignorant and insensitive, but it's hard to see malice there.

According to Sharpton, that doesn't matter. He was quoted by the Associated Press as saying, "What she said is racist. Whether she's a racist ... is immaterial."

I disagree.

The evidence suggests that Golf Channel broadcaster Kelly Tilghman is simply someone who put her foot in her mouth.

All of us who communicate for a living, and particularly those who work in the field of live broadcast, walk a tightrope. There is a daily danger that you will – through misstatement, miscommunication or malaprop – communicate something you did not intend. If that something reveals some shabby sentiment you have heretofore hidden, c'est la vie. The public has a right to know.

But what if what you communicate is antithetical to your beliefs? What if it is, finally and only, a mistake? I don't know Tilghman. Maybe she's David Duke in pumps. But the evidence suggests that she is simply someone who put her foot in her mouth – tried to use a loaded word generically, forgetting the heritage of the man to whom she referred.

In which case, what point is served by trying to take her professional life? Seems to me an apology and suspension are enough to square the books.

Mind, I am all for coming down like bricks on those who truly denigrate African-American people. But someone who just had a brain cramp? I don't see the purpose. So my advice to Reverend Al: Move on.

And take the high road. There's less traffic.

WHITE MEN CAN'T JUMP

Don Lewis thinks white men can't jump.

What else explains the bizarre statement he issued last week? According to the Chronicle newspaper of Augusta, Georgia, Lewis is the commissioner of something called the All-American Basketball Alliance, which hopes to set up shop in 12 cities. "Only players that are natural born United States citizens with both parents of Caucasian race are eligible to play in the league," his statement said.

Yes, we're talking about a whites-only basketball league.

But Lewis, you'll be relieved to hear, is no racist. Shucks no, he says. It's just that white fans are tired of black players (cover your eyes, Kobe, D-Wade, LeBron) who rely on "street-ball" athleticism to make up for their lack of fundamental skills.

The AABA (Affirmative Action Basketball Association?) has an ice cream cone's chance in the Georgia sun of ever becoming a reality or, if it does, of surviving its first legal challenge. Success in any field is not some birthright of skin color, but, rather, a function of how hungry you are and how hard you work.

A reader on the Chronicle website wonders if the players would play in white robes with or without hoods. But this story, silly as it is, affords a chance to make a serious observation about excellence and expectation.

Back in 1997, Sports Illustrated ran a groundbreaking story, "Whatever Happened to the White Athlete?" which quantified the declining prominence of white players in mainstream sports. SI found a creeping sense of inferiority among young white student athletes.

Whether they ascribed it to physiological superiority or to being hungrier and harder working, most seemed to accept that black athletes were simply better than they – so why go out for the team?

The obvious irony is that, well into the 20th century, it was an article of faith in this country that blacks were physically inferior, lacking the strength, speed and intelligence to compete with white athletes. Now, we come into an era where white kids see themselves as the athletic bumblers.

But the new stereotype is as false as the old. Any list of basketball's all-time greats, after all, would be incomplete without the
snow-white likes of George Mikan, Larry Bird, John Stockton,
Jerry West, "Pistol" Pete Maravich and Kevin McHale, to name a
few.

Tellingly enough, if you put together a list of today's white
basketball elite, you'd find it dominated by international stars like
Manu Ginobili (Argentina), Dirk Nowitzki (Germany), Steve Nash
(South Africa, Canada) and Pau Gasol (Spain).

The common denominator, I think, is that they grew up in
places where they didn't get the memo that white men can't jump,
grew up unburdened by their supposed athletic impotence.

Their ability to thrive in a sport where black men dominate
suggests that sometimes, excellence is a question of expectation, of
how you see yourself.

That should be a message of hope to young white athletes –
and to young black scholars. Their plight, after all, is the mirror
image of that faced by the white kid who fears to go out for the
team, i.e., an academic achievement gap in which people who look
like them are perennially on the short end and there is a dearth of
role models to suggest it could ever be otherwise.

One often hears black kids speak in ways that suggest they
have internalized the inevitability of academic failure in much the
same way white kids internalize the idea that they can't run or
jump. But success in any field is not some birthright of skin color,
but, rather, a function of how hungry you are and how hard you
work – a function of what you deem possible.

That's why people who expect to fail usually do. So here is the
question we should ask our white kids struggling to hold on to the
ball and our black ones struggling to master the equation:

What if you expected to succeed?

Sunday, November 28, 2010

POSITIVE STEREOTYPES ARE NOT HELPFUL

A few words about black supremacy.

Such words seem necessary in light of a minor controversy
now roiling the sports world after boxer Bernard Hopkins, who is

black, declared that boxer Manny Pacquiao, who is Filipino, is scared to face an African-American fighter.

Pacquiao, considered by many the best fighter in the world, has fought – and dispatched – a black fighter from Ghana, but Hopkins stressed to the website Fanhouse.com that he's speaking specifically of a black American boxer, such as Floyd Mayweather.

Mayweather, said Hopkins, represents "the kind of fighter Pacquiao has yet to face: A big guy with tremendous speed and quickness as well as punching power, defensive skill and a quality chin."

Pacquiao, he said, would be helpless against "the styles that African-American fighters [use] – and I mean, black fighters from the streets or the inner cities ..."

"Listen, this ain't a racial thing," said Hopkins. "But then again, maybe it is."

For the record, this kind of thing is hardly new in boxing. As a sport predicated on one man's physical dominance of another, it has often served as a kind of surrogate warfare among races and tribes. From Jack Johnson to Joe Louis to Jake LaMotta to Muhammad Ali, boxers have always borne our various racial, ethnic and even national aspirations.

Indeed, Pacquiao himself, dubbed the "Mexicutioner" for his dominance of Mexican fighters, called his latest such victory "a testament that the Filipino race can rise above all odds and be the best in their chosen fields."

All that duly noted, though, there is something discomfiting in Hopkins' certitude that Pacquiao would meet his comeuppance at the hands of a black fighter. We live, after all, in a culture in which black athletic supremacy is frequently taken as a given.

Consider the old hit movie, "White Men Can't Jump." Consider Shaquille O'Neal once writing of how embarrassing it is to get dunked on by "a white boy." Consider Vince Carter once reportedly telling an opposing player's coach – Carter denied this – "You better get this white guy off me, or I'm going to score 40."

Taken in that context, Hopkins' assessment speaks less to harmless racial chauvinism than to enduring racial stereotype. Granted, he nods toward environmental factors ("... from the streets or the inner cities ..."), but it's still hard to escape a sense

Hopkins thinks there is something in the very fact of being black that confers athletic superiority.

He would not be the only one. A 1997 Sports Illustrated poll found about one-third of young white males saying that blacks simply outclassed them as athletes, and a roughly similar number of blacks agreeing.

And while it's understandable that many blacks would validate a flattering stereotype, what we fail to appreciate is that it is, nevertheless, a stereotype. And it is a short hop from a stereotype that says we are born athletes to those that say we are born criminals, malcontents, sluggards and academic incompetents. How do you embrace one without embracing them all? Why would you even try?

A stereotype – even a "good" one – imposes limitations upon the way we are seen by others and, more critically, upon the way we see ourselves.

I've spoken before thousands of school kids, and it has been my experience that when you ask a black boy what he wants to be when he grows up, you will most often get one of two answers: entertainer, athlete. Ask a white boy the same question and you'll find they see themselves as writers, cops, shark experts, vets.

Something to remember next time someone says white men can't jump. A child aims for goals he deems possible. When we embrace the stereotype of physical superiority, we as black people send our kids a clear message about what we deem possible for them.

And what we do not.

ENTERTAINMENT

Sunday, August 10, 1997

ELVIS CUT ACROSS RACIAL DIVIDE

Twenty years ago this week, Elvis Presley died and I didn't care.

It wasn't antipathy I felt, but ambivalence. In those days I was associate editor of SOUL ("America's Most Soulful Newsmagazine"), a tabloid covering black entertainment. As far as I was concerned, Presley's death had nothing to do with me or my readers; he was irrelevant.

Nor was I alone in that estimation. Indeed, I was, at 19, part of that post-Civil Rights school of black thought whose rejection of Elvis was pure reflex. We had a sense that Elvis Presley was an interloper who raided black culture and exploited it to a degree that blacks, being black, never could. It was like being made to live on the back porch of your own house and it raised a mighty resentment. Calling Presley the King of Rock 'n' Roll was, we felt, not unlike calling Jimmy Carter the president of Bolivia.

And then, there was this quote: "If I could find a white man who had the Negro sound and the Negro feel, I could make a billion dollars."

So said Sam Phillips, the man who would soon catapult Presley to glory in the mid-'50s. His words stung all the more for being true and for saying what they did about a black man's place in

America. Stung so much that two, three, four decades later, we still felt the pain. What else explains the visceral hostility the black hip-hop community lavished on a man named Vanilla Ice, a white rap star of modest talents?

Presley's talents, on the other hand, were prodigious, which always made it tougher to dismiss him out of hand. Besides which, there's an inescapable irony in the fact that he has come to be called an icon of white cultural imperialism and racial division: In his years of greatest creative power, Elvis Presley brought black and white together, often at professional risk. Motown, disco and even rap, whose fan base is as much white as it is black, all grew out of that precedent he helped to set: the revolutionary idea that black and white could be brought together in – and by – the groove.

It's worth remembering that Presley arrived during the last – and in some ways, the fiercest – years of legally mandated separation of the races. It was a time when dance organizers might stretch a rope down the center aisle of an auditorium to keep black and white dancing apart. A time when police broke up white teen parties because it was thought the kids were swinging with too much abandon, swinging too much like Negroes. A time when sweaty white men with sledgehammers smashed open juke boxes containing music by Negro artists, music variously described as "animalistic," "jungle-like" and "savage."

What might they have thought to learn that "juke" itself was an old African word meaning to jab or poke, in a sexual sense? It's probably best they didn't know: The poor men were already outraged enough, their sense of decency, their sense of place and self, all under assault by a new sound emanating from the shanties on the wrong side of the track. Because this was a time of fire.

And Elvis Presley came not to cool that fire, but to stoke it, to make it higher and hotter until it razed the old order and swept away the old men with the sledgehammers where they stood. He married black and white, made country more rhythmic and rhythm more country until what he had sounded like neither and sounded like both. He challenged what had never been challenged before, and the fact that he was a good-looking white boy born among the temples of the old Confederacy only made the act that much more seditious. And subversive. And daring.

Small wonder the establishment reacted to him with such unbridled revulsion. "Unspeakably untalented," said The New York Herald Tribune. "Nightmare," said Look magazine. Frank Sinatra called him "deplorable," Jackie Gleason promised that he wouldn't last, Billy Graham said, "I wouldn't let my daughter walk across the street" to see him. And then there's this sign, spotted on a used car lot in Cincinnati: "We guarantee to break 50 Elvis Presley records in your presence if you buy one of these cars today."

It wasn't simply the music that frightened them. It was what the music meant.

Elvis Presley brought separations together, resolved in one grand sweep the irresolution and interdependence of the black and white South. And he revealed segregation as a lie, unmasked white men doing what white men had done since the days of Thomas Jefferson and before: standing at the fence hole spying on black culture, taking notes. Unable to turn away, they stood there conjuring fantasies that blasted and offended their puritanical souls. The thing is, Elvis dared to live what he had conjured. With every throbbing quiver of his leg, every percolating note of rhythm guitar, with every whisper of loss, hymn of grace, thunder of righteousness from his outsized voice, he spoke what was then an officially unspeakable truth: that black and white are intertwined, entangled, woven together like braids.

Which is why James Brown's observation that Elvis "taught white America to get down" comes short of ultimate truth. What Elvis taught didn't stop with getting down, or even with white America.

Consider: According to Billboard magazine, Presley was the third most popular black music artist of the 1950s, after Fats Domino and Dinah Washington. Between 1956 and 1963, he posted 24 Top 10 hits on the R&B chart. "Hound Dog," Presley's version of Big Mama Thornton's 1953 hit, spent six weeks at No. 1 in 1956.

And black people, antennae preternaturally attuned to currents of culture and nuances of behavior, sensed something in him the charts could not quantify. Something sweet and genuine, something that respected and admired them. And they responded in kind. Upon spotting Presley one day, black girls on storied Beale Street in Memphis took off after him "like scalded cats," according to a black reporter. The black press noted with approval the way

Elvis profusely and publicly thanked a Memphis friend, B.B. King, for "the early lessons."

In his book, "Last Train To Memphis," Peter Guralnik recalls how Jet magazine once undertook to verify Presley's rumored disparagement of black people ("The only thing Negroes can do for me is buy my records and shine my shoes.") Presley denied making the statement and Jet found no end of black acquaintances willing to vouch for him.

They seem small gestures now. Even Presley's black chart success has been repeated (though less spectacularly) by such white performers as Teena Marie, the Doobie Brothers and Hall and Oates. But in its time, in the days of fire, this was revolution.

And on the anniversary of Presley's death, it seems that the least we can do is remember these things and honor him for them. Elvis Presley has, after all, become rather a foolish figure these last years – a tabloid mainstay kept alive by kitsch, an army of impersonators in rhinestone jumpsuits and the unwillingness of the easily gulled to believe him truly dead.

So it seems only fair to remind ourselves that whatever else he was, he was also this: one of the most dangerous men of a very dangerous time, a performer who dared integrate the two pieces of a disparate whole and tell the truth about what it means to be American. He forced raw-boned, hill-country white to look into kinky-haired, son-of-Africa black and see its own reflection. More, he forced us all to see a shared legacy of hardscrabble days and sweltering nights, of loving and longing and guitar twang, of train whistle and mule-drawn plow and front porch lemonade, of pea-picking and Moon Pie and the kind of yearning you can't speak, the kind that starts high in the throat as a keening sound and ends up low in the soul as a weary sigh.

This was music, yes. But it was also miracle.

Twenty years ago Elvis Presley died and I thought it didn't matter.

I was wrong.

BLACK IS MANY THINGS

The rappers are mad at Oprah again.

Just one rapper, actually: the gentleman who calls himself 50 Cent, but whose 1994 mug shot identifies him as prisoner No. 94R6378: Jackson, Curtis. Mr. Cent – "Fiddy" – to the cognoscenti – was one of a trio of rappers (Ice Cube and Ludacris were the others) who lambasted the Queen of All Media last summer for being insufficiently willing to promote hip-hop. Now, Mr. Cent renews the attack.

In an interview in Elle magazine(!), he charges Winfrey with being not black enough. Winfrey, he says, "started out with black women's views but has been catering to middle-aged white American women for so long that she's become one herself." He also calls her an "Oreo, " which, for those not fluent in black-on-black insult, means black on the outside, white on the inside.

Mr. Cent, should it not be painfully obvious from the foregoing, is an idiot. Worse, he's an idiot with a painfully transparent need for approval from the woman he has spent so much energy denigrating. I'll leave it to the mental-health community to explain what that means. I'm here only to make one point:

It's not easy being O.

Yeah, I know: Cry me a river. And $1.5 billion (the reported size of Winfrey's fortune) buys a lot of Kleenex.

I'm not trying to engage your sympathy for the most powerful woman (sorry, Hillary, beg pardon, Condi) in America. I'm only trying to say it's a hard trick to manage, being both famous and black. Or, at least, famous to the degree that Oprah Winfrey is – i.e., to the degree that you are recognized as readily in white homes as in black.

To reach that level of renown is to find yourself pulled between competing expectations. On the one side, they praise you for "transcending race" – whatever that means – and they get resentful if you remind them of the ways you are not like them. On the other side, they are alert to any sign that you have Forgotten Where You Came From, and they will call you out if they think you're suffering racial amnesia.

I've always thought Oprah Winfrey handled those competing pulls with a rare grace. She produces programming ("The Legends Ball") that celebrates the passages of great black women, she promotes black authors (full disclosure: I was once one of them), she speaks out on racial issues, she makes a movie ("Beloved") on the horror of slavery, she builds a school in South Africa – and yet, somehow, white women don't fear her, still love her. Even when she rebukes them for racial insensitivity.

I remember when one of those women, intending a compliment, told Winfrey she didn't think of her as black. And Oprah said, Whoa. Black, she explained, gently, but emphatically, is exactly what she is. And her predominantly white audience, as I recall, cheered. That's a minor miracle.

Granted, I watch daytime television infrequently. So maybe in those dozens of Oprah shows I haven't seen, Winfrey proves herself the black man hater and white woman worshipper that black critics often depict. But you'll forgive me if I doubt. You'll forgive me if I suspect that the "Oprahs" I haven't seen track pretty closely to the ones I have: celebrity interviews, pop psychology and self-actualization strategies for women of a certain age and station in life.

It's hard for me to understand what's wrong with that, or inherently "not black" about it. 50 Cent makes the mistake a lot of white people do: assuming that there is but one monolithic black experience and that it is street, poor and hard-core.

Which doesn't insult just Oprah Winfrey. It insults all of us because it denies a simple fact: Black is many things. That's something Mr. Cent should consider next time he's holed up in his mansion in Farmington, Connecticut (median income $67,000, black population 1.5 percent), writing rhymes about how hard life is for poor black folks on mean streets.

Tuesday, May 11, 2010

A SINGER WHO CHANGED THE WORLD

Lena Horne was one of the last links to an era fading slowly from living memory.

A singer and actress of café au lait skin, lively eyes and an irrepressible smile, she came to fame in the 1940s, a time when

African Americans could not vote in the South or gain admittance to most hotels, when southern trees still bore strange fruit.

Thus the African-American performer who climbed out of obscurity became, wittingly or not, a de facto symbol, a stand in representing millions of other African Americans shut out of the mainstream by custom and by law. She bore all their hopes and aspirations. It was unfair; it was ridiculous. It was the way things were. Lena Horne, who died Sunday at 92, had to represent. And she did – spectacularly.

Not simply because she was beautiful, though she was. Not simply because she sang in a satiny, deceptively agile voice, though she did. In the end, the thing for which Lena Horne may be most justly celebrated is simply that she did all of the above with a sense of weightless grace, a wordless insistence upon her dignity and carried herself with a refined sophistication the nation simply was not used to equating with African-American people. In so doing, she became a hero in a way that went far beyond her beauty.

Although, in the end, everything always came back to that beauty. Horne was ambivalent about it.

"I was unique in that I was a kind of black that white people could accept. I was their daydream. I had the worst kind of acceptance because it was never for how great I was or what I contributed. It was because of the way I looked."

African-American men did not share her ambivalence. Indeed, African-American men of a certain age will testify that while the white guys went to war with posters of Betty Grable to remind them of what they were fighting for, black men climbed into their tanks, hefted their rifles, knowing that they were fighting for Lena Horne.

They were smitten by an elegance that seemed effortless. But she would tell anyone who asked that it never really was.

Lena Mary Calhoun Horne was born in Brooklyn on June 30, 1917. Her parents split up when she was still a toddler, and her childhood was itinerant, spent touring with her performer mother. For a time, they lived in Overtown, a thriving mecca of African-American culture before the freeway pierced its heart.

At 16, at her mother's behest, she quit school and auditioned as a chorus dancer at the Cotton Club, the famous Harlem nightspot where whites went to be entertained by black performers (only the light-skinned need apply) but which blacks were not allowed to patronize. In 1938, she made her film debut in "The Duke Is Tops," a black musical. But her film career would always be stunted by the bizarre racial politics of the era.

Because of her refusal to play maids — the stereotypical role that was pretty much all Hollywood offered black actresses at the time — she was reduced to cameo appearances in movies starring white performers. She was typically depicted in a lavish evening gown leaning against a pillar, singing a musical interlude. Her performance was never part of the main action, allowing film companies to edit her out completely when films were shown in the South.

Among the few exceptions was "Stormy Weather," a frothy, 1943 musical in which she and famed dancer Bill "Bojangles" Robinson headed an all-black cast. The movie's title number became her signature.

Otherwise, the movies simply did not know what to do with Lena Horne, a fact of which she was acutely aware. "They didn't make me into a maid," she wrote in her 1965 autobiography, "Lena," "but they didn't make me into anything else, either. I became a butterfly pinned to a column singing away in Movieland."

She was always outspoken like that, particularly in confronting the racism that hemmed in her career and life. She expressed herself with her funds, contributing generously to the civil rights movement.

She also expressed herself with her deeds. In 1945, Horne was incensed to walk onstage and find herself singing to an audience of German POWs and African-American soldiers; the soldiers were required to sit in the back, behind the enemy prisoners. Horne left the stage, turning her back on the Germans and singing for the black men. In 1960, she threw an ashtray, several glasses and a lamp at a white patron of a Beverly Hills restaurant who addressed her by a racial slur.

There was no such drama when Horne broke the color barrier in Miami in 1952. Her engagement at the Clover Club on Biscayne Boulevard went exceptionally well, according to contemporary accounts, though Horne's manager would admit they were initially "hesitant" about accepting the gig.

The singer was married twice. The first wedding came when she was just 19. Her husband was Louis Jones, a friend of her father who was nine years older; the union lasted nine years and produced her children, Gail and Teddy. In 1947, she married Lennie Hayton, a musician. They kept the marriage a secret for three years. He was white, and they feared the controversy that would — and eventually did — erupt. Hayton died in 1971.

Horne continued recording well into the 1990s. In 1978 she appeared as Glinda the Good in the big-screen adaptation of "The Wiz." In 1981, she mounted a one-woman Broadway show: "Lena Horne — the Lady and Her Music." It won her a Tony.

Still, she never quite outpaced the irony of her career: She made it possible for the likes of Halle Berry, Beyoncé, Taraji P. Henson and Angela Bassett to have the sort of unfettered career Horne herself never did. In her later years, she became philosophical about that.

As she said in an interview when she was 80, "My identity is very clear to me now. I am a black woman. I'm free. I no longer have to be a 'credit.' I don't have to be a symbol to anybody; I don't have to be a first to anybody. I don't have to be an imitation of a white woman that Hollywood sort of hoped I'd become. I'm me, and I'm like nobody else."

PUNDITS

Wednesday, August 18, 2010

WHEN CONSERVATIVE PUNDITS TALK RACE

Asking a conservative pundit for advice on race is like asking an ayatollah for advice on preparing the Christmas ham.

There are exceptions, yes, but by and large, this terrain is the dark side of the moon for conservatives. They don't know it well, so they tend to go there rarely, reluctantly and seldom voluntarily. And when they do, they not infrequently make Patrick Buchanan-size jackasses of themselves.

So the train wreck of a radio segment that generated unwelcome headlines for talk show host Laura Schlessinger last week was predictable the moment she took a call from an African-American woman named "Jade." See, Jade, inexplicably, sought Dr. Laura's advice on what to do when her white husband's family and friends make "racist comments" in front of her.

And that's when the train took a header into the gorge. First, there was Jade's mention of a neighbor who can't drop by without asking her how black people like this or black people like that. Dr. Laura said that wasn't racist — which is arguably fair, but ignores the fact that a person gets tired of constantly being treated as an emissary from the planet Negro.

Then there was Dr. Laura's non sequitur rant about how blacks voted for Barack Obama "without giving much thought" — the brainless, easily swayed black voter being a fiction beloved by many conservatives, and never mind that it was Queen of Soul Hillary Clinton who had the black vote sewn up and Obama who was forced to earn it.

There is much more, but we are running out of page and still haven't gotten to the part that made headlines and forced Dr. Laura into an apology the next day. Jade asked, "How about the N-word?"

"Black guys use it all the time," snapped Dr. Laura. "Turn on HBO, listen to a black comic and all you hear is nigger, nigger, nigger."

When Jade challenged her casual use of that word, Schlessinger doubled down. She repeated her N-word trilogy and at one point told Jade, "I think you have too much sensitivity ..."

Oh, my stars and garters.

There is, should it need saying, a big hole in Dr. Laura's reasoning. Comics do all sorts of obnoxious things. They call women by a synonym for female dogs. They talk about menstruation, masturbation, nose-picking, gas-passing and other subjects generally avoided in polite company.

Does Schlessinger really think comedians should be our standard on matters of decorum? Does she really think comedians' — or for that matter, rappers' and street kids' — choice of language justifies her use of a noxious epithet loathed by the vast majority of the 38 million people against whom it is routinely hurled? Or that calling her on that is evidence of hypersensitivity?

Too bad I already used that stars and garters line. It would go nicely here.

Suffice it to say, I bet you Dr. Laura never thought about it like that. I bet you she never thought about it at all. And therein lies the problem — not simply for her, but for conservatives in general who seek to contribute to a constructive racial dialogue.

See, I'd argue the most offensive thing about Schlessinger's gaffe wasn't her use of the N-word, but the air of smug entitlement with which she did so. Conversing with a woman who lives a reality about which she can only theorize, Dr. Laura brushed away

Jade's every effort to dissent or explain. She was not there to engage. She already knew all she needed to.

One finds that often when conservative pundits talk race. They seem trapped within their own baseless narratives, loath to listen to, much less credit, anything that contradicts what they chose long ago to believe.

Small wonder they seldom contribute anything of value to the discussion. They don't know what they don't know. And they are unwilling to learn.

Wednesday, October 27, 2010

RUSH TO JUDGMENT

I probably should not be surprised that the Juan Williams story got as big as it did.

There are, after all, few topics in public life more dangerous than race and culture. And the fact that the liberal-leaning National Public Radio fired Williams for comments made on Fox News about that topic provides irresistible ammunition for conservatives who see liberals as hypocritical on matters of free speech.

The surprise, I guess, would've been if the story had been allowed to quietly die.

Williams got in trouble for his response to a question from Fox's Bill O'Reilly about whether the nation faces "a Muslim dilemma." Said O'Reilly, "The cold truth is that in the world today jihad, aided and abetted by some Muslim nations, is the biggest threat on the planet."

Williams agreed. "I mean, look, Bill, I'm not a bigot. You know the kind of books I've written about the Civil Rights Movement in this country. But when I get on the plane, I got to tell you, if I see people who are in Muslim garb and I think, you know, they are identifying themselves first and foremost as Muslims, I get worried. I get nervous."

Two days later, he was informed – by phone – that his years of service at NPR had come to an end.

I happen to think O'Reilly was mostly right. The attempt by some – the qualifier is important – Islamic nations and groups to intimidate and destabilize the rest of the world is, if not "the biggest threat on the planet" (North Korea and global warming might have something to say about that), certainly in the top three. And no, nothing in that observation is inconsistent with the demand that the vast majority of peaceful Muslims be left alone to worship and live as they see fit.

I also think Williams was mostly wrong. Seems to me your average terrorist is unlikely to dress in a way that screams Muslim. I'm thinking T-shirt, ball cap and jeans. He may not have a Middle Eastern appearance. He may not even be a he.

That said, my concern isn't whether the comments were right or wrong, but whether they were inbounds, whether they crossed that subjective but critical line between fair commentary and rank bigotry. I don't believe they did, especially given that Williams went on to decry the tendency to smear all Muslims with the misdeeds of a few. That context suggests his intent was to question – not justify – his own paranoia.

And in firing him, NPR shows not the commitment to journalistic guidelines it has cited, but rather, a capacity for hair-trigger response. There's a lot of that going around.

For every Don Imus, Rick Sanchez or Mel Gibson who deserved the censure and sanction their words brought down, we lately seem to have a Juan Williams, a Shirley Sherrod or a Harry Reid whose crime is not what they said but that they said and that someone felt no obligation to listen before passing judgment. Indeed, in matters of racial and cultural difference, some of us seem to feel it a sin even to acknowledge the existence thereof.

Joe Biden was pilloried in many forums, including this one, for seeming to call Barack Obama the first black presidential candidate "who is articulate and bright and clean and a nice-looking guy." Except that if you actually listen to what he said – most transcripts mis-edited the quote – it becomes clear he was making another point entirely.

There's a moral to that experience: Few issues are more in need of serious discussion than race and culture. And while we should be vigilant against those who would drag that discussion into the mire of bigotry, we also owe people the courtesy of listening to what they've said before judging it. After all, a subjective line is still a line.

And if you keep fooling around with a hair trigger, sooner or later, someone is going to get hurt.

Chapter 5

CRIME AND PUNISHMENT

Wednesday, April 20, 2016

JUSTICE IS BLIND

Friday is a day of reckoning for Duane Buck.

That's the day the Supreme Court will determine whether to hear his appeal for a new sentencing hearing. Buck is on Death Row in Texas.

It is important to emphasize that he is not seeking a new trial. There's no question of Buck's guilt in the 1995 shooting deaths of his ex-girlfriend, Debra Gardner, her friend, Kenneth Butler, and Buck's stepsister, Phyllis Taylor. No, all he's asking is to be re-sentenced for the crime.

There is, you see, a law in Texas that says you can't be sentenced to death unless a jury finds that you represent a future danger, i.e., that you are likely to hurt someone else if left alive. In Buck's case, psychologist Walter Quijano, a supposed expert testifying for the defense, no less, told jurors Buck represented just such a danger.

Because he is black.

If any of this rings a bell, it's because I wrote about the case three years ago. If you read that column, you may recall that one of the researchers on whose writings Quijano based his testimony says his work supports no such conclusion. Indeed, Quijano's claim was so outrageous that even Buck's surviving victim and one of his prosecutors think he should get a new hearing. In 2000, Senator John Cornyn, who was then Texas' attorney general, conceded the state was wrong in allowing race to be used as factor in sentencing.

Quijano had given similar testimony in six cases. The other five defendants, all black or Hispanic, got new hearings. Buck was denied, based on a flimsy legalism. Namely that the offending testimony came not on "cross," but on direct examination. In other words, it was first elicited by the defense.

People keep telling me I'm wrong to believe the justice system is riddled with racial bias. They tell me the system has nothing against people of color, and that it is only evidence of their own native criminality that such people are stopped, frisked, arrested, tried and incarcerated in wildly disproportionate numbers. People keep promising me the system is just.

And I keep being sickened by stories like this. I keep finding studies like the 2012 report by University of Maryland criminology professor Raymond Paternoster, which said that at the time of Buck's sentencing, the local DA was three times more likely to seek death for a black defendant than for a white one.

It's worth noting, by the way, that these predictions of future dangerousness are not exactly unerring. The Texas Defender Service, a nonprofit law firm specializing in capital cases, studied the records of 155 Death Row inmates and found that only 5 percent went on to commit assaults serious enough to warrant more than a Band-Aid. In a place where you can get written up for saving a seat in the cafeteria or having too many postage stamps, Buck has a clean disciplinary record dating back to 1998.

So Quijano's testimony was not only racist, but also – pardon the redundancy – wrong.

Look, I don't like the death penalty. If you know me, you already know that. But even if I did, I would want to be sure this severest of sanctions was imposed fairly. Plainly, it is not.

And the fact that it is not cannot help but undermine the credibility of the entire system. If we countenance bias at this extremity, what confidence can anyone have in the system's fairness at any level, down to and including parking tickets?

The racism here is not subtle. To the contrary, it is neon. To deny Buck a new sentencing hearing untainted by bizarre suppositions about the future danger he poses because of his skin color would shred even the pretense of equality before the law. So let us hope the Court does what it should.

Because, yes, Friday is a day of reckoning for Duane Buck. But it's a day of reckoning for justice, too.

THE JUSTICE SYSTEM

Wednesday, September 19, 2007

DIFFERENT RULES

Scenes from America, circa once upon a time.

White men taking sledgehammers to the door of the jailhouse in Marion, Indiana, intending to murder three African-American prisoners. The sheriff orders his men not to interfere.

White men hearing testimony tying two white defendants conclusively to the kidnap, torture and murder of a black boy in Money, Mississippi. The jury takes less than an hour to set them free.

White men with badges arresting three civil rights workers for an alleged traffic violation in Neshoba County, Mississippi. Forty-four days later, the workers' bodies are dug out of an earthen dam.

There are other examples – literally thousands – but let three suffice to make the point. Which is that African Americans have frequently found the justice system to be about anything but justice. From the day slavery ended, that system has often been its surrogate, a tool used specifically for the suppression and control of black people.

There was no artifice about it. This conspiracy of beat cops and county sheriffs and DAs and judges and senators and attorneys general operated openly and with impunity. Everyone knew there were simply different rules, different enforcement and different punishment for blacks.

Maybe your impulse is to seal all that off in a mental box called history, interesting, lamentable, but hardly relevant. In which case, what will you say about Jena?

Meaning, of course, the tiny Louisiana town now infamous for a series of events that began a year ago when a black high school student asked the principal if it was OK for him to sit under a shade tree white kids claimed as theirs. The principal told him yes. But the next day, nooses were found hanging in the tree.

The principal wanted the white kids who did it expelled, but the superintendent overruled him, briefly suspending them instead. Expulsion, he felt, was excessive for this "prank."

There followed weeks of racial brawls and even an arson fire. A black student, Robert Bailey, was hit in the head with a beer bottle by a white kid who was later charged with simple battery and released on probation.

After a white student, Justin Barker, supposedly taunted Bailey about it, six black kids allegedly jumped him, kicking and stomping. Barker was knocked out and had a black eye. He was treated and released at the hospital and felt well enough to go out that same night.

Yet the DA called it attempted murder.

Yes, charges against five of the six were eventually reduced. Yes, an appeals court just overturned the aggravated battery conviction of the only student whose case has been adjudicated.

But it is hard to be sanguine. This unjust justice is hardly unique. Consider Genarlow Wilson, 17, sentenced to 10 years for consensual sex with a 15-year-old. And Marcus Dixon, 18, who drew 10 for having sex with an underage white girl. And Shaquanda Cotton who shoved a white teacher's aide and got seven years from a judge who had earlier given probation to a white girl who burned down her family's house. A 2000 study co-sponsored by the Justice Department codifies the obvious: People of color receive starkly unequal treatment in the "justice" system.

Where blacks are concerned, it seems, that system often still exists not to enforce the law and protect order, but to intimidate and compel. But at least they care enough about appearances these days to lie.

"Race? This has nothing to do with race. Oh, no." Prosecutors justifying the unjustifiable. Utterly convinced of their own blamelessness.

One might ask why it is that black justice so seldom looks like real justice, even today.

The answer is that history does not fit in a box. And once upon a time is now.

Wednesday, June 22, 2011

DOUBLE STANDARD

Consider two recent examples of American justice.

In 2009, after a night of bar hopping, a man named Ryan LeVin plowed his speeding Porsche into two British tourists in Fort Lauderdale, killing them. He fled the scene, lied to the cops, tried to pin the crime on someone else.

About three weeks ago, Tyell Morton, a kid from Rushville, Indiana, sneaked into his school wearing a hooded sweat shirt and left a mysterious package in the girls' restroom. It turned out to be a blow-up doll.

LeVin was recently sentenced: he got house arrest at his oceanfront condo. Morton, who is 18, was jailed with a $30,000 bond and faces trial on charges that could put him away for eight years. Morton has no record. LeVin was on probation, has a string of traffic violations and a cocaine conviction. It ought not surprise you to learn that LeVin is white and fabulously wealthy, while Morton is black, and not.

Jaye Davis would reject the implications of that observation. She wrote a letter to the editor of the Rushville Republican that said in part, "I want and need someone to PLEASE tell me this case is not going to become a huge deal because of RACE! I feel very strongly that skin color had nothing to do with these charges..."

Morton's father doesn't want it to be about race, either. Several times during a telephone conversation with me, Walter Nelson, a barber who owns a shop near Joliet, Illinois, repeated that he does not want to "cloud" matters by framing his son's experience in racial terms.

Rushville, he explained, is a small, predominantly white town. Most of his son's homeboys are white. Many of those who contributed to pay his son's bond are also white. "My son's life is more important than some racial issue that people can't seem to get over. That's what I want to focus on, man."

Tyell, he said, is a good kid who brings home A's and B's and the occasional C. He dreams of going to college. He wants to be a doctor – or a video-game tester.

"He's a teenager," his dad said. "He's a young man trying to find his way in life."

Nelson knows Tyell pulled a knuckleheaded stunt. But the overreaction to that stunt frustrates him. Once upon a time, a Tyell Morton might have suffered only a chewing out by the cops and his folks. But, said one official, things are different post-Columbine. Indeed, the initial charge was "terroristic mischief."

"They labeled my son as a terrorist," said Nelson. "They referenced Columbine with my son. Columbine, those guys had intent to harm. My son did not have any intent to harm anybody at all. That's what angers me." He wonders how six days spent in shackles with car thieves and drug dealers might scar his child.

And Jaye Davis is right, after a fashion. This is not an issue of race. It is an issue of race and class. To believe otherwise is to believe a Ryan LeVin would now be facing eight years in jail, and that requires a level of naïveté inaccessible to me.

I asked Nelson if he thought his son would be in this jeopardy if he were wealthy and/or white instead of a black kid whose family had to pass the hat to raise the $3,000 the bondsman required. This man who doesn't want to cloud matters with side issues snorted a bitter laugh. "That question has been answered way before this happened to my son. Do I need to even answer that? Come on."

Sunday, April 29, 2012

BETRAYED BY JUSTICE

Twenty years ago today, my hometown burned. I had moved to Miami the year before and there is, let me tell you, something surreal about watching on television from a continent away as places you've been and streets you know are smashed and burned.

The Los Angeles riots happened because justice did not. They happened because a predominantly white jury in the far flung suburb of Simi Valley looked at video of four white cops bludgeoning a black drunk driving suspect, Rodney G. King, so viciously that even Chief of Police Daryl F. Gates said it made him sick – and yet, pronounced them not guilty of any crime.

To acknowledge this is not to lionize the rioters. You do not lionize 54 deaths and a billion dollars in property damage. You do not lionize what almost killed Reginald Denny, beaten nearly to death for the "crime" of being in the wrong place at the wrong time with the wrong color skin.

But one need not lionize the rioters' method of expression to empathize with the message they expressed. Namely, a certain frustration, a certain sickness at heart, a certain outrage at being betrayed by justice – again.

It is an experience far older than the L.A. riots – and as relevant as the shooting of Trayvon Martin. On the surface, perhaps, the two incidents have little in common: the then-27-year-old drunkard beaten so badly after a high speed chase that his body and mind still bear the scars, and the unarmed 17-year-old boy shot to death by a neighborhood watchman who thought him suspicious because he was dawdling and looking around.

They are not dissimilar, however, in one telling aspect: delay. It took a ruinous riot and a new federal trial for Rodney King to receive anything approaching justice. It took 46 days, uncounted public demonstrations and the appointment of a special prosecutor for that process even to begin for Trayvon Martin. Historically, that has always been the problem when African Americans seek redress of grievances pregnant with racial overtones. Justice comes slowly, grudgingly, and grumblingly, when it comes at all.

I hear all these warnings not to "rush to judgment" in the Martin case, and it is sage advice. Yet I find myself wondering: when is the last time I saw anyone who is not black look at one of those episodes where the justice system failed African-American people – look at Trayvon, look at Jena, Louisiana, look at Tulia, Texas, look at Amadou Diallo, look at Abner Louima – and say, unprompted and unambiguously, that thus and so happened because of race. Outside of the most far-left liberals, they seldom do.

Even when it is as obvious as a cockroach on white satin, it is something most cannot bring themselves to admit.

And yes, I know someone wishes I should just shut up about it. I hear that a lot. Indeed, more than once, someone has actually told me there'd be no racial problems in this country "if you didn't talk about it." What a piece of logic that is: ignore it and it will go away.

Such people, Martin Luther King once observed, mistake silence for peace. Silence is not peace.

As we count the lessons we have learned since L.A. burned, count that as one of the lessons we have not. Here is another: Justice too long delayed is justice denied. As protesters often put it: "No justice, no peace."

Sometimes, I wonder if some of us really understand what that means. With the L.A. riots now 20 years behind us and the Martin case before us, it is a good time to consider those words afresh, consider them in light of our noble ideals and too-frequent failings, consider them as if it were you, looking for recourse after justice failed you – again.

Because, you see, that slogan is not a threat. It's not a prediction. It's not even a warning.

"No justice, no peace" is a certainty.

Wednesday, May 9, 2012

THE GREATEST JAILER ON EARTH

I promised Russell I would ask you something.

We met last week in a medium security correctional facility. There, I spent a couple hours talking with a group of men who are studying for their GEDs. I stressed to them the need for long-term goals, the criticality of education in an era where good-paying, low-skill jobs are going away and the importance of refusing to allow oneself to be defined by whatever box of race or class society has placed you in. It was toward the end that Russell asked a question whose exact wording I can't recall, but whose gist was a simple challenge:

What are you going to do to help me when I get out?

He meant me, personally. And he meant you, personally.

Perhaps the question makes you indignant. This would not surprise me. A generation of conservative "reform" on issues of criminal justice has encouraged many of us to believe the only thing we "owe" those who break the law is punishment, followed by punishment, along with punishment and then punishment. It is a seductive line of reasoning. Who among us is not made furious by those men and women who break and enter and steal and damage and violate and maim and kill and thereby rob us of the right to feel secure in our own persons?

Small wonder, then, that harsh, endless punishment has come to seem such an absolute good that politicians of both the right and the left stumble all over themselves to prove they are "tough on crime." And none of them dare speak a word about rehabilitation, for mortal fear of being declared that hated other thing: "soft" on crime.

Thus, you get mandatory sentencing guidelines that give a man 25 years for stealing a slice of pizza or kicking down a door. Thus, you get Joe Arpaio, the cartoonish Arizona sheriff, feeding his prisoners moldy bologna and rotten fruit and housing them in tents where the temperature reaches 140 degrees. Thus, you get Troy Davis executed despite substantive doubts about his guilt.

Maybe such things leave you feeling righteous and tough. They should actually leave you feeling concerned, if not from moral questions, then from pragmatic ones. America is now the greatest jailer on Earth. Prison overcrowding is a growing problem; we literally cannot build facilities fast enough. As CBS News recently reported, the United States has less than 5 percent of the world's population, but about 25 percent of its prisoners. As CNN recently reported, at 760 prisoners per 100,000 citizens, the United States jails its people at a rate 7 to 10 times higher than most any other developed nation.

Either Americans are much more crime prone than, say, the Japanese or the British or this "reform" is insane. Worse, in a system of punishment followed by punishment, the insanity does not end with locking up our citizens in obscene numbers. No, after we set them "free," we deny them re-entry into the mainstream of society with laws barring them from jobs, housing, loans, voting, schooling. How can you fix your life – why even try? – if you are denied the reward that should follow, i.e., the dignity of full citizenship? We close doors of advancement and opportunity to ex-felons, then wonder why so many end up walking back through the door to prison.

Once upon a time, there was an ideal that held that once a person had paid his "debt to society," he was owed a second chance. That seems to have gone the way of vinyl albums and 69-cent gas. But our new ideal – punishment and then punishment – is short-sighted and unsustainable.

Maybe you find Russell's question impertinent. Actually, it could not be more pertinent. What are we going to do to help him when he gets out?

It would be good if we had an answer for him. We might not like the answer he finds for himself.

Wednesday, July 22, 2015

'INJUSTICE SYSTEM'

The United States does not have a justice system.

If we define a justice system as a system designed for the production of justice, then it seems obvious that term cannot reasonably be applied to a system that countenances the mass incarceration by race and class of hundreds of thousands of nonviolent offenders. Any system that vacuums in one out of every three African-American males while letting a banker who launders money for terrorist-connected organizations, Mexican drug cartels and Russian mobsters off with a fine is not a justice system.

No, you call that an injustice system.

This is something I've been saying for years. Imagine my surprise when, last week, President Obama said it, too. "Any system that allows us to turn a blind eye to hopelessness and despair," he said in a speech before the NAACP in Philadelphia, "that's not a justice system, that's an injustice system." He called for reforms, including the reduction or elimination of mandatory minimum sentencing and the repeal of laws that bar ex-felons from voting.

This was the day after Obama commuted the sentences of 46 nonviolent drug offenders, and two days before he became the first president to visit a prison, Federal Correctional Institution El Reno, near Oklahoma City. "There but for the grace of God," he said, minutes after poking his head into an empty 9 by 10 cell that houses three inmates.

It was more than just an acknowledgment of his personal good fortune. Given that Obama, his two immediate predecessors, and such disparate luminaries as Sarah Palin, John Kerry, Newt Gingrich, Al Gore, Jeb Bush and Rick Santorum are known to have used illicit drugs when they were younger, it was also a tacit acknowledgment that fate takes hairpin turns. And that the veil separating drug offender from productive citizen is thinner than we sometimes like to admit.

Welcome to what may be a transformational moment: the end of an odious era of American jurisprudence. Meaning, the era of mass incarceration.

Apparently, the president has decided to make this a priority of his final 18 months in office. Even better, the call for reform enjoys bipartisan support. Republican Senators Rand Paul and Ted Cruz, among others, have embraced the cause. And the very conservative Koch brothers have chosen to "ban the box" (i.e., stop requiring ex-offenders to disclose their prison records to prospective employers on their job applications).

All of which raises the promise that, just maybe, something will actually be done.

It is long past "about time." Our color-coded, class-conscious, zero-tolerance, punishment-centric, mandatory minimum system of "justice" has made us the largest jailer on earth. One in four of the world's prisoners is in an American lockup. This insane rate of imprisonment has strained resources and decimated communities.

It has also shattered families and impoverished children, particularly black ones. So many people bewail or condemn the fact that a disproportionate number of black children grow up without fathers, never connecting the dots to the fact that a disproportionate number of black fathers are locked up for the same nonviolent drug offenses for which white fathers routinely go free.

The "get tough on crime" wave that swept over this country in the '80s and '90s was born of the unfortunate American penchant for applying simplistic answers to complicated questions. But bumper sticker solutions have a way of bringing unintended consequences.

We will be dealing with these unintended consequences for generations to come. But perhaps we are finally ready to take steps toward reversing that historic blunder.

And giving America a justice system worthy of the name.

RACIAL PROFILING

Sunday, December 2, 2012

BLACK BLINDNESS

Call it black blindness.

It is a kind of myopia that afflicts some of us – too many of us – whenever we gaze upon a dark-skinned man. It causes some of us – too many of us – to see things that are not there, and to miss things that are. Sometimes, it is fatal.

Such was the case for Amadou Diallo, the African immigrant who died in a hailstorm of gunfire in 1999 after police mistook his wallet for a gun.

We cannot yet know if black blindness was the cause of death for Jordan Davis, a 17-year-old black kid who was killed the night after Thanksgiving. But there is reason to suspect it was. Davis was shot by a 45-year-old white man, Michael David Dunn, who says he saw a rifle. At this writing, police have recovered no such weapon.

The altercation began with an argument in a gas station in Jacksonville. Dunn had pulled in so his girlfriend could go to the convenience store. In an SUV next to him were Davis and three other teenagers playing their music too loudly. Dunn told them to turn it down. An argument ensued. Dunn's attorney, Robin Lemonidis, says the teenagers peppered him with obscenities and insults. Then, she says, Davis poked a rifle through an open window, threatened her client and began to open the door of the SUV. Dunn reached for his pistol and came up firing. The SUV peeled out. Dunn kept shooting at it because, his lawyer says, he feared the teenagers might come back after him.

"There is no racial motivation here whatsoever," she told The New York Times. But even if you buy that, Dunn's story still has holes in it you could drive a shot-up SUV through.

Consider: someone's got a gun trained on you, about to shoot, yet you have time to reach for your glove box, open it, unholster your own weapon and bring it up? Not even Little Joe Cartwright was that fast on the draw.

Then there's the fact that afterward, Dunn and his girlfriend went to a hotel. You've been threatened, you had to shoot to save your life ... and you go to a hotel? You don't alert authorities about this SUV full of dangerous kids roaming the streets?

Dunn, says Lemonidis, did not realize he had killed Davis until he saw the news the following morning. Yet, he still did not contact authorities, instead driving home to Satellite Beach, about 175 miles south, intending to turn himself in to a neighbor who has law enforcement ties. Police, who had gotten his license plate number from witnesses, soon arrived to arrest him.

So Dunn's story is shaky without the overlay of race.

With it, with the obvious comparisons to the killing of Trayvon Martin, one can only wonder if black blindness has not claimed yet another victim. That is a danger all over the country, but particularly in Florida, whose misbegotten Stand Your Ground law essentially licenses any citizen to use deadly force against any other citizen so long as the first citizen claims he or she felt threatened.

Sure enough, Lemonidis is considering just such a defense for her client.

The frightening thing, if you are a young African-American man, is that you know nothing makes some folks feel more "threatened" than you. Nor do you threaten by doing. You threaten by being. You threaten by existing. Such is the invidious result of four centuries of propaganda in which every form of malfeasance, bestiality and criminality is blamed on you.

In such an environment Florida's law inevitably becomes a potential "Get Out Of Jail Free" card for anyone who shoots a young black man. So this death, besides being a tragedy for the grieving family of one boy, is a sobering reminder for the family of every boy who looks like him.

And until or unless there is a definitive answer, they – we – must ponder with heartsick urgency one simple question:

What did Michael Dunn really see? And why?

POLICE

Wednesday, July 29, 2015

POLICE VIOLENCE

This will not be a column about Sandra Bland, although it could be.

Certainly there is cause for outrage over the way a Texas state trooper escalated the routine traffic stop of an indignant African-American woman into a violent arrest; she died of an apparent jail cell suicide three days later. But Chuck would say that in habitually defining police violence as a black problem, we make it smaller than it is.

Chuck is a reader who responded to a question I passed on in this space a few months back from another reader, a white woman named Tracy. "What can I do?" she asked, as a private citizen, to fight police brutality against African Americans?

"My suggestion may seem counter-intuitive," wrote Chuck, "but here goes: Stop focusing on the racial component and focus on the larger problem ... Of course, the disparity in how people are treated by the police – based on their race – is real. It is shameful. It is deadly. Still, though, it remains a subset [however horrible and painful] of the bigger problem."

Chuck goes on to say, "No country on earth is policed as we are. We have too many law enforcement agencies and individuals. They are too heavily armed. They are too militarized. They are too quick to violence. They are rarely held accountable. The false narrative that exists regarding the dangers of police work creates an inordinate sense of fear. Mix that with guns and too much authority and you have a problem. We – all of us – have this problem.

"The hyper-violent policing that is practiced in this country is a disgrace. Yes, African Americans face it at higher rates, but that is all it is ... a higher rate of the larger problem."

By way of illustration, Chuck points to video – you can find it online – of the 2013 arrest of a man he says he knows: David Connor Castellani. The clip, which has no audio, shows Castellani, then 20, yelling and pointing at officers, who are posted down the street, after his ejection from an Atlantic City casino for being underage. Four officers rush him, take him down and begin beating him – a fifth officer soon joins in.

It is after they've got him under control, lying on the curb with five officers on top of him, that a sixth officer arrives with a police dog and sets it loose on the young man's head and neck. Castellani's injuries required over 200 stitches.

The officers – big surprise – were cleared, while Castellani – shocking! – was indicted on charges that could have put him away for 10 years. Last week, according to his attorney, Jennifer Bonjean, he entered a pretrial diversion program that will leave his record clean. She has filed a federal civil suit on his behalf. Bonjean wants to force Atlantic City, where, she says, "They don't discipline their officers," to either stop using canines, or accept some kind of oversight. "This isn't the 19-frickin'-50s," she says.

So yes, Chuck has a point, the argument over police brutality sometimes misses the proverbial forest for the proverbial trees. Not that it is invalid to frame the problem in its racial dimensions; as Chuck himself says, when it comes to police violence, people of color seem to get it first and worst, and that deserves discussion. Still, it is too often the case that we – and I include myself – forget that the racial dimension is not the only dimension.

In the process, we exclude from the conversation those who ought to be part of it and forfeit the strength that comes with their numbers. So perhaps one answer to "What can I do?" is this:

Broaden the discussion, recognize that this "black" problem is in fact a human rights problem, help those who may feel removed – or safe – from police violence to understand that they are neither.

Maybe David Castellani felt that way once. If so, he probably changed his mind when that dog began biting his head.

Wednesday, November 1, 2015

NOTHING TO DO WITH RACE

It had nothing to do with race.

So said Sheriff Leon Lott, last week, in discussing a violent arrest by one of his officers, a white deputy named Ben Fields, of a black female student at Spring Valley High in Richland County, South Carolina. Fields, a school resource officer, was called in when the girl reportedly ignored a teacher's instruction to stop using her cellphone and leave the classroom. He ended up overturning her desk and slinging her across the floor like a sandbag or a sack of dog food.

His actions, caught on cellphone video, have detonated social media, many observers expressing visceral fury over this treatment of a black child. But Lott, who later fired his deputy, said he doesn't think Fields acted from racial prejudice because he has an African-American girlfriend.

It is a statement of earnest, staggering obtuseness that sheds no light on the officer's overreaction, but reveals with stark clarity the simplistic way many of us perceive the all-American conundrum of race. Granted, it is not inconceivable a white girl could have been subjected to the same brutality in a similar situation. But it is a matter of statistical fact that it's more likely to happen to a child of color.

Multiple studies have shown that those kids are subjected to harsher discipline in school than their white classmates. Indeed, numbers released last year by the federal government show that this begins in preschool where the "students" are little more than toddlers, yet black kids, who account for 18 percent of the population, get 42 percent of the suspensions.

Nothing to do with race?

The people who habitually say that operate under the misapprehension that racial bias requires intent or awareness and that it leaves obvious evidence of itself: a tendency toward racist comments, let's say, or membership in the Ku Klux Klan. In that worldview, racial bias is incompatible with having a black girlfriend.

But that worldview is naive. Bias is frequently subterranean, something you carry without meaning to or knowing you do. In a country that has used every outlet of media, religion, education, politics, law and science for over two centuries to drive home that black is threatening, black is inferior, black is bad, it is entirely possible Fields could have acted from unconscious racial bias and yet had a black girlfriend. For that matter, he could have acted from unconscious racial bias and had a black face; African-American people are no more immune to the drumbeat of negativity surrounding them than is anyone else.

So "nothing to do with race" is a reflexive copout many of us embrace against all reason because to do otherwise is to face a mirror whose reflection does not flatter. Which is why the usual suspects – Steve Doocy, Mark Fuhrman, Glenn Beck and et cetera – have attempted to fix the blame for what happened here on the girl.

Let's be very clear in response. It doesn't matter if she was disruptive. It doesn't matter if she was disobedient. It doesn't matter if she was disrespectful. Those things justify discipline, but they emphatically do not justify this child being lifted and flung by a grown man as if she were an inanimate object. If she were white, that would likely go without saying.

One is reminded of all the other African Americans we have seen in just the last few years brutalized and even killed for no good reason. One is reminded of Trayvon Martin and Walter Scott and Eric Garner and Charnesia Corley and Oscar Grant and Tamir Rice and Sean Bell and Levar Jones and more names than this column has space to hold, more blood than conscience can contain. And how many times have we been offered the same simplistic assurance in response?

This had nothing to do with race, they say.

Of course not. It never does.

IMPLICIT BIAS

I once read a question that went as follows:

Two groups of young men are walking on opposite sides of the street. One group is black, the other, white. Both are loud and swaggering, both have baseball caps turned to the back, both are brandishing bats.

Which one is the baseball team and which one, the street gang?

The truth is, many of us – maybe most of us – would decide based on race, giving benefit of the doubt to the white group, leaping to the harshest conclusion with the black one. Some will resist that notion, but the reality of implicit bias has been exhaustively documented.

Dr. Angela Bahns, an assistant professor of psychology at Wellesley College who describes herself as a "prejudice researcher," wanted to push the question further. Earlier this year she published a study testing what she says is the prevailing theory: Prejudice arises from threat, i.e., you perceive those other people over there as dangerous and that's what makes you biased against them.

"My research," she said in a recent interview, "tests whether the opposite is true, whether prejudice can precede and cause threat perception." In other words, is it actually pre-existing bias that causes us to feel threatened? It's a question with profound implications in a nation grappling with what has come to seem an endless cycle of police brutality against unarmed African-American men, women and children.

Reliably as the tides, people tell us race played no role in the choking of the man, the arrest of the woman, the shooting of the boy. But Bahns' research tells a different story. She conditioned test subjects to feel negatively toward countries about which they'd previously had neutral feelings, including Guyana, Mauritania, Surinam and Eritrea. "And I found," she said, "that when groups were associated with negative emotion, they came to be perceived as more threatening in the absence of any information about what the people are like objectively."

This column, by the way, is for a woman named Tracy from Austin who wrote earlier this year to ask, "What can I do?" to fight police brutality against African-American people. I promised her I would seek answers. Well, Bahns' research suggests that one answer might be to encourage police departments to incorporate bias training in their regimens.

According to Bahns, this training can help people overcome implicit prejudice and the heightened perception of threat it brings, but there is an important caveat: They have to be motivated and willing, and have to leave their defensiveness at the door. "Before any change can happen, the first step ... is that the perceivers – in this case, the white perceivers, or police officers – have to be open to admitting that they might be influenced by bias. I think we're not getting anywhere when there's this defensive reaction ... [We're] all prejudiced, and until we admit that, we're not going to get anywhere in terms of reducing its effects."

Not that people's defensiveness is difficult to understand. "Everyone's motivated to see themselves in a positive light," said Bahns. "People that genuinely hold egalitarian values and desperately do not want to be prejudiced are very motivated not to see bias in themselves."

The thing is, we cannot wait passively for their conundrum to resolve itself. Some of us are dying because of this inability to tell the ball club from the street gang. And frankly, if people really do hold egalitarian values and desperately don't want to be prejudiced, those deaths should push them past defensiveness and on to reflection.

As Bahns put it, the idea "that threat causes prejudice assumes that something about them – the out group – makes them threatening rather than assuming there's something about us that makes us see them that way."

Sunday, August 14, 2016

SYSTEMIC RACISM

We will get to Baltimore in a moment. First, let's talk about innocence.

That's the unlikely ideal two great polemicists, writing over half a century apart, both invoked to describe America's racial dynamic. It's a coincidence that feels significant and not particularly coincidental.

In 1963's "The Fire Next Time," James Baldwin writes, "... and this is the crime of which I accuse my country and my countrymen, and for which neither I nor time nor history will ever forgive them, that they have destroyed, and are destroying hundreds of thousands of lives and do not know it and do not want to know it ... But it is not permissible that the authors of devastation should also be innocent. It is the innocence which constitutes the crime."

In 2015's "Between the World and Me," Ta-Nehisi Coates muses about the possibility of being killed under color of authority. "And no one would be brought to account for this destruction, because my death would not be the fault of any human but the fault of some unfortunate but immutable fact of 'race,' imposed upon an innocent country by the inscrutable judgment of invisible gods. The earthquake cannot be subpoenaed. The typhoon will not bend under indictment."

It simplifies only slightly to say that what both men were describing is the phenomenon sometimes called institutional, structural, or systemic racism.

Which brings us to Baltimore and a scathing new Justice Department report on its police department. The government found that the city's police have a long pattern of harassing African Americans and that oversight and accountability have been virtually nonexistent.

Indeed, the Constitution must have been looking the other way when an officer struck in the face a restrained youth who was in a hospital awaiting mental evaluation, when police arrested people who were doing nothing more sinister than talking on a public sidewalk, when they tasered people who were handcuffed. Not to mention the time a cop strip-searched a teenager on the street as his girlfriend looked on and, after the boy filed a complaint, threw him against a wall and repeated the humiliation, this time cupping his genitals for good measure.

It's all outrageous stuff. But to understand the deeper outrage, you must realize that this happened in a city where 63 percent of the people – and 42 percent of the police – are African American.

You will seldom see a sharper picture, then, of systemic bias. If the term confuses you, ask yourself: Who is responsible for this? Who gave the order that let it happen?

No name suggests itself, of course, and that's the point. The assumption that black people are less educable, loan-worthy or deserving of their constitutional rights is baked into our systems of education, banking and policing. If you're a teacher, a banker, a cop – even a black one – you swiftly learn that there are ways this institution treats African Americans and that if you want to thrive, you will conform.

There is no longer a Bull Connor or Strom Thurmond preaching this, nor any need for them. Somehow, the racism just ... happens. Somehow, it just ... is.

Changing the way it is will require more than good intentions; it will require sustained and purposeful action. But the alternative is a world where a cop feels free to grope a bare-butt black boy on a public street. Yes, the cop is guilty of the groping, but who stands accountable for his sense of freedom to do so? On that point, many of us grow tellingly mute.

"The earthquake cannot be subpoenaed," writes Coates.

But Baldwin was right. It is, indeed, the innocence that constitutes the crime.

DEADLY FORCE

Wednesday, August 13, 2014

NOT JUST ABOUT MICHAEL BROWN

A riot can be many things.

It can be an act of communal madness, reflecting the emotional imbecility of those who believe the best way to express joy at their ball team's win is to overturn a car.

It can be an act of opportunism, a chance, under cover of darkness, influence of chaos, suspension of order, to smash and grab and run away, arms heavy with loot.

And it can be an act of outcry, a scream of inchoate rage.

That's what happened this week in Ferguson, Missouri. The people screamed.

To believe that this carnage – the windows smashed, the buildings torched, the tear gas wafting – is all about the killing of Michael Brown is to miss the point. Brown, of course, was the unarmed 18-year-old African-American man shot multiple times by a Ferguson police officer on Saturday.

St. Louis County Police Chief Jon Belmar – Ferguson Police asked his department, as an outside agency, to investigate the shooting – has said Brown was walking with another individual when a so-far unnamed officer sitting in a police car, stopped him. According to Belmar, the officer was trying to get out of his car when one of the two individuals pushed him back inside, where there was a struggle over the officer's weapon and at least one shot was discharged. He says the officer came out of the car and fired, striking Brown, who was about 35 feet away, multiple times.

Witnesses say Brown, who was to have started college this week, had his hands up when he was shot. Police have not said why the officer felt the need to stop him in the first place.

Details are still too sketchy for us to draw hard conclusions about what happened that afternoon. But it is all too easy to understand what happened afterward and why good people should be paying attention.

Because, again, this is not just about Brown. It's about Eric Garner, choked to death in a confrontation with New York City Police. It's about Jordan Davis, shot to death in Jacksonville because he played his music too loud. It's about Trayvon Martin, shot to death in Sanford because a self-appointed neighborhood guardian judged him a thug. It's about Oscar Grant, shot by a police officer in an Oakland subway station as cellphone cameras watched. It's about Amadou Diallo, executed in that vestibule and Abner Louima, sodomized with that broomstick. It's about Rodney King.

And it is about the bitter sense of siege that lives in African-American men, a sense that it is perpetually open season on us.

And that too few people outside of African America really notice, much less care. People who look like you are every day deprived of health, wealth, freedom, opportunity, education, the benefit of the doubt, the presumption of innocence, life itself – and when you try to say this, even when you document it with academic studies and buttress it with witness testimony, people don't want to hear it, people dismiss you, deny you, lecture you about white victimhood, chastise you for playing a so-called "race card."

They choke off avenues of protest, prizing silence over justice, mistaking silence for peace. And never mind that sometimes, silence simmers like water in a closed pot on a high flame.

One can never condone a riot. It is a self-defeating act that sells some fleeting illusion of satisfaction at a high cost in property and life.

But understanding this does not preclude recognizing that the anger we see in Ferguson did not spring from nowhere, nor arrive, fully-formed, when Michael Brown was shot. It is the anger of people who are, as Fannie Lou Hamer famously said, sick and tired of being sick and tired.

Silence imposed on pain cannot indefinitely endure. People who are hurting will always, eventually, make themselves heard.

Even if they must scream to do so.

Sunday, April 12, 2015

HOW PRIVILEGE WORKS

What follows is for the benefit of one William James O'Reilly, Jr. – "Bill" to his fans.

Last summer, Mr. O'Reilly, a pundit for Fox "News," spent time talking about white privilege and his contention that no such thing exists. He debated this with colleague Megyn Kelly, and sparred about it with Jon Stewart of "The Daily Show." Part of Mr. O'Reilly's reasoning is that because Asian Americans (according to him) make more money and are better educated than whites, what we really should be talking about is "Asian privilege."

Except, of course, that privilege is not a direct function of income or education. The inability – or, more aptly, the unwillingness – of Mr. Reilly and others of his ilk to get this, to understand what privilege is and how it works, is an ongoing source of exasperation for your humble correspondent. The good news is, O'Reilly and his ilk can now educate themselves for the price of a couple mouse clicks.

With the first click, they should play video of Joseph Houseman, a 63-year-old white man who, back in May, stood with a rifle on a street in Kalamazoo, Michigan. When police arrived, he refused to identify himself, grabbed his crotch, flipped them the bird and cursed. They talked him down in an encounter that lasted 40 minutes. Houseman was not arrested. The next day, he got his gun back.

With the second click, O'Reilly should play video of Tamir Rice, a 12-year-old black boy who, last month, was playing with a realistic-looking toy gun in a Cleveland park. When police arrived, an officer jumped out of the car and shot him at point-blank range.

There was no talking him down. Indeed, the entire encounter, from arrival to mortal wounds, took about two seconds.

It should be noted that anyone who waves a real – or real-looking – firearm in an encounter with police risks getting shot. We should also question who, if anyone, was irresponsible, inattentive or immature enough to allow Tamir to play – outside, yet – with that deadly toy. The resultant tragedy was all too easy to foresee.

That said, anyone looking to define white privilege would be well advised to ponder the 40 minutes police spent sorting things out with the white man and the two seconds it took them to shoot the black boy.

Privilege, you see, is not about being born with a silver spoon in one hand and a scholarship in the other. One can be poorer than dirt and a sixth-grade dropout and still enjoy white privilege. Because privilege is about the instant assumptions people make about you – your worth, your honesty, your intelligence – based on color of skin.

Nor is privilege defined only by race.

Some years back, my wife took the car back to a certain national tire shop, because one of the tires we'd just bought there had developed a bulge. The guy at the counter said the bulge was her fault. He refused to put the car up on the rack, refused to call his manager. He dismissed her, curtly and rudely.

So I go up there with her to have it out with this guy. Next thing I know, we're dealing with the manager, he's got the car up on the rack and is apologizing for some "rare defect," in the tire, which he will replace while we wait.

What I had experienced was male privilege, the ability to be taken seriously at an auto shop because of my gender. Now, to unwittingly benefit from misogyny does not make one a misogynist. But to pretend said benefit did not exist would be profoundly boorish.

Which is, not incidentally, an excellent description of Mr. O'Reilly's behavior here. So he and those like him who find it so difficult to understand what white privilege means should study those videos closely.

For a white man with a gun in Kalamazoo, white privilege meant the privilege of not being instantly shot. Sadly, that's a privilege Tamir Rice did not enjoy.

Sunday, April 12, 2015

JUST AN ISOLATED INCIDENT

" ... You foolish and senseless people, who have eyes, but do not see, who have ears, but do not hear." – Jeremiah 5:21

So here we are with another isolated incident.

That, at least, is how the April 4 police killing of 50-year-old Walter Scott will play in those conservative enclaves where the notion that there is such a thing as systemic racism is regarded as deluded and absurd. Those enclaves will not, of course, be able to claim innocence for now-fired North Charleston, South Carolina, police officer Michael Slager. As cellphone video captured by a passerby makes brutally clear, Slager repeatedly shot the fleeing, unarmed African-American man in the back after a traffic stop.

They will likewise find it difficult to defend a police report that claims officers administered CPR to the dying man. The video shows them doing no such thing. Finally, they will find it problematic to support Slager's claim that he shot Scott after the suspect seized his Taser. The video shows Slager picking up a small object and dropping it near Scott's body, fueling strong suspicion that he planted the Taser.

The video, in other words, will make it impossible to deny Slager did wrong. But conservatives will dispute with vehemence the notion that the wrong he did has larger implications.

Indeed, Bill O'Reilly of Fox "News" has already invoked misleading statistics to assure his audience that, "There doesn't seem to be, as some people would have you believe, that police are trying to hunt down young black men and take their lives."

In other words, move on, nothing to see here.

We ought not be surprised. It is only human that a Bill O'Reilly would want to think of himself and of the culture in which he has flourished as decent and good. To acknowledge that there is bias in that culture is to put oneself into an unenviable moral squeeze: One must either bestir oneself to say or do something about it – or else stop thinking of oneself as decent and good.

It is easier simply to deny the bias, to say that what is, is not. Small wonder that's the default position of conservatism on matters of race: Absent burning crosses and pointy white hoods, nothing is ever racism to them. And the more fervently one denies self-evident truth, the more emotionally invested one becomes in doing so.

Thus, every incident that illustrates the racism of our system, every statistic that quantifies it, every study that proves it, becomes just another "isolated incident." There is never an accumulation of evidence pointing toward an irrefutable, irredeemable conclusion. They are a thousand trees, but no forest, a million raindrops, but no storm.

Rodney King, Amadou Diallo, Abner Louima? Isolated incidents.

Oscar Grant, Eric Garner, Tamir Rice? Isolated incidents.

Sean Bell, Levar Jones, Trayvon Martin? Isolated incidents.

A study co-authored by law professor David Baldus, a 1991 study by the San Jose Mercury News, a 1996 report from the National Criminal Justice Commission, a 2000 study co-sponsored by the Justice Department, a 2004 report by The Miami Herald, a 2010 book by reporter Joseph Collum, all documenting profound and pervasive racial bias in the justice system? Isolated incidents.

Sometimes, you have to wonder at our conservative friends: Where is conscience? Where are intellectual integrity and moral courage? Where is simple, human decency?

Because if you are a decent person, you are up in arms right now. You are demanding solutions – not making excuses.

And if you are not up in arms yet, then pray tell: How many more "isolated incidents" do you need? How much more obvious must this be? How many more bodies will it take?

Wednesday, July 13, 2016

OUR BEHAVIOR PROVES US LIARS

This is not about the police.

At least, not solely. Granted, the police are the reason we are heartbroken today, the reason cable news networks are assembling panels to talk about black and blue, the fraught intersection between African Americans and the law.

Last week, after all, saw two more African-American men shot by police under questionable circumstances and then, five Dallas police officers assassinated by a sniper at a Black Lives Matter rally.

But ultimately another tragedy overarches both of those: America's ongoing struggle to reconcile itself along lines of race. We are still fighting over what being black means – and should mean – in a nation that ostensibly holds equality as a foundational belief.

We say that's what we stand for, yet in virtually every field of endeavor, our behavior proves us liars.

In education, for instance, the federal government issued data in 2014 documenting that even as early as preschool, African-American kids are suspended far more frequently than others.

In medicine, a 2016 study by researchers from the University of Virginia found that white med students were sometimes less aggressive in assessing and managing the pain of African-American patients.

In labor, a 2003 study by the National Bureau of Economic Research found that job seekers with perceived "black" names were significantly less likely to get callbacks from prospective employers.

And in justice, oh, dear God. Multiple studies have documented a system that, from arrest to incarceration, is heavily stacked against African-American people.

This is not abstract. This is blood and bone reality, life as experienced by over 40 million Americans. And can any thinking or compassionate person blame them if they are sick and tired of it?

Yet rather than respond to expressions of that frustration and anger in constructive and compassionate ways, too many of us seek every cowardly avenue of avoidance they can find.

Some take refuge in defensiveness, answering complaints about subconscious and systemic biases as if you'd just accused them, personally, of membership in the KKK. As if their feelings were what this is all about. Others try to shout down the messenger, often using the absurd formulation that to talk about race is racist.

Go online if you're not there already and read the message board beneath this column; chances are good you'll see examples of both.

Then, there are those who try to change the subject. As in Bill O'Reilly, the TV pundit, who recently proclaimed that Martin Luther King would never march with Black Lives Matter, a movement O'Reilly accuses of fomenting violence. King would probably find that laughable, given how often he was accused of the selfsame thing.

But again, to make this all about Black Lives Matter – or policing – is to make it too small.

Granted, inequality becomes more visceral, visible and urgent when police are concerned, when we are called upon to tease out the role color played in some split-second decision to pull the trigger. But the point is, color also plays a role in the decision to punish a toddler, call back a job applicant, prescribe a drug, approve a loan, rent an apartment, or just extend the benefit of the doubt.

The police do not stand apart from society – they reflect it. And our society is riven by race, defensive about race, terrified of race. We say we seek understanding and light, yet too often generate only noise and heat. If America is ever to reconcile itself, that has to change.

It's fine to demand better training, more body cams, more community liaisons. But to lay the onus entirely on the men and women in blue is to delude ourselves. Ultimately, the police are not the problem.

We are.

Wednesday, August 17, 2016

ANGER BEYOND RECONCILIATION

As racial martyrs go, you could hardly do worse than Sylville Smith.

He was no Trayvon Martin or Tamir Rice, no unarmed innocent gunned down. No, Milwaukee police say Smith was an armed 23-year old with a lengthy arrest record – drugs, weapons, robbery – who bolted from a traffic stop Saturday afternoon. They say he ran a short distance, then wheeled around, gun in hand, refusing orders to drop it. Whereupon the police officer shot and killed him.

"I'm not going to say he was an angel," Smith's godmother, Katherine Mahmoud, told the Milwaukee Journal-Sentinel.

The officer who killed him was a year older than Smith and black, like him. Though perceptions are obviously subject to change once body-cam footage is released, there is at this writing no reason to believe the officer acted improperly and, indeed, no serious allegation that he did. As such, this incident seems an un-likely focal point for public outrage.

That it became one anyway, that Smith's death sparked two nights of arson, shooting and general unrest, is an ominous sign. It suggests the rise of a species of anger inimical to any hope of racial reconciliation in Milwaukee – and cities far beyond.

A certain amount of anger in the face of injustice is not neces-sarily a bad thing. Such anger – defined as a passionate impatience with unfair status quo – is often a necessary catalyst for progress. But when there is no progress even after long years, anger can intermix with frustration and despair and become something much less constructive.

It can become something that doesn't listen, doesn't reason, doesn't even hope. Something that simply explodes.

African Americans in Wisconsin's largest city say Smith's death was the last straw after years of racially stratified policing. It is hardly immaterial that an officer was not charged just two years ago in the controversial shooting death of a mentally ill black man. Or that the department is under Justice Department review which, to its credit, it requested.

Who will be shocked if that probe finds what other probes have found in cop shops around the country: patterns of institu-tionalized racism that corrode public trust and impinge the ability of police to do their jobs.

Unfortunately, there is a tendency, when such probes are done, to treat the affected department as unique, an outlier. Think of the person who sees a drop of water here, a drop of water there, another drop over there, yet somehow never perceives the storm.

It's worth noting, too, that Mike Crivello, president of the Milwaukee police union, issued a statement after the shooting to "denounce" the idea of racism in the department's ranks. Of course, no institution of any size can credibly make a blanket claim of freedom from bias, but that didn't stop him. That should tell you something.

Here's the thing: You get tired of being treated as an unreliable witness to your own experience. You get sick of not being heard. Black Milwaukee has complained for years about biased policing. Yet the police chief pronounced himself "surprised" by this uprising.

Apparently, he hasn't been listening.

The rest of us would do well to avoid that mistake. If this unrest is an omen, it is also an opportunity – for civic self-examination and accountability, for giving the people a voice, for listening to what they have to say. For making change.

This violence, following what might well have been a justified shooting, was tragic and troubling. But it also made one thing starkly clear. African Americans have been demanding justice a very long time.

And they're getting tired of asking nicely.

WAR ON DRUGS

Sunday, June 27, 2010

NEW LEGAL CASTE SYSTEM

"You have to face the fact that the whole problem is really the blacks. The key is to devise a system that recognizes this all while not appearing to." – Richard Nixon as quoted by H.R. Haldeman, supporting a get-tough-on-drugs strategy.

"They give [black people] time like it's lunch down there. You go down there looking for justice, that's what you find: just us." – Richard Pryor.

Michelle Alexander was an ACLU attorney in Oakland, preparing a racial profiling lawsuit against the California Highway Patrol. The ACLU had put out a request for anyone who had been profiled to get in touch. One day, in walked this black man.

He was maybe 19 and toted a thick sheaf of papers, what Alexander calls an "incredibly detailed" accounting of at least a dozen police stops over a nine-month period, with dates, places and officers' names. This was, she thought, a "dream plaintiff."

But it turned out he had a record, a drug felony – and she told him she couldn't use him; the state's attorney would eat him alive. He insisted he was innocent, said police had planted drugs and beaten him. But she was no longer listening. Finally, enraged, he snatched the papers back and started shredding them.

"You're no better than the police," he cried. "You're doing what they did to me!" The conviction meant he couldn't work or go to school, had to live with his grandmother. Did Alexander know how that felt? And she wanted a dream plaintiff? "Just go to my neighborhood, " he said. "See if you can find one black man my age they haven't gotten to already."

She saw him again a couple months later. He gave her a pot-ted plant from his grandmother's porch – he couldn't afford flowers – and apologized. A few months after that, a scandal broke: Oakland police officers accused of planting drugs and beat-ing up innocent victims. One of the officers involved was the one named by that young man.

"It was," says Alexander now, over 10 years later, "the begin-ning of me asking some hard questions of myself as a civil rights lawyer. ... What is actually going on in his neighborhood? How is it that they've already gotten to all the young African American men in his neighborhood? I began questioning my own assumptions about how the criminal justice system works."

The result is a compelling new book. Others have written of the racial bias of the criminal injustice system. In "The New Jim Crow," Alexander goes a provocative step further. She contends that the mass incarceration of black men for nonviolent drug of-fenses, combined with sentencing disparities and laws making it legal to discriminate against felons in housing, employment, edu-cation and voting, constitute nothing less than a new racial caste system. A new segregation.

She has a point. Yes, the War on Drugs is officially race-neutral. So were the grandfather clause and other Jim Crow laws whose intention and effect was nevertheless to restrict black free-dom.

The War on Drugs is a war on African-American people and we countenance it because we implicitly accept certain assump-tions sold to us by news and entertainment media, chief among them that drug use is rampant in the black community. But. The. Assumption. Is. Wrong.

According to federal figures, blacks and whites use drugs at a roughly equal rate in percentage terms. In terms of raw numbers, whites are far and away the biggest users – and dealers – of illegal drugs.

So why aren't cops kicking their doors in? Why aren't their sons pulled over a dozen times in nine months? Why are black men 12 times likelier to be jailed for drugs than white ones? Why aren't white communities robbed of their fathers, brothers, sons?

With inexorable logic, "The New Jim Crow" propounds an answer many will resist and most have not even considered. It is a troubling and profoundly necessary book.

Please read it.

Monday, January 21, 2013

DISMANTLE THE WAR ON DRUGS

Dear Mr. President:

Congratulations on your second inauguration. Let's talk about drugs.

As it happens, today's festivities fall on Martin Luther King Day. This isn't the first time you and Dr. King have encountered one another on the calendar. You first accepted your party's nomination for the presidency on the 45th anniversary of his "I Have a Dream" speech.

Though King is a hero for you, one suspects you find mild annoyance in that confluence of dates, given that it draws attention to that which you have assiduously ignored. Meaning, of course, race and the milestone your presidency represents.

Not that anyone should blame you for this. Your predicament is reminiscent of a fairly obscure comic book character named Black Bolt. Because his merest whisper can shatter mountains, he is doomed to live as a mute. That's an apt description of you with regard to race. The social and political dynamics of your unique position are such that whatever you say on the subject is magnified a hundredfold, reverberates through the echo chamber of media until it drowns out everything else. And any racially related action you take is magnified beyond even that, as your opponents will surely use it in an effort to shrink and delimit your presidency.

On the other hand, when have they ever needed an excuse to do that?

Mr. President, one should always be cautious in speculating what might happen "if so-and-so were alive today," if only because it is unfair to "so-and-so," who gets used like an advertising mascot and has no say in the matter. But, that said, one cannot help but believe that if your hero Martin – our hero Martin – were with us today, he would be deeply concerned about the inequities and iniquities of the so-called War on Drugs.

For over 40 years, it has fallen on African-American men like a hammer, a litany of selective enforcement and incarceration funneling white drug offenders into diversion programs or otherwise giving them the benefit of judicial discretion, while locking up black ones in numbers that are nothing less than a national scandal. In some states, a black drug offender is as much as 50 times more likely than a white one to be incarcerated

For the African-American community, it is a state of affairs that has implications far beyond the injustice system. It touches on poverty (former felons are often denied employment); father absence (it is hard to be a father from behind a glass barricade); housing (former felons can be banned from public housing); education (drug offenders can be denied student loans); voting rights (former felons often lose the ballot).

A handful of your predecessors, Mr. President, at significant political risk, struck away most of the legal strictures binding African-Americans to lives of paltriness, penury and pain. But this one remains, and it falls to you.

Granted, you have other things on your plate as your second term begins: immigration reform, gun control, war, the economy. Put this there, too.

African-Americans gave you 93 percent of their vote. Yes, conservatives often read into that number some conspiracy of racial solidarity against them. And yes, like so much of what conservatives say these days, that's both silly and anti-factual. John Kerry got 88 percent of the black vote, Al Gore got 90 and neither man has ever sung an Al Green song at the Apollo Theater.

Still, it is obvious there is in the African-American community a great affection for you and pride in you. If that holds any meaning for you, you must address this issue. At some point, the failure to do so amounts to nothing less than moral cowardice.

Dismantle the failed War on Drugs, Mr. President. In so doing, you would honor Dr. King's legacy. And help ensure your own.

CAUTIOUSLY OPTIMISTIC

It's been a war on justice, an assault on equal protection under the law.

And a war on families, removing millions of fathers from millions of homes.

And a war on money, spilling it like water.

And a war on people of color, targeting them with drone-strike efficiency.

We never call it any of those things, though all of them fit. No, we call it the War on Drugs. It is a 42-year, trillion-dollar disaster that has done nothing – underscore that: absolutely nothing – to stem the inexhaustible supply of, and insatiable demand for, illegal narcotics. In the process, it has rendered this "land of the free" the biggest jailer on Earth.

So any reason to hope sanity might assert itself is cause for celebration. Monday, we got two of them, a coincidental confluence of headlines that left me wondering, albeit, fleetingly: Did the War on Drugs just end?

Well, no. Let's not get carried away. But it is fair to say two of the biggest guns just went silent.

Gun 1: In a speech before an American Bar Association conference in San Francisco, Attorney General Eric Holder announced that federal prosecutors will no longer charge nonviolent, low-level drug offenders with offenses that fall under mandatory minimum sentencing guidelines. Those Kafkaesque rules, you may recall, got Kemba Smith, a college student with no criminal record, sentenced to almost 25 years without parole after she carried money for her abusive, drug-dealing boyfriend.

Gun 2: A federal judge ruled New York City's stop-and-frisk policy unconstitutional. The tactic, more in line with some communist backwater than with a nation that explicitly guarantees freedom from random search and seizure, empowered cops to search anyone they deemed suspicious, no probable cause necessary. Unsurprisingly, 84 percent of those stopped were black or Hispanic, according to the Center for Constitutional Rights, a civil rights group, which says illegal drugs or weapons were found in less than 2 percent of the searches.

Michelle Alexander wrote the book on the drug war – literally. "The New Jim Crow" documents in painful, painstaking detail how policies like these have been directed disproportionately against communities of color with devastating effect.

She told me via email that Monday's headlines leave her "cautiously optimistic" they reflect an emerging national consensus that "war on certain communities defined by race and class has proved to be both immoral and irrational, wasting billions of dollars and countless lives."

But, she warned, "tinkering with the incarceration machine" is not enough.

These are important first steps, but only that. She'd like to see the resources that have been wasted in this "war" redirected to help the communities it decimated.

"We've spent more than a trillion dollars destroying those communities in the War on Drugs; we can spend at least that much helping them to recover. We must build a movement for education, not incarceration; jobs, not jails. We must do justice by repairing the harm that has been done. In that process, perhaps we will finally reverse the psychology that brought us to this point and learn to care about poor people of all colors, rather than simply viewing them as the problem."

We can only hope. At the very least, Monday's headlines suggest maybe a sea change is underway. Maybe we're ready to stop using criminal-justice tools to solve a public health problem. Maybe we're ready to end this "War."

It's about time.

Indeed, it is past time. Our stubborn insistence on these foolish, unworkable policies has left families bereft, communities devastated, cops and bystanders dead, money wasted, foreign governments destabilized, distrust legitimized and justice betrayed.

We call it a War on Drugs. Truth is, drugs are about the only thing it hasn't hurt.

SEXUAL ASSAULT

Friday, April 21, 2006

THE DANGEROUS INTERSECTION OF SEX AND RACE

And so we come again to the place where race and sex intersect.

It's an intersection we never seem to quite escape, one ever present in our news and our history, whether it be Kobe Bryant accused of rape or O.J. Simpson accused of murder or back through antiquity to a black woman in a slave cabin, knees pressed together at the sound of her door opening at midnight and the white man who owns her stepping through, unwelcome.

This time, it's Duke University, where three students, all members of the lacrosse team, are accused of raping a stripper hired to perform at a team party. Two have been indicted.

African Americans are watching the case with keen interest, amid accusations that the district attorney, campaigning for reelection, initially dragged his feet because the accuser was black and the accused were white kids at an elite school in the South.

And if that seems overwrought, imagine the response if the woman were white and reported being raped by three black members of the basketball team. You'd have to call out the National Guard.

Because race and sex mix like dynamite and fire.

But the thing I keep coming back to is this: If some woman reported being raped by three men of the same race, we wouldn't even be having this discussion. That would "only" be rape and as such, it wouldn't qualify as national news, much less news with the potential to explode.

And yet. Did you know that 300,000 women are raped each year in this country? Did you know that one woman in six can expect to be raped, or to face an attempted rape, in her lifetime? This, according to the Centers for Disease Control and Prevention.

Which makes you marvel that it takes race to make this a story.

I don't mean to minimize the importance of race and, for that matter, class, to what allegedly happened here. If – and right now it's only an if – a black woman was indeed raped by white men at an elite private school, the echoes of white privilege, white entitlement and white brutality will be too loud to ignore.

My point, though, is that there are other issues here, too.

The unnamed alleged victim is a 27-year-old single mother working her way through school by undressing for men. Since the news broke, there have been whispers of her supposed drunkenness on the night of the alleged assault and reports about her reputedly troubled past. Both of which come uncomfortably close to slandering the victim.

Then there's the e-mail sent from the account of one of the lacrosse players: "Tomorrow night, after tonights show, ive decided to have some strippers over. However there will be no nudity. I plan on killing bitches as soon as they walk in and proceeding to cut their skin off."

Doug Clark, a columnist for The News & Record in Greensboro, has expressed sympathy for the writer of that note, saying he was young and dumb and indulging in "the sort of crude talk teenage boys sometimes exchange when they're sure no adults are listening."

I disagree. Healthy minds of whatever age don't harbor such fantasies. More to the point, woman-hating is hardly confined to some college kid's e-mail. Rather, that note reflects sentiments that have seeped like sewage into our culture, showing up in that video game where you kill prostitutes and rob them, in that music video where a credit card is swiped through a woman's backside, in the defamation and death threats that greeted the young woman who accused Kobe Bryant of raping her.

So it's all well and good to make this a story about sex and race or class.

But I believe it's about more than that. And I suspect that one in six women would agree.

O. J. SIMPSON

O. J. Simpson, February 9, 2001

Wednesday, September 13, 1995

POLICING IN AMERICA

A few of you have taken issue with my recent suggestion that Mark Fuhrman's racial animus was no rarity among law officers. A blonde woman wanted me to know that blonde women often get pulled over for no apparent reason. A concerned parent pointed out that young white men frequently face unwarranted police scrutiny.

It's not about race, more than one correspondent said gently, as if to help this paranoid black man see beyond his own patch of earth.

Perhaps they have a point. Perhaps more often than paranoia will allow a black man to admit, it's not about race.

But, much more often than naiveté and denial will allow some white people to admit, it is.

And here, for them, is the ultimate content of character question. What do you do when it is? Do you grow angry or weary or sad? Do you fight against it or gripe about it or try to keep it from touching your life?

Or, do you simply cocoon yourself in naiveté, pile your denial to the sky, and tell yourself that what is, is not?

To my knowledge, it is not routine police procedure to pull guns on blonde women caught driving in brunet neighborhoods. To my knowledge, there is no long and painful history of unarmed young white men being shot to death, choked to death, or otherwise mysteriously expiring while in police custody. To my knowledge, these things are, historically and indisputably, about race.

For as long as I can remember, African Americans have been saying that – complaining of the special treatment they receive from officers of the law. But no matter how much evidence is piled up in support of this claim, the wall of denial is always higher.

There is never, it seems, evidence enough.

Yet you keep hoping that someday there will be. Each time you add a new piece of evidence to the pile, you figure maybe this is the one that proves the case.

I thought that in 1988 when baseball Hall of Famer Joe Morgan was thrown to the floor and handcuffed at Los Angeles International Airport by police who accused him of being a drug courier.

I was wrong.

I thought it in 1991 when Jamaal Wilkes, a former All-Star forward for the Lakers, was stopped by L.A. police and handcuffed on the curb because, he says, the tags on his expensive car were about to expire.

I was wrong.

I thought it when Rodney King's head was bashed in during a drunk-driving arrest and we all stood witness.

I was wrong.

I thought it when Mark Fuhrman was condemned by his own words and in his own voice as a perjurer, a manufacturer of evidence and a racist.

But wouldn't you know it? I was wrong.

The other day I was talking to a friend, a black LAPD officer, about racism and the police. My friend – call him Joe since he doesn't want his real name used – told me how, in one L.A. division, blacks and whites sat on opposite sides of the room during roll call. He told me how the old-timers brag of taking black boys in gang colors off the street and dropping them deep in the territory of rival gangs. And he told me of partners he's had who routinely stopped people for no cause deeper than skin color.

White officers, he said, are often "more aggressive" in policing blacks.

The one good thing about the Fuhrman debacle, added Joe, is that black officers are feeling "vindicated for what we've been saying for years."

I suspect my friend ought not count his vindications before they hatch. No matter what he says, or what I say or what Mark Fuhrman himself says, some people will continue to insist that ignorance and hatred play no part in the policing of America.

Proof is a tower that looks down on the trees.

But denial blots out the sun.

Wednesday, October 4, 1995

RACE IS A CANCER ON OUR NATIONAL SOUL

It's always about race, isn't it?

Even when it shouldn't be, even when you don't want it to be, even when you flee it like a back alley mugger, it's always there.

In America, we sprinkle race on our breakfast cereal. And lace up race to go jogging. We snap our fingers to race on the radio and curl up with race in bed at night. Wherever you go, there it is – race in your face.

I'm choking on it.

Or maybe that's just my naiveté going down hard for the umpteenth time. Because I still remember what I said to myself on the day O.J. Simpson was identified as a suspect in his ex- wife's murder.

Can we make this not about race? Can we treat this as a man who happened to be black accused of the murder of an ex-wife who happened to be white? What maturity it would show if we resisted the urge to make this tragedy a racial litmus test.

But of course, it became exactly that. Worse, we failed it. Utterly, completely, and at every relevant stratum of society. Media failed by their early inability to leave race be. From a "Time" cover photo featuring an electronically darkened mug shot of Simpson to portentous think pieces portraying him as Icarus, flown too close to the sun of white acceptance, print and broadcast media were pandering practitioners of racial politics. They imagined what wasn't there and magnified what was. And will somebody tell me, what the hell is a "race card" and where can I buy one?

The police failed by having Mark Fuhrman on the payroll. Not to mention all the little Fuhrmans still running around shielding bigotry with a badge. Am I to believe no one in LAPD saw this man for the pig he was?

White Americans failed by their denial of the Fuhrmans among us. The fact that they were surprised when Fuhrman was revealed as the sort of mendacious, evidence-planting cop-racist of whom blacks have often complained, spoke volumes about how blind, deaf and dumb white Americans have willed themselves to be. Mark Fuhrman is many things. A surprise is not one of them.

Black Americans failed by adopting O.J. Simpson as some sort of racial cause celebre. Excuse me, but this is not poor old Rodney King, getting his drunken butt kicked from here to eternity by LAPD storm troopers. This is not a slam-dunk case of justice denied on account of race. Not even close.

Rather, it's a case of a millionaire ex-jock who had money enough to buy a brand of justice about which most blacks – indeed, most Americans – can only dream. More to the point, he's a man about whose guilt or innocence good people can reasonably disagree. Even now.

I was insulted by the suggestion black people might riot if Simpson were found guilty. Shamed by the cheers of celebration that suggested this was some great victory for African America. Disappointed by word that black prosecutor Chris Darden has been branded some sort of Uncle Tom for doing his job to the best of his ability. And I am appalled by an NBC News report that one or more black jurors raised the power sign to Simpson as the jury left the courtroom.

Unity is fine, but if by unity you mean I must stand shoulder to shoulder with those among us who kill, loot, rape and pillage, then I decline the offer. Evil comes in black face as well as white and we ill serve ourselves when we deny or discount that.

For the record and for whatever it's worth, I thought O.J. Simpson was guilty. I also thought he would be acquitted. To my mind, his lawyers raised enough reasonable doubt that I, for one, would have had difficulty voting for conviction.

In any case I'm glad, with apologies to Gerald Ford, that this long national nightmare is over.

We did not acquit ourselves well here. From Senator Alfonse D'Amato's jibes at Japanese-American judge Lance Ito to constant media fretting over the racial makeup of the jury, we once again demonstrated ourselves obsessed, controlled, consumed by the great American bogeyman, race.

And so it goes. Race is clothing, race is sex, race is crime, race is the environment, race is music, race is money, race is a cancer on the national soul.

"The problem of the 20th Century is the problem of the color line, " said W.E.B. DuBois, the great black scholar, in 1900. It's a bedeviling bit of prescience, especially as viewed from the cusp of the millennium.

DuBois died in 1963. But I find myself wondering what it might be like if we could dig him up and reanimate him on this day. If we could let him walk around a little, and give him a taste of the O.J. Simpson trial.

How long do you think it would be before he recognized America?

The next litmus test is coming and we still are not ready.

Chapter 6

EDUCATION

Sunday, May 23, 2010

WHAT WE TEACH OUR CHILDREN ABOUT RACE

Last week, Soledad O'Brien made a young mother cry. It came in the midst of a special series, "Black or White: Kids on Race" on CNN's "Anderson Cooper 360." The series was based on a new version of the famous "doll tests" pioneered by husband and wife psychologists Kenneth and Mamie Clark in the 1930s and '40s, and recreated in 2005 by Kiri Davis, a teenage filmmaker.

In the tests administered by the Clarks and Davis, black children were presented two dolls, identical in appearance except that one was dark and the other, light.

Asked which doll was bad, stupid, or ugly, most of the black kids picked the black doll. Asked which was good, smart, or pretty, they chose the white one.

CNN's study was similar, except that children were presented with pictures, not actual dolls, and the images ran a color gamut from very light to very dark. One other difference: CNN tested white children along with black ones.

Which is how this little 5-year-old white girl in Georgia came to be sitting at a table facing an unseen researcher as her mother sat with O'Brien and watched on video. Asked to point out the "good child," she touched one of the lighter skinned figures. Why is that the good child, she was asked. "Because I think she looks like me," the little girl said.

Asked to point out the "bad child," she touched the darkest image on the paper. And why is that the bad child? "Because she's a lot darker," the little girl said.

And watching, her mother softly wept.

Your heart broke for her, because you just knew she never saw that coming. Your heart broke because you just knew she had bought into the myth that children are not soiled by the prejudices that stain their elders. Your heart broke, because how many times have you heard it said that, since they are growing up in the era of Oprah and Obama, our children will live beyond the belief that character is a function of color.

But children are not idiots. They hear us and see us. They watch television, they listen to radio, they read magazines, they live in our world. So very early on, they know what we think. And often enough, it becomes what they think, too.

Thus, it is no surprise that CNN found both black and white kids maintain a decided bias toward whiteness. For instance, 76 percent of younger white kids pointed to the darker figures when asked to identify "the dumb child." Because this is a pilot study, those results are not definitive. But they are instructive.

So is this: A few months ago, a white teacher brought a black girl up to me as I was preparing to give a speech. The teacher wanted me to talk to her. She doesn't think she is beautiful, said the teacher, because she is dark. I asked the girl if this was true and in a soft voice, with eyes averted, she said that it was.

And man, what do you say to that? How do you explain the psychology of self-loathing and the futility of judging oneself by someone else's beauty standards, and the cumulative psychological weight of 400 years of being told you are not good enough and the need to embrace and love and value yourself just as you are? How to explain all that in 90 seconds or less while people are pulling at you, and the event is about to begin and you've got a speech to give and this little girl won't even look up?

I did the best I could. It was not nearly good enough.

As I watched her walk away, I was troubled by my failure to make the case. And by the enduring need to do so. We are over 40 years beyond the Civil Rights Movement, 40 years beyond a burst of pride and racial consciousness that transfigured our very understanding of what it means to be black, 40 years into a future where Michael Jordan is an icon, Oprah Winfrey is a media queen and a Kenyan's son is president of these United States.

Forty years. And still...

And still.

AFFIRMATIVE ACTION

Monday, October 20, 2003

WHITE AFFIRMATIVE ACTION

I guess I touched a nerve. That much seems apparent from the dozens of responses to my recent column about a hospital in Abington, Pennsylvania, where a white man asked that no black doctors or nurses be allowed to assist in the delivery of his child. The hospital agreed, a decision I lambasted.

Which has produced the aforementioned dozens of critical e-mails. The tone varies from spittle-spewing bigotry to sweet reason, but they all make the same point: that affirmative action entitles white people to question black people's competence.

As a reader who chose to remain nameless put it, many people wonder if a given black professional "is there because of his/her skills and abilities, or because of affirmative action. Unfortunately, affirmative action policies leave many unanswered questions about a black person's education and training, as well as skills and abilities. ... How do we answer these questions?"

I will try my best to answer them with a straight face. It's going to be difficult.

Because there's an elephant in this room, isn't there? It's huge and noisy and rather smelly, yet none of these good people sees it. The elephant is this simple fact:

White men are the biggest beneficiaries of affirmative action this country has ever seen.

That's not rhetoric or metaphor. It's only truth.

If affirmative action is defined as giving someone an extra boost based on race, it's hard to see how anyone can argue the point. Slots for academic admission, for employment and promotion, for bank loans and for public office have routinely been set aside for white men. This has always been the nation's custom. Until the 1960s, it was also the nation's law.

So if we want to talk about achievements being tainted by racial preference, it seems only logical to start there. After all, every worthwhile thing African Americans achieved prior to the mid-'60s – Berry Gordy's record label, John Johnson's publishing company, Alain Leroy Locke's Rhodes scholarship, Madame C.J. Walker's hair care empire, Dr. Daniel Hale Williams' pioneering heart surgery – was done, not just without racial preference, but against a backdrop of open racial hostility.

By contrast, nothing white men have ever achieved in this country was done without racial and gender preferences. Affirmative action.

I know that will be hard for some folks to hear. I know it will leave some white brothers indignant. And I expect many recitations of "up by my bootstraps" and "know what it's like to be poor." We all want to feel that we made it on our own merits, and it's not my intention to diminish the combination of pluck, luck, hard work and ability that typically distinguishes success, whether white, black or magenta.

On the other hand, there's a word for those who believe race is not a significant factor in white success: delusional.

It is not coincidence, happenstance or evidence of their intellectual, physical or moral superiority that white guys dominate virtually every field of endeavor worth dominating. It is, rather, a sign that the proverbial playing field is not level and never has been.

My correspondents feel they should not be asked to respect the skill or abilities of a black professional who may or may not have benefited from affirmative action. They think such a person should expect to be looked down upon. But black people have spent generations watching white men who were no more talented, and many times downright incompetent, vault to the head of the line based on racial preference.

So, here's my question:

Would African Americans be justified in looking down on white professionals? In wondering whether they are really smart enough to do the job? In questioning their competence before they had done a thing?

Yeah, you're right. That would take one hell of a nerve.

Sunday, November 25, 2012

CAN'T FIX IT BY LOWERING THE BAR

I take this one personally. Let me tell you why.

As I recall, I scored 960 on my SAT. This was good enough for second best in my class and many congratulations and backslaps from teachers and administrators. Based on that, I thought I'd done pretty well.

So I'm in college, right? Freshman year, and I get to talking with my roommate, this white guy named Reed, about our SAT scores. Reed's kind of sheepish, finally confessing that he scored "only" about 1,200.

That's when I realized I had not done pretty well. I had done pretty well for a student of John C. Fremont High, in the poverty, crime and grime of South Los Angeles. I had done pretty well for a black kid.

As it happens, I started classes at the University of Southern California at 15 years of age, got good grades and came out four years later with my degree. So there was nothing wrong with my brain. I've always suspected my modest SAT score and the fact that I was encouraged to celebrate it said less about me than about the expectations others had of me – and kids like me.

So yes, it touches me in a raw spot, this news that two states – Florida and Virginia – have adopted new education standards under which they would set different goals for students, based on race, ethnicity and disability.

Like many other states, Florida and Virginia requested waivers from the No Child Left Behind Act's unrealistic goal of having every child at grade level in reading and math by 2014. But these states used their waivers to create separate and unequal performance standards for their black, white, Hispanic, Asian and disabled children.

Last month, for example, Florida set a goal of having 86 percent of white kids at or above grade level in math by 2018. For black kids, the goal is 74 percent. Virginia is wrestling with similar standards.

In fairness, both states would want you to know a couple of things. First, that these dissimilar standards reflect the achievement gap, the fact that kids do not start toward the goal from the same place. Black kids may have to cover more ground to reach a lower benchmark because they are starting from further behind. The second thing is that these are interim goals and the ultimate goal remains the same: close the achievement gap and educate every child to her fullest potential.

Understood. But if that's what these standards are, can we talk for a moment about what they feel like? The best analogy I can give you is based in the fact that some coaches and athletic directors have noted a steep decline in the number of white kids going out for basketball. They feel as if they cannot compete with their black classmates. What if we addressed that by lowering the rim for white kids? What if we allowed them four points for each made basket?

Can you imagine how those white kids would feel whenever they took the court? How long would it be before they internalized the lie that there is something about being white that makes you inherently inferior when it comes to hoops, Steve Nash and Dirk Nowitzki notwithstanding?

Indeed, for all the talk about the so-called "reverse racism" of affirmative action, I have long argued that the real problem with it – and the reason it needs an expiration date – is that it might give African-American kids the mistaken idea they carry some inherent deficiency that renders them unable to compete with other kids on an equal footing.

We should be wary of anything, however well-intentioned, however temporary, which conveys that impression to our children. I am proof we have been doing just that for a very long time. And it burns – I tell you this from experience – to realize people have judged you by a lower standard, especially when you had the ability to meet the higher one all along. So this "interim" cannot end soon enough.

Because ultimately, you do not fix education by lowering the bar. You do it by lifting the kids.

Wednesday, March 26, 2014

RACIAL BIAS BEGINS IN PRESCHOOL

What excuses will they make this time?

Meaning that cadre of letters to the editor writers and conservative pundits who so reliably say such stupid things whenever the subject is race. Indeed, race is the third rail of American conscience; to touch it is to be zapped by rationalizations, justifications and lies that defy reason, but that some must embrace to preserve for themselves the fiction of liberty and justice for all. Otherwise, they'd have to face the fact that advantage and disadvantage, health and sickness, wealth and poverty, life and death, are still parceled out according to melanin content of skin.

So they become creative in their evasions.

They use made up facts (Trayvon Martin was actually casing the neighborhood) and invented statistics (black men and boys commit 97.2 percent of all the crime in America), they murder messengers ("You're a racist for pointing out racism!") they discredit the source (Can you really trust a government study?).

One waits, then, with morbid fascination to see what excuse those folks will make as federal data released last week reveals that African-American children are significantly more likely to be suspended – from public preschool. Repeating for emphasis: preschool, that phase of education where the curriculum encompasses colors, shapes, finger painting and counting 10. Apparently, our capacity for bias extends even there. According to the Department of Education, while black kids make up about 18 percent of those attending preschool, they account for 42 percent of those who are suspended once – and nearly half of those suspended more than once.

Armed with that information, there are many questions we should be asking:

Are black kids being suspended for things that would earn another child a timeout or a talking to?

If racial bias pervades even the way we treat our youngest citizens, how can anyone still say it has no impact upon the way we treat them when they are older?

What does being identified as "bad" at such an early age do to a child's sense of himself, his worth and his capabilities?

Does being thus identified so young play out later in life in terms of higher dropout rates and lower test scores?

How can we fix this, build a society in which every one of our children is encouraged to stretch for the outermost limits of his or her potential?

Those are the kinds of smart, compassionate questions we should ask. But again, we're talking about the third rail of American conscience. So one braces for dumb excuses instead.

Maybe someone will claim African-American preschoolers are 73.9 percent more likely to fail naptime.

Maybe someone will contend that they thuggishly refuse to color inside the lines.

And you may rest assured someone will say that for us even to have the discussion proves hatred of white people.

What a long, strange road we have traveled from the high land of idealism and hope to which the human rights movement brought us 50 years ago, down to the swampy lowland of justification and circumscribed horizons we find ourselves slogging through now. It is noteworthy that this story of institutional bias against children barely out of diapers scarcely skimmed – much less penetrated – an American consciousness presently preoccupied by basketball brackets and the mystery of a doomed jetliner.

Small wonder. Those things ask very little of us, other than a love for sport and a capacity to feel bad for other people's misfortune. This, on the other hand, cuts to the heart of who we are.

Last week we learned that their schools routinely bend little black boys and girls toward failure. And the people who make excuses should just save their breath.

There are none.

TEACHING HISTORY

Sunday, May 16, 2010

HISTORY HURTS

History is not a Hallmark card. Sometimes, history breaks your heart.

I know this because I have often recounted history in this space, tales of black men and women bought and sold, cheated and mistreated, maimed and lynched. And whenever I do this, I can be assured of e-mails and calls of chastisement.

I still remember one of the first, an earnest lady who pleaded with me to leave this history behind. Telling such tales, she said, could not help but make black people resent white ones.

Her complaint presented a quandary. I find the same value in recounting those stories that my former boss Bert used to find in remembering Holocaust brutalities and my friend John finds in recalling Irish suffering at British hands. Understanding the past provides context to understand the present and predict the future. Moreover, history is identity. These stories tell me who I am.

But there's a difference, isn't there? Bert's history indicts Germans in Europe, John's indicts Britons in the United Kingdom. Mine indicts white people, here.

So I'm not without sympathy for people like that lady. This history hurts. But is requiring me not to speak it really the best response to that hurt? Should a hard truth not be uttered for fear it might cause somebody, somewhere to resent?

Her answer, I suspect, would be yes. In that, she would be much like the state of Arizona, where Governor Jan Brewer just signed a law restricting ethnic studies courses in public schools. Having apparently decided she had not done enough to peeve Latino voters by signing a Draconian immigration bill a few days back, the governor went after a Mexican-American studies program in Tucson. But the prohibitions in the new law seem to say more about the mind-set of the governor than about any real danger posed by ethnic studies.

Specifically, the law bans classes that "promote the overthrow of the United States government, promote resentment toward a race or class of people, are designed primarily for pupils of a particular ethnic group, advocate ethnic solidarity instead of the treatment of pupils as individuals." And you wonder: what sort of ethnic studies classes did she attend?

Is that really what people think those classes are about?

Worse, the restrictions are so broad, so void of legal precision, as to be meaningless. How does one decide to a legal certainty whether a class is "designed primarily for pupils of a particular ethnic group?" How can one know with legal exactness whether a class will "promote resentment?"

Like the lady who called me, the governor seems to prefer that hard stories not be told, that doing so detracts from American unity. As one online observer put it, "We need to focus on America instead of promoting everyone else."

The problem with that reasoning is obvious: America is everyone else, a nation composed of other nations, a culture made of other cultures, a history built of other histories. And yes, sometimes, those histories will be hard to hear.

But silence does not make a hard story go away. Silence only makes it fester, grow and, sometimes, explode.

It is in our narratives that we explain ourselves to ourselves. That's a crucial matter in a nation which is, after all, bound not by common blood or ancestry, but by common fealty to a set of revolutionary ideals that begins, "We hold these truths to be self-evident ..." To those ideals have flocked men and women from every other nation on earth, each with stories of their own.

Granted, the challenge of incorporating those stories into the larger American story is daunting. The governor seems to fear what kind of nation we'll be if we accept that challenge.

I fear what kind we'll be if we don't.

Sunday, September 28, 2014

'HAPPY HISTORY'

This is a tale of two countries.

The first country was built on a radical new promise of human equality and a guarantee of the right to life, liberty and the pursuit of happiness. That country made it possible for even those born in the humblest and most meager circumstances to climb to the pinnacle of prosperity and achievement. It helped save the world in a great global conflagration, fed and rebuilt the devastated nations of Europe, planted the first footprints on another world.

The second country was built on the uncompensated labor of human beings owned from birth till death by other human beings. That country committed genocide against its indigenous people, fabricated a war in order to snatch territory belonging to its neighbor, put its own citizens in concentration camps. And it practiced the "science" of eugenics with such enthusiasm that it inspired advocates of mandatory sterilization and racial purity all over the world. One was an obscure German politician named Adolf Hitler.

Obviously, the first of those countries is America. But the second is, too.

This would not come as a surprise to any reasonably competent student of American history. But that is a category that soon may not include students in Jefferson County, Colorado. The good news is, they are not taking it lying down.

To the contrary, hundreds of them staged mass walkouts from at least five area high schools last week. They chanted and held up signs in protest of a proposed directive from a newly elected conservative school board member that would require teachers of history to "promote citizenship, patriotism, essentials and benefits of the free enterprise system."

Teachers are further told to emphasize "positive aspects" of U.S. heritage and to avoid lessons that "encourage or condone civil disorder, social strife or disregard of the law."

Like, say, the Civil Rights Movement.

To the students' credit, they recognized this for the act of intellectual vandalism it was and did a very American thing. They protested. As of late last week, the board was promising to revise the proposal, claiming it had been misunderstood.

Actually, it was understood all too well. One frequently sees these efforts to whitewash the ugliness out of American history. The state of Virginia was ridiculed in 2010 for a history book which falsely claimed thousands of black soldiers fought for the Confederacy during the Civil War. The state of Arizona passed a law that same year restricting ethnic studies classes under the theory that they tend to "promote resentment toward a race or class of people."

Now, here are educators in Colorado promoting a "happy history" that will leave students positive, patriotic – and ignorant.

There is a reason courts require witnesses to tell "the truth, the whole truth." To tell half the truth is to tell a lie of omission. And in this tale of two countries, the whole truth is not summed up in the triumphs of the first country any more than in the sins of the second. America is both those nations. And American history, properly understood, is a story about the summit we sometimes reach and the sewer we too often tread, about the work of resolving the tension between America's dream and its reality.

Such complexity tends to frighten and confuse small-minded people who think you can't love your country and question it, too, can't celebrate its glories if you acknowledge its failures. So instead they embrace this "happy history" that is stagnant, barren and antithetical to progress. Why would you work to resolve the tension between the dream and the reality if you've been taught that the dream is the reality?

Censoring history is an act of cowardice. The Colorado demonstrations suggest that some of us, at least, are still brave enough for the truth.

Sunday, October 11, 2015

WHITEWASHING BLACK HISTORY

"This," says Roni Dean-Burren, "is what erasure looks like."

She's talking about something you might otherwise have thought innocuous: a page from "World Geography," a high school textbook. A few days ago, you see, Dean-Burren, a former teacher and a doctoral candidate at the University of Houston, was texted a caption from that book by her son Coby, who is 15. It said that the Atlantic slave trade "brought millions of workers from Africa to the southern United States to work on agricultural plantations." This was in a section called "Patterns of Immigration."

She says the words jumped out at her. After all, a "worker," is usually someone who gets paid to do a job. An immigrant is usually someone who chooses to come to a new country. Neither of which describes the millions of kidnapping victims who cleared America's fields and endured its depravities in lives of unending bondage that afforded them no more rights under the law than a dog or a chair.

As the Trail of Tears was not a nature walk and the Normandy invasion not a day at the beach, black people were neither workers nor immigrants, but slaves. Dean-Burren, who is black, took to social media to explain that. You can guess what happened next. The story went viral, and the embarrassed publisher, McGraw-Hill Education, scrambled to apologize and fix the mess.

That's all well and good. But let no one think this was incidental or accidental. No, there is purpose here. There is intent. In recent years, we've seen Arizona outlaw ethnic studies, Texas teach that slavery was a "side issue" to the Civil War, a Colorado school board require a "positive" spin on American history and Glenn Beck claim the mantle of the Civil Rights Movement.

We are witness to the vandalism of African-American memory, to acts of radical revision and wholesale theft that strike at the core of black identity. Once your past is gone, who are you? What anchor holds you? So Dean-Burren's word strikes a powerful chord: This is, indeed, erasure – like a blackboard wiped clean, all the inconvenient pain, sting and challenge of African-American history, gone.

It is, she says, "the saddest thought ever" that her grandchildren might not know Nat Turner's rebellion or Frederick Douglass' harsh condemnation of slavery. "The fact that they may not know what it was like for women to get the right to vote, the fact that they may not know that millions of Native Americans were slaughtered at the hands of 'Pilgrims' and explorers ... I think it says a lot about our society."

Nor is she persuaded by the argument that teaching the uglier aspects of American history would make students hate their country. She calls that "a crock of poo." And it is. America's ugliness defines its beauty as silence defines sound and sorrow defines joy.

"We tell our children that all the time: 'The reason you're standing here today ... and you have what you have and you can go to the schools you want to go to, and you can say out loud, 'I want to be an Alvin Ailey dancer ... 'or 'I want to go to Stanford,' ... is that you come from survivors. You come from people who said, 'I'm going to stick it out. I'm going to make it. I'm going to keep pushing.' If we don't know the ugly, I don't know how you can really love the pretty."

To put it another way: Black History Matters. So let us be alarmed at attempts to rewrite that history for the moral convenience of others or to preserve what James Baldwin and Ta-Nehisi Coates have described as the fiction of white American "innocence" where crimes of race are concerned. They keep trying to make it less painful, says Dean-Burren, like putting a document through a Xerox machine and making it lighter, lighter and lighter still.

"And then, when you look up, there's nothing on the page."

Chapter 7

EMPLOYMENT

Monday, January 20, 2003

RACE STILL CONTROLS EMPLOYMENT

Happy Martin Luther King Day.

Over at the White House, they're marking the day by the festive ritual of extending the middle finger to the civil rights community. Last week, President George W. Bush came out against a University of Michigan affirmative action program designed to foster racial diversity on campus. He's concerned that the policy, which is now before the Supreme Court, discriminates against white kids.

One wonders where all this concern over discrimination was when the president was campaigning in South Carolina at Bob

Jones University, which was infamous for its ban on interracial dating. But that's another column.

It has been suggested that the president chose this latest fight from a need to tack to his right, offer a sop to his conservative base, after being compelled to lambaste Trent Lott a few weeks ago. Without disagreeing with that suggestion, let me offer another:

I don't think the president thinks race matters.

You got a sense of that in Bush's statement on the Michigan case. The university's policy – a point system that rewards applicants for being members of a racial minority – may have good intentions, he said, "but its result is discrimination, and that discrimination is wrong." Like many foes of affirmative action, the president tacitly equates the decades of institutionalized exclusion the practice seeks to address with the relatively minor hurdle it represents to prospective white students.

That's an affront to history itself. But it is not a surprise.

Bush only echoes the so-called colorblind view that has crept into the mainstream of white thought in recent years, a view that treats even the mention of race as a lapse in decorum. In this view, it is never proper or necessary to take color into account. Just last week, a New York Times letter writer described as "dangerous and outmoded" the notion that race matters.

The writer is guilty of wishful thinking.

Yes, we've made great progress on this front. Indeed, for my money, racism isn't even the most pressing issue facing the black community in 2003. I'd rank black-on-black crime and fatherless homes above it.

And yet, racism is still the problem that undergirds all the others.

Consider a recent study conducted by professors at the University of Chicago Graduate School of Business and the Massachusetts Institute of Technology. They sent out 5,000 résumés in response to newspaper want ads. All the fictitious applicants had similar qualifications. But those in one group had "white-sounding" names: Emily, Gregg, Brett and so forth. The other group was full of people with names like Tameka, Ebony and Kareem.

It ought not surprise you to learn that the "white" group heard back from prospective employers half again as often as the "black" one. Not to put too fine a point on it, but any man who is shut out of the job market arbitrarily is, it seems to me, more likely to engage in crime or to leave his children fatherless.

And here, the usual people will make the usual weak attempts to rationalize race out of the equation. Somebody – bank on it – will fault black people for, as one of my readers once put it, choosing names that distance their children from "normal society." As if black parents, alone among all parents, should not have the right to pick baby names that reflect their creativity or heritage. What a stupid and arrogant view.

No, if you're honest with yourself, you know exactly what the study is telling us.

Of course, that's a big "if" in a nation where people from the president on down have convinced themselves that we've arrived at "someday." As in, "We shall overcome, someday."

Those people may be fooling themselves, but they're not fooling anybody with eyes. George may honestly feel that race no longer matters.

I'm sure Rasheed has a different view.

Chapter 8

POLITICS

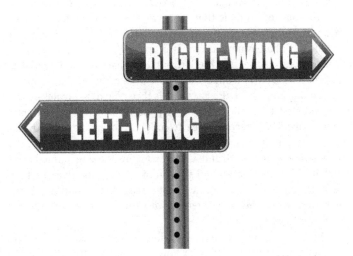

Sunday, April 19, 2015

'NORMAL' IS GONE FOR GOOD

Maybe, conservatives are done with dog-whistle politics.

After all, NRA chief Wayne LaPierre traded his dog whistle for an air horn at a recent gathering of the gun faithful in Washington, D.C. "I have to tell you," he said, "eight years of one demographically symbolic president is enough."

Subtle, it was not.

Still, as insults go, it was a rather neatly crafted two-fer. On the one hand, it demeaned the nation's first African-American president and welcomed the day the White House is, well ... de-

Negro-fied. On the other hand, it also demeaned the candidate seeking to become the nation's first female-American president and promised to save the White House from, well ... woman-ification. Evidently, LaPierre wants America to get back to normal, "normal" being defined as when the president is white and male.

So out come the air horns, blatting Woman! Woman! Woman! seeking to reduce a former senator and secretary of state to the sum of her chromosomes. Now the race is apparently on to see who will be first to tag the former law professor, senator and secretary of state with which crude, sexist epithet. Oh, the suspense.

The blazing irony is that conservatives have at least two "demographically symbolic" candidates vying for their favor: Marco Rubio, a Cuban-American senator from Florida and Ted Cruz (does no one else see Joe McCarthy staring back when they look at this guy?), a senator from Texas whose father was born in Cuba.

So the "normal" LaPierre seeks is threatened, regardless.

Not that he is the only one tripped up by Clinton's woman-ness. Consider, a recent piece from Time magazine that argued that Clinton is "the perfect age to be president" because, at 67, she is "postmenopausal." Granted, the essay, by a doctor named Julie Holland, flatters Clinton and women of her age, assuring us that, having been freed from the "cyclical forces" that "dominated" the first half of her life, she emerges with the "experience and self-assurance" to be president.

Still, could you not have happily gone the rest of your days without contemplating Hillary Clinton's "cyclical forces?" More to the point, can you imagine such an essay being written about a male candidate? Marco Rubio is 43, which means he's probably already had his first digital prostate exam. Will anyone analyze how that factors into his readiness for the presidency? Rick Perry is 65. If he jumps in, will anyone speculate on how possible issues of erectile dysfunction might inform his foreign policy?

Here's the thing about "demographically symbolic" presidents and candidates: They tend to function like Rorschach inkblots. Meaning that what we see in them reveals more about us than them. Where Barack Obama is concerned, the right-wing panic over birth certificates and fist bumps and the left-wing tendency to idealize and canonize his every exhalation revealed the rank bigotry and messy irresolution beneath our "post-racial" happy talk.

Where Clinton is concerned, these very early indications suggest her woman-ness will likewise be a minefield for friend, foe and media - even more, perhaps, than in 2008.

And that's not to mention Cruz and Rubio. Who do you think will be the first to wear a sombrero to a Cruz rally in misguided solidarity, or to tell the Miami-born Rubio to go back where he came from?

Point being that in America, markers of identity - gender, race, ethnicity - have a way of becoming identity itself, of blinding us to the singular, individual one in front of us. And campaigns tend to magnify that failing. To put that another way: Strap in. It's going to be a very long 19 months until the 2016 election. Even so, one thing is already clear, and it should please the rest of us, if not Wayne LaPierre.

"Normal" is gone for good.

BARRACK OBAMA

Friday, January 19, 2007

REASONABLE MAN

President Obama?

No, not yet. But, the intention of Senator Barack Obama, Democrat of Illinois, to move toward that goal seems clear with this week's news that he is forming an exploratory committee to raise money toward a possible White House bid. Count me among those who regard the bid as a foregone conclusion.

Strike while the iron is hot. Isn't that what the axiom says? And whose iron has ever been hotter than Obama's? The man is a rock star, a combination plate of handsome, intelligent and charismatic that has his supporters giddy. On the other hand, the battlefield of presidential politics is littered with the bones of rock stars for whom the giddiness of supporters was not enough. John Anderson and Ross Perot come to mind.

There are two obvious pitfalls facing Obama. One is his lack of experience. His two years in the Senate represent the sum of his federal résumé, though he also has under his belt many years in the Illinois statehouse and as a constitutional lawyer and community activist.

Obama has a ready answer for the experience question. As he told me in an interview in November: "I think the one thing the American people require of their president is good judgment. In most of our lives, we hope that more experience gives us better judgment – but not always. Dick Cheney and Donald Rumsfeld had an awful lot of experience, but displayed poor judgment in this Iraq War, in my mind. So part of the measure I have to take is, do I feel I have the judgment to take the toughest job on earth."

Touché. But one wonders if the question will be so easily put to rest this year. While his inexperience at the federal level certainly does not disqualify Obama from the presidency and while we've had politically inexperienced presidents before – Ulysses Grant and Dwight Eisenhower come to mind – I suspect experience is going to loom large as a factor in the next election, given the mess the new president will inherit from George W. Voters will be more wary than usual of a would-be chief executive who seems to require too much on-the-job training.

Which brings us to the second potential pitfall, the most obvious one. Race and culture. While mainstream media have seemed intrigued by, but not obsessed with, the senator's heritage, the same, unfortunately, cannot be said of the extreme right blogosphere. There, one seldom reads any reference to Obama that does not make reference to his middle name: Hussein. Then there are those who observe that only a single consonant separates his surname from the first name of the al-Qaida leader who launched the September 11 terrorist attacks.

It is such nakedly puerile slander that your first response is to laugh. Then you remember how that same blogosphere managed to turn the war hero John Kerry into a "traitor" and the Texas Air National Guardsman, George W. Bush, into a war hero – and it seems much less funny.

Barack Obama is an African-American man with a Muslim name who would be seeking the presidency in a historically racist nation currently at war against Muslim extremists. One wonders if there is enough handsomeness, intelligence and charisma in the world to overcome all that.

For my money, though, Obama's signature asset is not his brains, his looks, or his magnetism. Rather, it's this: He seems reasonable. Though unabashedly liberal, he does not come across as a prisoner of ideology. He seems a man who can be persuaded by logic. It's an attractive trait made more so by the fact that we have seen it so rarely in recent years.

The question is, whether it will be attractive enough to offset concerns about inexperience and transparent appeals to xenophobic fears.

Either way, this promises to be a fascinating political season. And a very long year.

Friday, February 2, 2007

HE'S BLACK

Apparently, it comes as quite a surprise to some people that Barack Obama is black.

I'm driven to this realization by the response to a recent column in which I referred to the senator as African American. Many people wrote to correct me on that. Among the most memorable was a guy who said: "I heard his dad was a radical Muslim from Africa and his mom was a white atheist from Kansas City. If that be the case wouldn't he be half a black man and half a white man? If he's a half breed, shouldn't you do a correction?"

Then there's the gentleman who wrote following Obama's mild criticism of a recent comment by Senator Joseph Biden to the effect that Obama was the first mainstream African-American presidential candidate "who is articulate and bright and clean and a nice-looking guy."

The e-mail writer saw Obama's response – he called the comment "historically inaccurate" – as a fatal misstep, sign of a philosophical alliance with the dreaded Jesse Jackson and Al Sharpton and it changed, he said, his view of Obama. "Up to now," he wrote, "I did not see him as an Afro American."

Most folks were less ... strident than these two, but the core concern was the same: Obama should not be identified as African American.

To which there is an easy answer: I call him African American because that's what he calls himself.

There is, however, another answer that is not so easy.

If Obama asked to be identified as biracial, I would accommodate him because I believe that, within broad limits, people should be allowed to define themselves as they please. But with that said, I must confess I've always found that term rather meaningless insofar as the African-American experience goes.

That's not to criticize anybody who feels compelled to honor a multiplicity of heritages. For the record, many – maybe most – African-Americans are multiracial. One of my ancestors was Irish. My wife has Japanese and Native American forebears. But my point is less about how one sees oneself than about how one is seen by the world at large. And I'm sorry: you can be as "biracial" as you want; so long as your features show any hint of Africa, that world is going to give you the treatment it reserves for "black."

Assume for a minute Obama didn't have a famous face. Assume he was just another brother tooling down Main Street. Do you really think the cop who pulls him over for no good reason is going to change his tune if he is told Obama's mama is white?

"Oh. Sorry, Mr. Obama. I didn't realize you were BIRACIAL. Have a good day."

No way. You may be many things, but if one of them is black, that trumps the rest in terms of how the world sees you. Black is definitive.

Granted, this is, at some level, a silly conversation: as a scientific construct, race is meaningless. But as a social construct, it's anything but. So Obama becomes, inevitably, a Rorschach inkblot of our racial maturity. Meaning that what people see when they look at him so far seems to say more about them than him.

Which brings us back to Biden's remarks. I'm not qualified to judge the "nice-looking" part. But articulate? Even their critics would concede that Shirley Chisholm and the Revs. Jackson and Sharpton – all black, all former contenders for the presidency – talk real good.

Bright? They seems intelligent enuf.

Clean? I stood near Jackson in an airport once. He didn't smell.

What Biden surely meant to say is that Obama is the first black presidential candidate who is potentially electable. But what he wound up saying is revealing and what it reveals is not pretty. Biden was not the first. He won't be the last.

Meantime, I've got two words of advice for those folks who are surprised to learn Barack Obama is black:

Eye. Doctor.

Wednesday, August 27, 2008

VISION OF A BETTER AMERICA

He spoke of the promise before he spoke of the dream.

In the first part of the momentous speech he gave at the Lincoln Memorial, the part school children don't memorize and pundits never quote, Martin Luther King, Jr. reminded a watching world that in writing the Constitution and the Declaration of Independence, the founders were "signing a promissory note to which every American was to fall heir.

"This note," said King, "was a promise that all men, yes, black men as well as white men, would be guaranteed the unalienable rights of life, liberty, and the pursuit of happiness." His evocation of this great American promise may be less well-known than King's description, moments later, of his great American dream, but there is, nevertheless, a straightforward clarity to it that compels.

Because where race is concerned, what is American history if not the story of how that promise was repeatedly broken? As King put it five years later in the last speech of his life, "All we say to America is, 'Be true to what you said on paper.' "

But America never did.

Except that now, here comes Barack Obama, son of a Kenyan and a Kansan, striding to the podium to accept the nomination of his party for president of the United States. It comes 45 years to the very day after King said he had a dream America's promise might someday be fulfilled, 100 years and a day after the birth of the president, Lyndon Johnson, who helped nudge that dream toward reality. The timing requires you, if you have any music in your soul, any soul in your soul, to reappraise both the promise and the dream.

That's what we've been doing lately in our various ways in our various Americas. On the sidewalk outside a Gladys Knight concert, a vendor sells a T-shirt depicting King and Obama shaking hands above the legend, "Sometimes, dreams come true." Meanwhile, they are passing around a "joke" on the Internet that has Obama picking Sylvester Stallone as his running mate: "Rambo and Sambo," goes the punch line.

The two extremes have one thing in common: slack-faced disbelief. Could it be? Could it really be?

Apparently, it could.

The realization coalesces something some of us never dared hope and others never dared fear: the idea that one day America would take its promise seriously.

And if that realization requires African-Americans to recalibrate their cynicism about what "they" will and will not allow black folks to achieve, it seems plain that the greater shock and sense of dislocation is borne by "they," who must now recalibrate their assessment of what black folks can achieve. Small wonder "they" have responded frantically, crying with ever more shrillness that this Obama character is something other, something foreign, something strange. Something not really, truly American.

They have grown used to defining "American" as a certain skin color, a certain religion and heritage. They have forgotten that "American" was, first and foremost, a certain ideal.

Thomas Jefferson stated it thusly: all men are created equal.

The Pledge of Allegiance says: liberty and justice for all. And King, in that speech 45 years ago, spoke of the day "all of God's children, black men and white men, Jews and Gentiles, Protestants and Catholics" would harmonize upon a song of freedom.

Not truly American, they say? On Thursday, a nation whose credo holds equality to be a birthright will see a brown-skinned man, son of Kenya and Kansas, assume leadership of a major political party. No, it is not the panacea, not the End of Race in America. But it is striking evidence of a promise fulfilled, a dream redeemed.

How could anything be more American than that?

'WE THE PEOPLE' INCLUDES AFRICAN AMERICANS

"For the first time in my adult lifetime, I am really proud of my country. And not just because Barack has done well, but because I think people are hungry for change." – Michelle Obama, February 18, 2008

I always thought I understood what Michelle Obama was trying to say.

You are familiar, of course, with what she actually did say, which is quoted above. It provided weeks of red meat for her husband's opponents, who took to making ostentatious proclamations of their own unwavering pride in country.

But again, I think I know what the lady meant to say. Namely, that with her husband, this brown-skinned guy with the funny name making a credible run for the highest office in the land, she could believe, for the first time, that "we the people" included her.

It is, for African Americans, an intoxicating thought almost too wonderful for thinking. Yet, there it is. And here we are, waking up Wednesday morning to find Barack Obama president-elect of these United States.

In a sense, it is unfair – to him, to us – to make last night's election about race.

Whatever appeal Obama may have had to African Americans and white liberals eager to vote for a black candidate, is, I believe, dwarfed by his appeal to Americans of all stripes who have simply had enough of the politics of addition by division as practiced by Karl Rove and his disciples, enough of the free-floating anger, the holiday from accountability, the nastiness masquerading as righteousness, the sheer intellectual dishonesty that have characterized the era of American politics that ends here.

But in the end, after all that, there still is race.

And it would be a sin against our history, a sin against John Lewis and Viola Liuzzo, against James Reeb and Lyndon Johnson, against Fannie Lou Hamer and Martin Luther King, against all those everyday heroes who marched, bled and died 40 years ago to secure black people's right to vote, not to pause on this pinnacle and savor what it means. It would be a sin against our generations, against slaves and freedmen, against housemen and washerwomen, against porters and domestics, against charred bodies hanging in Southern trees, not to be still and acknowledge that something has happened here, and it is sacred and profound.

For most of the years of the American experiment, "we the people" did not include African Americans. We were not included in "we." We were not even included in "people."

What made it galling was all the flowery words to the contrary, all the perfumed lies about equality and opportunity. This was, people kept saying, a nation where any boy might grow up and become president. Which was only true, we knew, as long as it was indeed a boy and as long as the boy was white.

But as of today, we don't know that anymore. What this election tells us is that the nation has changed in ways that would have been unthinkable, unimaginable, flat out preposterous just 40 years ago. And that we – black, white and otherwise – better recalibrate our sense of the possible.

There was something bittersweet in watching Michelle Obama lectured on American pride this year, in seeing African Americans asked to prove their Americanness when our ancestors were in this country before this country was. There was something in it that was hard to take, knowing that we have loved America when America did not love us, defended America when it would not defend us, believed in American ideals that were larger than skies, yet never large enough to include us.

We did this. For years unto centuries, we did this. Because our love for this country is deep and profound. And complicated and contradictory. And cynical and hard.

Now it has delivered us to this singular moment. Barack Obama is president-elect of the United States.

And we the people should be proud.

Sunday, February 22, 2009

THAT NIGHT IN CHICAGO'S GRANT PARK

On the day after the day we never thought we'd live to see, in the first dawn of what some regarded as post-racial America, historian Lerone Bennett Jr. awoke and turned on the television. There, he says, he saw "this great and beautiful sister, one of the great products of our tradition who has lived through all these disappointments and she saw triumph and she was crying and she was saying, 'America has changed. We won, we won.'

"I cried in that moment for the sister and with the sister, because I looked out my window and I looked to the east and I saw huge condominiums marching down the lakefront, far as I could see. White people are the primary occupants of those condominiums. I looked to the west and I could see evidence of the terrible housing, the terrible facilities prepared for black people in this country in 2008 and 2009. And I looked downtown and I saw these great cathedrals and skyscrapers. All that money, as far as I could see on the day after the election, controlled by white people."

You may, if you wish, call this a reality check. You know how, when there's a close play at the plate, the sportscasters will go to the instant replay to dissect what really happened? That's what this is.

In commemoration of Black History Month, I have engaged a group of African-American historians to tell us all, even as time closes over it like waters, what happened that night in November 2008 in Chicago's Grant Park.

We know what we saw, of course. We saw the photogenic African-American family come to the stage, waving to the many vibrant colors of us, saw Oprah Winfrey leaning on a stranger, her makeup running, saw memories of Selma and Birmingham glisten in Jesse Jackson's eyes, saw TV talking heads coughing into fists, voices snagging on the rough shoals of sudden feeling.

What is less obvious than what we saw is what it meant. All those people crying and sighing and saying over and over again, "I never thought I would live to see this day." All those learned people jousting over whether we had now entered a new, "post-racial America."

Occasionally, one is privileged to live through a moment when history doesn't just open wide like a door on a hinge, but you know it for what it is even then, even as it is happening, so you can fix the details in your mind, rehearse the stories you will tell your grandchildren someday. The night Barack Obama was elected president was one of those moments.

But what did that tell us about who we are, what we are, where we are on the road to racial reconciliation? What, indeed, will we tell the grandchildren about that moment we saw?

Dr. Donald Spivey, professor of history and Cooper Fellow at the University of Miami, says what he saw that night forced him to reconsider some basic assumptions. "One of my students said, 'You've written extensively on the racism of this nation and said we would never have a black president. So what do you say?' I said, 'I was wrong. And I was so glad to be wrong.' "

"I was totally, absolutely surprised at Obama," says Dr. Howard Lindsey, assistant professor of history at DePaul University. "If you talk to any black historian who said they could see this coming, tell them I said they're lying. Nobody, nobody I've talked to saw this coming. I live here in Chicago and I thought, 'Man, look here, what're you doing? You've got a funny name, you're half white, and for some racists that's even worse than being black. And you're going to go against Clinton? C'mon! I thought he would be another Jesse Jackson, he would be a protest candidate, and after a few weeks we'd all follow Hillary."

"It has to give you a sense of hope," says Spivey, who worked on Obama's South Florida campaign, "no matter how you analyze it and process it." America, he adds, deserves praise for being the kind of country where such a thing can happen. And yet, even this optimistic assessment is tempered, as if being both African and American has taught him that every hope has shadows. "I don't go too far," he is careful to add. "I don't go crazy. I still believe race and racism are a real problem in the USA."

Lindsey, too, cautions against interpreting Obama's victory too broadly. The election, he says, "caused me to recalibrate how white America looks at, or can look at, a single African American. But for the black masses, I'm still not convinced that America has changed its views that significantly."

That view is echoed by Dr. Robin Kelley, professor of American studies and ethnicity at the University of Southern California. "I don't think of African-American progress in terms of group progress," he says in an e-mail response. "African-American elites have been making significant progress in the electoral sphere for some time, and sometimes they exercise power in ways that put them at odds with other people of color – here in L.A. we have black city council people and other elected officials who are as oppressive as whites with regard to the treatment of Latinos, for example. I'm not sure that's progress."

And therein, of course, lies the glaring fallacy, not simply of the debate over What Obama Means, but of the way the nation has framed and approached the question of race from its inception – meaning the ancient tendency to believe black is black is black is black.

But when color of skin is treated as the sole significant indicator of personhood, trumping class, education, religiosity and anything else you care to name, it is inevitable that you end up with absurdities.

Like Oprah Winfrey being turned away from a tony dress shop because the proprietor feared one of the richest women in America was there to rob the place. Or like some lady handing John Hope Franklin, the eminent historian, her claim check and asking him to fetch her coat as he was en route to a dinner celebrating his Presidential Medal of Freedom.

One could argue that to expect Obama's election to bring about or signify radical change for all 36 million members of "the black community" is to perpetuate the same absurdity. Does the success of a Harvard-trained professor of constitutional law really speak to an illiterate high school dropout slinging dope on a street corner in Liberty City? Should we expect it to?

Or is that expectation part of the problem? Isn't part of our inability to solve the issue of race the fact that we habitually look for the knockout punch, the buzzer beater, the lightning bolt that changes everything everywhere all at once?

"In assessing the Magic Obama phenomena," says Bennett, retired editor for Johnson Publications in Chicago and author of "Before the Mayflower: A History of Black America," "I think we've got to remember the [other] times history turned on a dime and racism was solved forever. This is not the first time. Can we make that clear to people? This is not the first time the race problem has 'ended' in America."

It is a jolting realization, but he's right. We have been here before.

"In the great apocalyptic summer of 1865," he says, "black people marched up and down the roads of the South, singing for the first time in this country, free at last, and demanding their 40 acres and a mule. Several years later, when Congress passed the 14th and 15th amendments, commentators said the same things they said after Obama was elected, that race had been washed out of the Constitution and that there were 'no more Negroes in America.' "

"I'm an old cat," adds Bennett, who is 80. "I was here that great Monday when the Supreme Court ordered integration. I was here when Lyndon Johnson said, 'We shall overcome,' on prime-time TV. People said it was over. We were wrong. It wasn't over then, it wasn't over in 1965, it wasn't over when the 14th and 15th amendments were passed ... and it's not over now."

What happened that night in Grant Park? A milestone? Surely. A reason for joy? Certainly. America surprising itself again as America is wont to do? Yes. But not a buzzer beater, not a knockout punch, not a lightning bolt.

So on that day after the day we never thought we'd live to see, in that first dawn of post-racial America, when Bennett saw that black woman on television crying, "We won, we won," it made him sad for the shortness of historical memory, for a joy destined to be disappointed.

"Oh," he says, "I hope it comes true for her ..." But it won't, he adds, without mobilization, organization, confrontation. All four historians say this in some form.

That night in Grant Park, America celebrated a milestone. Lord knows America had reason. But that's not enough, says Bennett. "We've got to celebrate – and think." Because every hope is shadowed.

But every hope is still hope.

Wednesday, February 25, 2015

'NO SENSE OF DECENCY'

Amazing. Just ... amazing.

Here we are, six years later, six years of mom jeans and golf dates and taking the girls for ice cream. And yet, some of us are still hung up on the perceived "otherness," the "not like us"-ness, of Barack Obama.

The latest is Rudy Giuliani, speaking last week in New York at a fundraiser for Wisconsin Governor Scott Walker. "I do not believe," said Giuliani, "and I know this is a horrible thing to say, but I do not believe that the president loves America. He doesn't love you. And he doesn't love me. He wasn't brought up the way you were brought up and I was brought up, through love of this country."

In the entirely predictable firestorm that followed, Giuliani has tried out various defenses. He told the New York Times his remarks could not possibly be racist because the president had a white mother. It is a claim of such staggering obtuseness as to defy deconstruction and to which the only sensible response is to scream "Arghh!" while banging one's head against a wall.

In an op-ed for the Wall Street Journal, Giuliani wrote that he "didn't intend to question President Obama's motives or the content of his heart," a lie easily refuted. Quote: "I do not believe that the president loves America." End quote

The Giuliani defense tour also pulled in to Fox "News," where Giuliani claimed that while Obama frequently criticizes America, he expresses no love of country. But in the very first speech most Americans ever heard Obama give – at the 2004 Democratic Convention – he sang arias of American exceptionalism, noting that "in no other country on Earth is my story even possible." Since then, Obama has missed no opportunity to praise what he has called "the greatest country on Earth."

Nor is Obama the only president to criticize America. Yet somehow, when Jimmy Carter cited a "crisis of the American spirit" in which "too many of us now tend to worship self-indulgence and consumption," his country love went unquestioned.

There's a simple reason Giuliani is having such trouble defending what he said. What he said is indefensible. It was cloddish and, more than that, it was ugly

The man once dubbed "America's mayor" for his stirring response to the 9/11 attacks now seems, on matters of race, at least, more like "America's Batty Uncle." Remember, this is the same Giuliani who, in a discussion of police violence in black neighborhoods, told Michael Eric Dyson, "The white police officers wouldn't be there if you weren't killing each other."

Dyson is an author and academic. He is not known to have killed anyone.

Six years ago, there was wistful talk of a "post-racial America." But today, we find ourselves in the most-racial America since the O.J. Simpson debacle. It's not just income inequality, voter suppression and the killing of unarmed black boys. It's also the ongoing inability of too many people to see African Americans as part of the larger, American "us."

Most of them no longer say it with racial slurs, but they say it just the same. They say it with birther lies and innuendo of terrorist ties. They say it by saying "subhuman mongrel." They say it by questioning Obama's faith. They say it as Rudy Giuliani said it last week. They say it because they have neither the guts to say nor the self-awareness to understand what's really bothering them:

How did this bleeping N-word become president of the United States?

The day the towers fell, Giuliani seemed a heroic man. But he has since made himself a foolish and contemptible one, an avatar of white primacy struggling to contend with its own looming obsolescence.

And the question once famously put to Joe McCarthy seems to apply: "Have you no sense of decency, sir?"

But what's the point in asking? The answer is painfully clear.

Wednesday, February 17, 2016

DON'T BLAME HIM FOR GRIDLOCK

This was three days before Antonin Scalia died.

President Obama had just spoken before the Illinois General Assembly. Now, he and some old friends, all retired from that body, were being interviewed by the Los Angeles Times. Obama was talking about the legislative gridlock that has marked his terms and how he might have avoided it.

"Maybe I could have done that a little better," he said.

One of his friends wasn't having it. "They were afraid of you for a couple of reasons," said Denny Jacobs. "Number one, you were black."

Obama parried the suggestion, saying what he always says when asked about race and his presidency. "I have no doubt there are people who voted against me because of race ... or didn't approve of my agenda because of race. I also suspect there are a bunch of people who are excited or voted for me because of the notion of the first African-American president. ... Those things cut both ways," he said.

Jacobs, who is white, was unpersuaded. "That's what they were afraid of, Mr. President," he insisted.

Some might say his point was proven after the sudden death of the Supreme Court justice. The body was not yet cold when Republicans threw down the gauntlet. Senate Majority Leader Mitch McConnell said that the president should not even nominate a replacement and should leave it to his successor.

Judiciary Committee Chairman Chuck Grassley seconded this, saying his panel would not open confirmation hearings, although Politico reported Tuesday that Grassley told Radio IOWA he would not rule them out.

Understand: It's not uncommon for the opposition party to warn that a nominee better be to its liking. However, to declare before the fact that no person put forth by the president will receive even a hearing is not politics as usual, but rather, a stinging and personal insult without apparent precedent.

It is simply impossible to imagine another president being treated with such malign contempt.

But then, GOP contempt for Obama and his authority have been manifest since before Day One. McConnell's refusal to do his job is just the latest example. On Twitter, a person who tweets as "Josh@bravee1" put it like this: "Mitch McConnell just needs to admit that he thinks President Obama was elected to 3/5 of a term."

It's a great line, but what is happening here is more subtle than just racism. To be, as McConnell is, a straight, 73-year-old white male in America is to have come of age in a world where people like you and only people like you set the national agenda.

One suspects, then, that people like him see in Obama their looming loss of demographic and ideological primacy in a nation that grows more multi-hued and, on many vital social issues, less conservative every day. Some people can handle that. Others would rather cripple the country, leaving it without a functioning Supreme Court for almost a year, and never mind the will of the people as twice expressed in elections: Barack Obama is our president. He has the right and duty to nominate a new justice.

It's grating to hear Obama act as if the GOP's unrelenting campaign of obstructionism and insult were the moral equivalent of some African-American grandmother or young white progressive who were proud to cast their ballots for the first black president.

His attempt to shoulder blame for all the hyper-partisanship suggests a fundamental misreading of the change he represents and the fear it kindles in some of those whose prerogatives that change will upend.

It's well and good to be even-handed and reflective, but there is a point where that becomes willful obtuseness. Obama is there. "They were afraid of you for a couple of reasons," said his friend. "Number one, you were black." It's interesting that a white man in his 70s can see this, yet a 54-year-old black man cannot.

Sunday, February 28, 2016

HIS INFERIOR BLACKNESS

Today's column is for the benefit of one Dr. Benjamin Solomon Carson.

He shouldn't need what follows, but obviously does. No other conclusion is possible after his interview with Politico a few days ago.

The subject was Barack Obama and what the Republican presidential contender sees as the inferior quality of the president's blackness. "He's an 'African' American,' " said Carson. "He was, you know, raised white. I mean, like most Americans, I was proud that we broke the color barrier when he was elected, but ... he didn't grow up like I grew up ... "

Carson, the son of a struggling single mother who raised him in Detroit, and sometimes relied on food stamps to do so, noted that Obama, by contrast, spent part of his childhood in Indonesia. "So, for him to claim that he identifies with the experience of black Americans, I think, is a bit of a stretch."

Lord, have mercy.

Let's not even get into the fact that the man questioning Obama's racial bona fides once stood before an audience of white conservatives and proclaimed the Affordable Care Act "the worst thing that has happened in this country since slavery." Let's deal instead with Carson's implicit assertion that to be authentically black requires being fatherless and broke, scrabbling for subsistence in the 'hood.

If a white man said that, we'd call it racist. And guess what? It's also racist when a black man says it. Not to mention, self-hating and self-limiting. Carson denies the very depth and breadth of African-American life.

By his "logic," Kobe Bryant, who grew up in Italy, is not black, Shaquille O'Neal, who spent part of his childhood in Germany, is not black, Miles Davis and Natalie Cole, who grew up in affluent households, were not black and Martin Luther King, Jr., child of middle class comfort and an intact family, was not black. According to him, they were all "raised white."

Here's what Carson doesn't get: What we call "race" is not about neighborhood, class or family status.

Though the African hostages upon whose backs this country was built shared certain common approaches to music, faith and art, race ultimately isn't even about culture. Martin Luther King, for instance, was an opera buff; it's hard to get further from "black" culture than Lucia di Lammermoor.

No, race is something Europeans invented as a tool of subjugation. The people who came here from England, France and Spain did not initially see themselves as "white," after all. They declared themselves white – that is, a superior species of humanity – to justify in their own consciences the evil things they did to the people they took from Africa. Similarly, those Africans knew nothing about "black." They saw themselves as Fulani, Mende, Mandinkan or Songhay. "Black" was an identity forced upon them with every bite of the lash and rattle of the chains.

In other words, to be black is not to share a common geography, class or family status, but rather, the common experience of being insulted, bullied, and oppressed by people who think they are white.

Want to know if you're black? Try to rent a house in Miami. Try to hail a cab in Times Square. Try to win an Oscar in Hollywood. You'll find out real quick.

And there is something spectacularly absurd in the fact of Barack Obama being criticized as "not black" by a Republican.

Think about it: In the unlikely event he somehow managed to live the 47 years before his presidency without being insulted, bullied and oppressed by people who think they are white, Obama has sure made up for it since.

Members of Carson's party have called him "boy," "uppi-ty,"and "ape" and have gone to extraordinary and unprecedented lengths to block him from doing ... anything.

So the good doctor can relax. If Obama wasn't "black" before, he certainly is now.

THE DEMOCRATS

Wednesday, January 23, 2008

WHY MANY BLACKS VOTE DEMOCRAT

This is for John, who wants me to answer a question.

Two questions, actually. John's a reader in Port Orchard, Washington, who sent an e-mail the other day wondering: 1) "... why is it never mentioned that (Martin Luther King) was a Republican?" and, 2) given that Republicans were the party of abolition and that Democrats were the party of arch segregationists like George Wallace and Lester Maddox, "why do African-Americans support the Democrat (sic) Party?"

Frankly, I think John's just having a little fun at my expense, but I'm going to play along, because his questions give me an excuse to address an unspoken disconnect in modern American politics.

First of all, in regard to Dr. King's politics: John should note that this is the same King who declared himself neutral in the 1960 presidential campaign and said, "I feel that someone must remain in the position of nonalignment, so that we can look objectively at both parties and be the conscience of both – not the servant or master of either."

It's also the same King who said, "I have always argued that we would be further along in the struggle for civil rights if the Republican Party had risen above its hypocrisy and reactionary tendencies."

It is, however, true that African Americans tended to vote Republican for much of the last century, the simple reason being that the GOP was "the party of Lincoln." But as Lincoln receded in history, the GOP stranglehold on the black vote was broken by Franklin Roosevelt, John F. Kennedy, Lyndon Johnson and by the GOP's stubborn silence on civil rights.

It's disingenuous to pretend there is some philosophical coherence between the GOP of the 19th century and that of the 21st that should command African-American loyalty. Where race is concerned, Democrats and the GOP essentially exchanged ideologies in those years, the conservative Democrats becoming more moderate, the moderate GOP becoming more conservative. Black voters changed their loyalties accordingly.

And here's the disconnect: Large minorities of black voters actually side with conservatives on litmus test issues like abortion and the death penalty. So you'd think the GOP, the conservative party, would be more competitive among African Americans.

To understand why it is not, rephrase John's question a tad more honestly. Make it: Why do African Americans not support conservatism? Then the answer becomes simple: At no point in history when black folks were beset, bedraggled and fighting for their very existence have conservatives – whether you're talking Democrats of the 19th and early 20th centuries or Republicans now – been caught taking our side. From the abolition of slavery through Jim Crow through anti-lynching legislation through integration, through voting rights through civil rights through affirmative action, conservatives have always stood in opposition.

You'd think the GOP, the conservative party, would be more competitive among African Americans.

And no, it is not as if liberals have always been paragons of racial enlightenment. When President Bush decries "the soft bigotry of low expectations," he speaks insight and truth. But given the choice between the soft bigotry of low expectations and the hard bigotry of a cross burning on the lawn and silence in response, is it any wonder black voters choose the first?

I believe no ideology has a monopoly on truth. And that, to paraphrase Britain's Viscount Palmerston, black voters – like any other – ought to have no permanent friends or permanent enemies, only permanent interests. But where the permanent interest of race is concerned, conservatives are damned by their own history.

Now John wants to know why African Americans have never supported them. Here's a better question: Why haven't they ever supported us?

Sunday, August 10, 2014

'WAR ON WHITES'

At this point, you really have to wonder: Is it still news when a Republican says something asinine?

On the off chance it is, let us spend a few moments pondering the strange case of Alabama Representative Mo Brooks, who said last week that the Democratic Party is waging a "War on Whites."

Yeah, he actually said that. You can look it up if you want.

Brooks was responding to radio talk show host Laura Ingraham, who had asked him to comment on a remark from National Journal columnist Ron Fournier to the effect that the GOP cannot continue to be competitive in national elections if it continues to alienate voters of color. This is a truth so self-evident as to have been adopted by the GOP itself in its "autopsy" report after the 2012 election.

Yet here is what Brooks said in response: "This is a part of the war on whites that is being launched by the Democratic Party. And the way in which they're launching this war is by claiming that whites hate everybody else. It's a part of the strategy that Barack Obama implemented in 2008, continued in 2012, where he divides us all on race, on sex, greed, envy, class warfare, all those kinds of things."

"A War on Whites." Yet it's President Obama who is guilty of racially inflammatory rhetoric?

Brooks' words so alarmed Ingraham that she suggested his rhetoric was "a little out there." This woman belches fire on all things conservative; for her to suggest you've gone too far is like Charlie Sheen telling you to cut back on hookers and cigarettes.

But Brooks doubled down, repeating the claim in an interview with a website, AL.com: "What the Democrats are doing with their dividing America by race is they are waging a war on whites and I find that repugnant."

OK, so let's say the obvious first. There's something surreal and absurd about this lecture, coming as it does from a member of the party that invented the Southern strategy and birtherism and whose voters were last seen standing at the border screaming at terrified Guatemalan kids. But it's not the ridiculousness of Brooks' words that should be of greatest concern. You see, Fournier is right. If something does not arrest its present trajectory, the GOP seems destined to shrink into a regional party with appeal only to older white voters. It will be irrelevant in a nation where white voters will soon cease to be a majority – no group will be a majority – and appeals to racial and cultural resentments have less power to sway elections.

That should concern the GOP braintrust. It should concern us all. As a practical matter, this country has only two political parties; if one ceases to be competitive, we become a de facto single-party system. That is not democracy. No ideology has a monopoly on good ideas. So America needs a healthy Republican Party.

Yet for every Rand Paul trying – albeit in a fumbling and deeply flawed manner – to reach constituencies the party has written off and driven off, or to engage on issues it has disregarded, there seem to be five Mo Brookses doubling down on the politics of resentment and fear.

His party needs to realize once and for all that that day is done. It is critical for the GOP to wean itself from the cowardly belief that simply to discuss race and culture, to acknowledge disparity in treatment and outcomes, to put forward ways of addressing those things, constitutes "playing the race card" or "race-baiting" or fighting a "war on whites."

That idea was always wrongheaded and dumb. Very soon it will become electorally untenable as well. So the GOP must learn to speak a language it has shunned to people it has ignored.

Because its biggest threat is not the Democratic Party but demographic reality. And right now, that reality is winning, hands down.

THE REPUBLICANS

Sunday, June 7, 2009

CONFUSE THE DEBATE AND MUDDY THE WATER

So Newt Gingrich now says Sonia Sotomayor is not a "racist" after all. She must be trembling with relief.

Gingrich's backpedaling came last week in an article on HumanEvents.com. It leaves just two high-profile Republicans, former Representative Tom Tancredo and radio blowhard Rush Limbaugh, still clinging to that absurd allegation.

As you know unless you are just back from Antarctica, this sudden spasm of righteous Republican rage is because of a speech Sotomayor gave in 2001 about the role gender, ethnicity and other characteristics play in a judge's judgment. "I would hope," she said, "that a wise Latina woman with the richness of her experiences would more often than not reach a better conclusion than a white male who hasn't lived that life."

It is, yes, a wince-inducing statement. You might even call it a tone deaf and culturally chauvinistic one. But does it support comparisons to the Ku Klux Klan such as Tancredo and Gingrich have made? Not in a million years.

The attempt to paint Sotomayor as such represents more than political overreach. No, this is part and parcel of a campaign by conservatives to arrogate unto themselves and/or neutralize the language of social grievance. We've seen this before. They sullied the word "feminist" so thoroughly even feminists disdain it. They made "liberal" such a vulgarity you'd never know liberals fought to ban child labor, end Jim Crow or win women the right to vote.

Having no record of their own of responding compassionately to social grievance (ask them what they did during the Civil Rights Movement and they grow very quiet) conservatives have chosen instead to co-opt the language of that grievance. And if what they did to the language of women's rights and progressivism took some gall, what they are seeking to do to the language of race suggests a testicular circumference of bovine proportions. There is something surreal about hearing those who have historically been the enemies of racial progress define racial progress as looking out for the poor white brother.

And whatever comes beyond surreal is what describes these three men in particular, none of whom has ever been distinguished by his previous tender concern for racial minorities lied upon, denied upon and systematically cheated of their square of the American Dream, telling us "racism" is what happens when a Hispanic woman says something dumb about white men. We are, after all, talking about a man (Tancredo) who once called majority Hispanic Miami "a third world" country, and another man (Limbaugh) who advised a black caller to "take that bone out of your nose." These are fighters against racism?

You keep waiting for someone to break up laughing. You keep looking for Ashton Kutcher to say you've been punk'd.

But they are in earnest, and there is a pattern here: The forces of intolerance seeking to redefine the parameters of a debate they can win in no other way. Read the treatises that attempt to make Martin Luther King Jr. an icon of conservatism. Read the ones that claim the relative handful of black-on-white violent crimes occurring annually in this country constitutes "genocide." Read the mewling of white victimization that rises any time blacks or browns are perceived as having won some victory over discrimination.

There is to it a breathtaking cynicism and a willingness to manipulate for political gain one of the rawest places in the psyche of a nation. The goal is not to persuade. It is to muddy the water, confuse the debate. Because when you can't win the argument, confusing it works almost as well.

Based on one foolish quote, we have spent a week asking if Sotomayor is a racist. I'd call that mission accomplished. And I wish Kutcher would come out already.

It's not funny anymore.

WHO SPEAKS FOR THE POOR?

If he'd said it of Jews, he would still be apologizing.

If he'd said it of blacks, he'd be on BET, begging absolution.

If he'd said it of women, the National Organization for Women would have his carcass turning slowly on a spit over an open flame.

But he said it of the poor, so he got away with it.

"He" is South Carolina Lt. Gov. André Bauer, running for governor on the GOP ticket. Speaking of those who receive public assistance, he recently told an audience, "My grandmother was not a highly educated woman, but she told me as a small child to quit feeding stray animals. You know why? Because they breed. You're facilitating the problem if you give an animal or a person ample food supply. They will reproduce, especially ones that don't think too much further than that. And so what you've got to do is you've got to curtail that type of behavior. They don't know any better."

You read that right. The would-be governor of one of the poorest states there is likens the poor to stray animals.

And though it drew some newspaper notice, a riposte from "The Daily Show" and rebukes from Bauer's opponents, it never quite rose to the level of national controversy, as it would've had Bauer compared, say, women or Jews to the dogs one feeds at one's back door. The relative silence stands as eloquent testimony to the powerlessness and invisibility of the American poor.

One is reminded how earnestly shocked news media were at the poverty they saw five years ago when New Orleans drowned. "Why didn't they get out?" observers kept asking – as if everyone has a car in the driveway and a wallet full of plastic.

The poor fare little better on television. The Evanses of "Good Times" and the Conners from "Roseanne" aside, television has been heavily weighted toward fresh-scrubbed middle- and upper-class families for 60 years.

Politicians? They'll elbow one another aside to pledge allegiance to the middle class; they are conspicuously less eager to align with those still trying to reach that level.

Who, then, speaks for the poor? Who raises a voice when they are scapegoated and marginalized? Who cries out when they are abused by police and failed by schools? Who takes a stand when they are exploited by employers and turned away by hospitals?

As near as I can tell, no one does.

Unfortunately, poor people have never learned to think of and conduct themselves as a voting bloc; historically, they have proven too readily divisible, usually by race. As Martin Luther King once observed: "If it may be said of the slavery era that the white man took the world and gave the Negro Jesus, then it may be said of the Reconstruction era that the Southern aristocracy took the world and gave the poor white man Jim Crow. And when his wrinkled stomach cried out for the food that his empty pockets could not provide, he ate Jim Crow, a psychological bird that told him that no matter how bad off he was, at least he was a white man, better than the black man."

It takes some helluva psychology to get two men stuck in the same leaking boat to fight one another. You'd think their priority would be to come together, if only long enough to bail water. But the monied interests in this country have somehow been able to con the poor into doing just that, fighting tooth and nail when they ought to be standing shoulder to shoulder.

One hopes André Bauer's words will provide a wakeup call – in Carolina and elsewhere – for people who have been down too long and fooled too often, that it will encourage them to organize their votes, raise their voices, push their issues into the public discourse. In America, one is invisible and powerless only so long as one chooses to be.

And the Bauers of this world need to know: sometimes stray animals bite.

Wednesday, March 24, 2010

TEA PARTY AND RACISM DON'T MIX

So it turns out that, contrary to what I argued in this space a few weeks back, racism is not "a major component" of the so-called tea party movement. I am informed of this by dozens of tea party activists indignant and insulted that I would even suggest such a thing.

In other news tea party protesters called John Lewis a "nigger" the other day in the shadow of the U.S. Capitol.

For the record, Lewis wasn't their only target.

Representative Emanuel Cleaver was spat upon.

Representative Barney Frank, who is gay, was called "faggot."

But it is Lewis' involvement that gives the Saturday incident its bittersweet resonance. The 70-year-old representative from Georgia is, after all, among the last living icons of the Civil Rights Movement. Or, as Lewis himself put it, "I've faced this before."

Indeed. He faced it in Nashville in 1960 when he was locked inside a whites-only fast-food restaurant and gassed by a fumigation machine for ordering a hamburger.

He faced it in Birmingham in 1961 when a group of Freedom Riders was attacked and he was knocked unconscious for riding a Greyhound bus.

Most famously, he faced it on the Edmund Pettus Bridge in Selma 45 years ago this month when his skull was fractured by Alabama state troopers who charged a group of demonstrators seeking their right to vote.

In the very arc of his life, Lewis provides a yardstick for measuring American progress. The fact that he rose from that bridge to become a member of Congress says something about this country. But the fact that people demonstrating against healthcare reform chose to chant at him, "Kill the bill, nigger!" well, that says something, too.

Which is why tea party leaders have spent much of the last few days spinning the incident, deflecting renewed suggestions that their stated fears – socialism, communism, liberalism – are just proxies for the one fear most of them no longer dare speak. Some even faxed the McClatchy news bureau in Washington to suggest, without offering a shred of evidence, that the episode was sparked by Democratic plants within the crowd.

Amy Kremer, coordinator of the Tea Party Express, went on Fox News to dismiss what she called an "isolated" incident. Your first instinct may be to cede the benefit of the doubt on that one. It seems unfair to tar nine reasonable people with the hateful behavior of one lunatic.

But ask yourself: When is the last time organizers of protests on other hot-button issues – say, abortion rights or globalization – had to apologize for "isolated incidents" like these?

Moreover, given how often tea party leaders have been forced to disavow hateful signs and slogans and even the presence of organized white supremacist groups in their midst, is it really fair to use the word "isolated?"

Is there not a rottenness here? And is not the unwillingness to call that rottenness by name part and parcel of the reason it endures?

No, my argument is emphatically not that every American who opposes healthcare reform is a closet Klansman. Certainly, people can have earnest and honest disagreements about that.

But by the same token, as these "isolated" incidents mount, as the venom and the vitriol increase to the point where even proxy words no longer suffice, it insults intelligence to deny that race is in the mix.

Not that the denial surprises.

Often we tell ourselves lies to spare ourselves truths. Had you asked them, the people who locked John Lewis inside that restaurant, the ones who mauled him at that bus station and smashed him down on that bridge, would not have said they acted from a rottenness within.

No, like the ones who called him "nigger" half a century later, they would have told you they were good people fighting for principle, trying to save this country from the liberals, the socialists and the communists.

They would not have said they were racists. Racists never do.

Wednesday, October 5, 2011

PERRY'S ROCK

A few words about Rick Perry's rock.

This would be the one at the entrance to a remote Texas hunting ground used by Perry for decades, the one painted with the name of the camp: "Niggerhead." The Texas governor says his father painted over the ugly name almost 30 years ago, though some locals interviewed by the Washington Post in a story that ran Sunday claimed to have seen it there much more recently.

That same day, Herman Cain, who is competing with Perry for the GOP presidential nomination, called the word on the rock "vile," and accused Perry of being "insensitive." He was pretty much the only candidate to go after Perry about the rock though he was backpedaling a day later.

"I really don't care about that word," he said, after being accused of playing the "race card."

It was difficult to escape a suspicion that, though he is African American, he never cared about the perceived insult as much as he cared about the opportunity to inflict damage on Perry. Cain thus managed to make both his attack and retreat feel calculated and cynical.

Meanwhile, the rock becomes the latest outrage du jour, meaning the momentary controversies through which what passes for discussion of race and privilege in this country are carried. Think Bill O'Reilly and Don Imus shooting their mouths off. Think Andrew Breitbart sliming Shirley Sherrod. Periodically, the news delivers these neatly-packaged, self-contained dustups that allow political leaders and others to line up on the side of the angels, harrumphing the necessary condemnations, while never venturing too deeply into what the dustups tell us about us.

Where race is concerned, people sometimes act as if the past is a distant country, a far, forgotten place we ought never revisit, unless it be for the occasional purpose of congratulating ourselves on how far we have come.

But the past has this way of crashing the party. Usually, it does so with the relative subtlety of statistics quantifying ongoing racial bias in hiring, education and criminal justice. Occasionally, it does so with the bluntness of a sign reading "Niggerhead."

The name is not unique. To the contrary, the map of the United States was once dotted with similar words. For example, there is still a Negrohead Point in Florida and a Negro Cove in Maryland, both changed from the original slur in a fig leaf of decency. There is also Dago Peak in Idaho, Jew Hill in Pennsylvania and Redskin Mountain in Colorado.

Not to let the Texas governor off too easily, then, but to make this all about Perry is to miss the point. It is also about us. What does it say about America, about fairness in hiring, education, justice, that such place names were ever acceptable – or that some people don't understand why they no longer are?

"It's just a name," a man named David Davis told the Post. He is a Texas judge, a man to whom, we may suppose, African Americans periodically come seeking justice. "Like those are vertical blinds," he said, looking at a window in his courtroom. "It's just what it was called."

That rationalization ought to tell you that that rock is not the political football Cain sought to make it. Rather, it is a reproach to the unearned smugness of modern days. And a reminder that the past is closer than we think.

Sunday, October 16, 2011

EXPLAINING HERMAN CAIN

This is for those who keep asking what I think of Herman Cain. In particular, it's for those who want to know what the tea party's embrace of this black businessman turned presidential candidate says about my claim that the tea party is racist.

I might eat the plate of crow those folks proffer if I'd ever actually made that claim. What I have said, fairly consistently, is something more nuanced: racial animus is an element of tea party ideology, but not its entirety. As I once noted in this space, the tea party probably would not exist if Condoleezza Rice were president.

Modern social conservatives, in my experience, do not hate black people en masse. To the contrary, there are two kinds of blacks they love. The first is those, like Rice, who are mainly mute on the subject of race, seldom so impolite as to say or do anything that might remind people they are black. The second is those who will engage on race, but only to lecture other blacks for their failures as conservatives conceive them. And that, friends and neighbors, is Herman Cain all over.

"I don't believe racism in this country today holds anybody back in a big way," he told CNN recently. Had he contended too many African Americans use racism as an excuse for failure to succeed and even failure to try, Cain would have gotten no grief from me; I've made that argument often.

But what he said was that racism is no longer a factor. He surely warmed the hearts of his conservative fellow travelers who swear blacks have the same opportunity to succeed as whites if they'd only get off their lazy so-and-sos and do it.

It is a claim spectacularly at odds with reality, given that African-American unemployment runs twice that of whites, given that the Agriculture Department admits to systematically discriminating against black farmers, given documentation of a "justice" system engaged in the mass incarceration of young black men.

But what made the claim truly bizarre is that two days later, Cain branded himself a victim of racism. Specifically, he said some black people are "racist" because they disagree with his politics. So blacks aren't held back by racism, but Cain is?

Lord, give me strength.

He thus neatly encapsulates what has become an article of faith for many white conservatives; namely, that it is they, not black and brown people, who are the true victims of bigotry. Mind you, they have not a shred of a scrap of a scintilla of evidence to support this cockamamie idea, but they believe it anyway. And now they find support for their idiocy in this Negro from Atlanta.

One of the least-discussed impacts of the black experience in America is its emotional toll. African Americans were psychologically maimed by this country, the expression of which can still be seen in the visceral self-loathing that afflicts too many.

Meaning the black child who equates doing well in school with "acting white." Meaning the famous black man who bleaches his skin. Meaning the famous black woman who rationalizes her use of a certain soul-killing racial epithet. Meaning Herman Cain.

In his diminution of African-American struggle, he comes across as a man profoundly at odds with the skin he's in. He seems embarrassed he's black.

For what it's worth, I suspect black folks aren't real happy about it, either.

Sunday, November 6, 2011

OUR BLACKS ARE BETTER THAN YOURS

Do you think it gives Clarence Thomas a warm, fuzzy feeling to know he is one of Ann Coulter's blacks?

That is how Coulter put it on Fox "News" while defending Herman Cain against sexual harassment charges that threatened to engulf his campaign last week. Liberals, she said, detest black conservatives, but the truth is, "our blacks are so much better than their blacks."

"Our" blacks? Really?

Social conservative pundits tend to be astonishingly obtuse when discussing race, so it is good they rarely do so. Last week was an unfortunate exception, as one of "their" blacks struggled to frame a coherent response to allegations that he harassed female colleagues in the 1990s when he headed the National Restaurant Association. Though accusations of sexual impropriety have beset a bipartisan Who's Who of black and white politicians, the right wing came out in force to argue that people are only questioning Cain because he is a black conservative.

This would be the same Cain who not so long ago said racism was no longer a significant obstacle for African Americans. This would be the same right wing that is conspicuous by its silence, its hostility or its complicity when the injustice system imposes mass incarceration on young black men, when the number of hate groups in this country spikes to over a thousand, when the black unemployment rate stands at twice the national average, when the president is called "uppity" and "boy."

But they scream in pious racial indignation when Cain is asked questions he doesn't want to answer.

A "high tech lynching," said blogger Brent Bozell.

"Racially stereotypical," sniffed Rush Limbaugh.

"I believe the answer is yes," said Cain himself when asked on Fox if race was the cause of his woes, adding honestly, if hilariously, that he has no evidence whatsoever to back that up.

If you didn't know better, you'd think Cain was some hybrid of Emmett Till and Kunta Kinte. Nobody knows de trouble he's seen.

The candidate has spoken of how he left the Democratic "plantation," the implication being that more blacks should vote Republican. It would seem on the surface to make sense. As a 2008 Gallup Poll proved – and simple observation reiterates – African Americans tend to be as conservative as your average Republican on some key moral issues and are more religious than the average Republican, to boot.

So why don't blacks vote Republican? The answer is simple. Black people are not crazy. Being not crazy, they understand a simple truth about conservatives: They have never stood with, or up for, black people. Never.

Forget modern controversies like mass incarceration. Social conservatives, then based largely in the Democratic Party of the early to mid-20th century, opposed the Voting Rights Act. They opposed the Civil Rights Act. They opposed school integration. They opposed the Montgomery Bus Boycott. They opposed a law to crack down on lynching.

These are the people for whom African Americans are now supposed to vote? To make the argument is to betray a stunning contempt for the intelligence – and memory – of black voters.

In talking about race, conservatives have all the moral author-ity of a pimp talking about women's rights. Granted, "their" blacks might disagree.

Sunday, July 24, 2016

A CLEAR AND PRESENT DANGER

Well, that was sure ugly.

Last week's Republican conclave in Cleveland came across less as a nominating convention than as a four-day nervous break-down, a moment of fracture and bipolarity from a party that no longer has any clear idea what it stands for or what it is. Every-where you turned, there was something that made you embarrassed for them, something so disconnected from fact, logic or decency as to suggest those things no longer have much mean-ing for the party faithful.

Did the convention really earn rave reviews from white su-premacists, with one tweeting approvingly that the GOP "is becoming the de facto white party?"

Did Florida Governor Rick Scott really say he could remember "when terrorism was something that happened in foreign coun-tries" – as if four little girls were never blown to pieces in a Birmingham church, and an NAACP lawyer and his wife were nev-er killed by a bomb in Scott's own state?

Did Silicon Valley entrepreneur Peter Thiel really say, "It's time to end the era of stupid wars" as if it were Democrats who dragged Republicans into Iraq with promises of flowers strewn beneath American tanks?

Did Ben Carson really link Hillary Clinton to Satan? Did the crowd really chant, repeatedly and vociferously, for her to be jailed? Did at least two Republicans actually call for her execution?

No, you weren't dreaming. The answer is yes on all counts.

Then there was the party's nominee. Donald Trump's "acceptance speech" was a 75-minute scream as incoherent as everything that preceded it. He vowed to protect the LGBTQ community from "a hateful foreign ideology" as if his party's platform did not commit it to support so-called "conversion therapy," an offensive bit of quackery that purports to "cure" homosexuality.

He accused President Obama of dividing the nation as if he were not the one recycling Richard Nixon's racist Southern strategy with unsubtle cries of "law and order," and George H.W. Bush's infamous Willie Horton ad with tales of "illegals" out to kill us.

Trump painted a bleak picture of a nation in decline and under siege, and he offered a range of responses: fear or fright, fury or rage. But glory be, he promised to fix everything that ails us, down to and including long lines at the airport. Trump gave few specifics, mind you, beyond a guarantee that he can do all this "quickly." Any resemblance to a guy hawking magical elixir from the back of a wagon was surely unintentional.

This gathering made one thing clear, if it had not been already. The battle between left and right is no longer a contest of ideas, no longer about low taxes versus higher ones, small government versus big government, intervention versus isolation. No, the defining clash of our time is reason versus unreason, reason versus an inchoate fear and fury growing like weeds on the cultural, class, religious and racial resentments of people who cling to an idealized 1954 and wonder why the country is passing them by.

The Republicans, as presently constituted, have no ideas beyond fear and fury. And Lord help us, the only thing standing between us and that is a grandmother in pantsuits.

The Democrats have their gathering this week in Philadelphia. Ordinarily, you'd call on them to present a competing vision, but the GOP has set the bar so low you'd be happy to see the Democrats just present a vision, period, just appeal to something beyond our basest selves, just remind us that we can be better and our politics higher than what we saw last week.

This has to happen. Because, you see, the Republicans were right on at least one point: The nation does face a clear and present danger, a menace to our values, our hopes and our future. If the GOP wants to see this threat, there's no need to look outward.

Any good mirror will do.

ELECTION 2016

Sunday, November 29, 2015

A SELF-INFLICTED PLAGUE

"You got to give the people what they want." – O'Jays.

Even by his standards, it was an astounding performance.

Over the course of just two days last weekend, Donald Trump spewed bigotry, venom and absurdity like a sewer pipe, spewed it with such utter disregard for decency and factuality that it was difficult to know what to criticize first.

Shall we condemn him for retweeting a racist graphic on Sunday filled with wildly inaccurate statistics from a non-existent source ("Whites killed by blacks – 81 percent")?

Or shall we hammer him for tacitly encouraging violence when an African-American protester was beaten up at a Trump rally in Birmingham on Saturday? "Maybe he should have been roughed up," Trump told Fox "News."

Shall we blast him for telling ABC on Sunday that he would bring back the thoroughly discredited practice of waterboarding – i.e., torturing – suspected terrorists?

Or shall we lambaste him for claiming – falsely – at the Birmingham rally that "thousands and thousands" of people in Jersey

City, New Jersey, applauded the September 11 attacks and reiterating it the next day, telling ABC that "a heavy Arab population ... were cheering."

Trump is a whack-a-mole of the asinine and the repugnant. Or, as a person dubbed "snarkin pie" noted on Twitter: "Basically, Trump is what would happen if the comments section became a human and ran for president."

Not that that hurts his bid for the GOP nomination. A Washington Post/CNN poll finds Trump with a double-digit lead (32 percent to 22 percent) on his nearest rival, Ben Carson, who is his equal in nonsense, though not in volume. Meantime, establishment candidate Jeb Bush is on life support, mired in single digits.

And the party is panicking. In September, Bobby Jindal called Trump "a madman." Two weeks ago came reports of an attempt to lure Mitt Romney into the race. Candidate Jim Gilmore and advisers to candidates Bush and Marco Rubio have dubbed Trump a fascist. Trump, complains the dwindling coven of grownups on the right, is doing serious damage to the Republican "brand."

Which he is. But it is difficult to feel sorry for the GOP. After all, it has brought this upon itself.

Keeping the customer satisfied, giving the people what they want, is the fundament of sound business. More effectively than anyone in recent memory, Trump has transferred that principle to politics. Problem is, it turns out that what a large portion of the Republican faithful wants is racism, xenophobia, Islamophobia, the validation of unrealistic fears and the promise of quick fixes to complex problems.

That's hardly shocking. This is what the party establishment has trained them to want, what it has fed them for years. But it has done so in measured tones and coded language that preserved the fiction of deniability. Trump's innovation is his increasingly-apparent lack of interest in deniability. Like other great demagogues – George Wallace, Joe McCarthy, Huey Long, Charles Coughlin – his appeal has been in the fact that he is blunt, unfiltered, anti-intellectual, full-throated and unapologetic. And one in three Republicans are eating it up like candy.

Mind you, this is after the so-called 2013 "autopsy" wherein the GOP cautioned itself to turn from its angry, monoracial appeal. Two years later, it doubles down on that appeal instead.

And though candidate Trump would be a disaster for the Republicans, he would also be one for the nation, effectively rendering ours a one-party system. But maybe that's the wake-up call some of us require to end this dangerous flirtation with extremism.

"You got to give the people what they want, " says an old song. Truth is, sometimes it's better if you don't.

Wednesday, June 22, 2016

CAN'T KILL AN IDEA WITH A BULLET

On Saturday, someone tried to kill Donald Trump.

You may not have heard about it. The story didn't get much play, the attempt wasn't well planned and the candidate was never in jeopardy.

Still the fact remains that authorities arrested one Michael Steven Sandford, 19, after he allegedly tried to grab a gun from the holster of a Las Vegas police officer with the idea of using it to kill Trump at a campaign rally. Authorities say Sandford, who carried a U.K. driver's license but who had been living in New Jersey for about a year and a half, had visited a nearby gun range to learn how to handle a firearm. They say he has wanted to kill Trump for a year.

Let us be thankful he was not successful. The assassination of Donald Trump would have been a new low for a political season that is already the most dispiriting in memory. It would have deprived a family of its father and husband. It would have traumatized a nation where political murder has been a too-frequent tragedy.

And it would have imparted the moral authority of martyrdom to Trump's ideas. That would be a disaster in its own right.

Like most would-be assassins, what Sandford apparently did not understand is that you cannot kill an idea with a bullet. Even bad ideas are impervious to gunfire.

Trump, of course, has been a veritable Vesuvius of bad ideas in the year since he took that escalator ride into the race for the presidency. From banning Muslim immigrants to building a wall on the southern border to punishing women who have abortions to advocating guns in nightclubs to judging judicial fitness based on heritage, to killing the wives and children of terror suspects, if there has been a hideous, unserious or flat-out stupid thought floated in this political season, odds are, it carried the Trump logo.

It is understandable, then, that even people who wish Trump no bodily harm might feel as Sandford presumably did: that if he were somehow just ... gone, the stench of his ideas – of his anger, nativism, coarseness and proud ignorance – might somehow waft away like trash-fire smoke in a breeze.

But it doesn't work that way. Martin Luther King's dream of racial equality did not die on the balcony of the Lorraine Motel. Nor did Adolf Hitler's dream of racial extermination perish with him in that bunker beneath Berlin. Ideas, both transcendent and repugnant, are far hardier than the fragile lives of the men and women who given them voice.

So any hope that Trump's disappearance would somehow fix America is naive. America's problem has nothing to do with him, except to the degree he has made himself a focal point.

No, America's problem is fear. Fear of economic stagnation, yes, and fear of terrorism. But those are proxies for the bigger and more fundamental fear: fear of demographic diminution, of losing the privileges and prerogatives that have always come with being straight, white, male and/or Christian in America. It was the holy quadfecta of entitlement, but that entitlement is under siege in a nation that grows more sexually, racially and religiously diverse with every sunrise.

Trumpism is only the loudest and most obvious response to that, and it will not disappear when he does. There is no instant cure for what has America unsettled. There is only time and the hard work of change.

In a sense, we are bringing forth a new nation, conceived in liberty and dedicated to the proposition that all men and women really are created equal. If, for some of us, that fires the imagination, it is hardly mysterious that for others, it kindles a sense of displacement and loss. The good news is that their Trumpism cannot survive in the new nation.

In the end, you see, only one thing can kill a bad idea.

And that's a better one.

Sunday, August 28, 2016

THEY LOVE TRUMP BECAUSE HE SEES THEM

His name doesn't even appear in the book.

But make no mistake. "Hillbilly Elegy," the new bestseller by J.D. Vance, is, in a very real sense, about Donald Trump. More to the point, it's about the people who have made his unlikely run for the presidency possible.

It is also, not coincidentally, a book about being invisible. Not H.G. Wells invisible, with objects seeming to float in mid-air. Rather, Ralph Ellison invisible, when you are right there in three dimensions, but somehow, unseen.

First and foremost, though, Vance's book is a memoir about growing up hardscrabble and white in clannish, insular communities in Kentucky and Ohio. It was a tough, unstable life. Vance was in and out of his mother's house – she was a drug user with a procession of boyfriends and husbands – and was raised mostly by his grandparents – "Papaw" and "Mamaw."

Mamaw was no June Cleaver. A gun-toting "lunatic" with a menthol cigarette forever dangling from her lips, she was rumored to have once almost killed a man who stole from her family. Her favorite descriptive term was the verb form of the F-word. But her love for her grandson was iron.

That grandson did a hitch in the Marines, went to college, went to law school at Yale. But he never lost a certain tough-minded pride of people and place.

"I may be white," writes Vance, now a Silicon Valley investment executive, "but I do not identify with the WASPs of the Northeast. Instead, I identify with the millions of working-class white Americans of Scots-Irish descent who have no college degree. To these folks, poverty is the family tradition – their ancestors were day laborers in the Southern slave economy, sharecroppers after that, coal miners after that, and machinists and mill workers during more recent times. Americans call them hillbillies, rednecks, or white trash. I call them neighbors, friends and family."

In other words, Vance's people are Trump's base. And the book is a must-read for anyone seeking to understand Trump's appeal. "Hillbilly Elegy" is a compelling and compassionate portrait of a people politicians seldom address and media seldom reflect.

They love Trump because he sees them.

Yes, he's a racist clown who lies like bunnies copulate. Yes, he appeals to their lowest selves, to their hatreds and fears. But he sees them and speaks to them, something neither Democrats nor Republicans do. When you feel yourself forgotten, when work and hope have fled, when you live by a tough-minded pride of people and place, yet also by a whisper of embarrassment that your people and place are so often sick, unschooled and hungry, the simple fact of being seen and spoken to is powerful.

The one great flaw in Vance's book is a disingenuous near-silence on his kinsmen's attitudes about race. And a passage wherein he claims their antipathy toward Barack Obama has "nothing to do with skin color" but rather, with the fact that he is "brilliant, wealthy, and speaks like a constitutional law professor" is flat out intellectually dishonest.

Obama is hardly the first politician to be smart, rich and well-spoken. He is, however, the first to be hounded into producing his long form birth certificate.

Still, that flaw does not outweigh Vance's triumph, which is to give substance and dimension to those America has made invisible. Democrats, Republicans and media struggling to comprehend the forces that have upended politics should be asking themselves a question. Donald Trump shattered the paradigm because he sees J.D. Vance's people.

Why is he the only one who does?

Chapter 9

ISSUES AND EVENTS

SEARCHING FOR ANSWERS

"There comes a time when people get tired."
Martin Luther King, Jr., December 5, 1955.

Tracy is tired. She was tired even before Baltimore burned this week.

I received an email from her on April 12. She wanted me to know she is a 55-year-old white lady from Austin, Texas, who is tired unto tears by incident after incident of police violence against unarmed African-American men – including a 2013 shooting in her own hometown. "What can be done?" she asked. "What can I do? I'm sincere in this question. I want to DO something. What can that be? I'm embarrassed to have to ask; I feel like I should KNOW what to do, but I don't."

There comes a time when people get tired. And then what?

In Baltimore, the answer some people gave was to break windows, smash cars, set fires and loot stores.

In so doing, they gave aid and comfort to every enemy of justice who would just as soon not look too closely at what happened in that city. Meaning, of course, the death of Freddie Gray, a 25-year-old African-American man who mysteriously suffered fatal injuries – on April 12, no less – while in police custody.

As Martin Luther King noted after young people in Memphis broke windows and looted stores during the last march he ever led, violence has a way of changing the subject.

He lamented that he was now forced to talk about the vandalism rather than the exploitation of dirt-poor working men that had brought him to Memphis in the first place.

Similarly, we are now required to take time out from demanding justice for Freddie Gray to discuss the sacking and looting of Baltimore and to say the obvious: The road to better policing does not go through a burned-out CVS pharmacy. So the rioting – whether motivated by genuine anger or craven opportunism – was not just thuggish, short-sighted and self-defeating.

It was also tactically stupid, ceding the moral high ground and giving media, politicians and pundits permission to ignore the very real issues here.

Not that they ever need much of an excuse, particularly over at Fox "News" and other citadels of conservative denialism. Indeed, on Monday night even as Baltimore burned, Fox's Lou Dobbs was, predictably enough, blaming the violence on President Obama.

Apparently, the death of Gray, whose spine was partially severed in some still unexplained way, had nothing to do with it. Repeated incidents of police violence against men and boys who somehow always happen to be black and unarmed, had nothing to do with it. No, it was Obama's fault. Amazing.

It has reached a point where you can't keep the atrocities straight without a score card. Besides Gray, we've got Eric Harris, an unarmed black man shot in Tulsa who cried that he was losing his breath, to which a cop responded "F-- your breath."

We've got Levar Jones, a black man shot by a state trooper in South Carolina while complying with the trooper's commands.

We've got Oscar Grant, Sean Bell, Eric Garner.

We've got video of a black man named Walter Scott, wanted for a traffic violation and back child support, running from a police officer and being shot to death.

We've got video of a white man named Michael Wilcox, wanted for murder, running toward a police officer, threatening him, daring him to shoot, refusing to remove his hands from his pockets, yet somehow not being shot.

We've got all this plus statistical proof. Yet the same people who cry "War on Christmas!" every time some city hall in Podunk erects a menorah on the lawn can discern no racial disparity in police violence against unarmed men.

So if there comes a time when people get tired, who can blame them?

POVERTY

Friday, January 13, 2006

POVERTY ISN'T ALL BLACK

The barber leaned close so the white folks couldn't hear.

How are you adjusting to the culture shock, he asked? Takes some getting used to, I replied.

We were two black men in a place – the Appalachian foothills where Ohio abuts West Virginia – that is home to very few people like us.

But the culture shock he spoke of wasn't about race so much as economics. It's a strange thing, he said, still leaning close, to see white people, poor.

It is strange, indeed.

Not that I didn't know there are white poor. To the contrary, I knew that while poverty on a percentage basis is far greater among blacks than whites, there are, in terms of raw numbers, more poor whites than poor anybody. And this region, where I will be teaching journalism until June, is among the poorest and whitest in the country.

Still, it's one thing to read statistics and quite another to see with your eyes. But my sojourn here makes seeing inevitable. And I find myself fascinated by how markers of poverty can be simultaneously so familiar and yet so unknown: the unmarried teenage dropout soon to be a mother, the service worker missing teeth, the uneducated woman dying of emphysema, sneaking a smoke in her hospital bed, the rough man who lives between scrapes with the law, the young guy buying a 40-ounce bottle of malt liquor before noon. All white.

We are so comfortable thinking of people like them as archetypes of black dysfunction. It's jarring to be reminded that they are, in fact, archetypes of dysfunction, period, and that dysfunction, no matter its color, should trouble us all.

Martin Luther King understood this. Which is one of the things we understand least about him.

Monday will be the 20th King Day. It will bring the 20th round of interfaith prayer breakfasts, recitations of I Have a Dream, assessments of progress toward racial equity and the lack thereof. I suspect there won't be much discussion of white poverty.

This is not a surprise. We like our heroes and their heroism simple, unencumbered by that which doesn't fit neatly into a box. We like our commemorations simpler still, a self-congratulatory excuse for a three-day weekend or a used car sale.

But the man who said, "I have a dream," also said, "All life is interrelated," and came to believe his mission as a moral leader encompassed more than race. Encompassed, among other things, class.

It is instructive to remember that in his last days, King was planning what he called the Poor People's Campaign, a multiethnic march on Washington to demand action against poverty. "At Canaan's Edge," the final chapter of Taylor Branch's epic retelling of the civil rights years, recounts a summit meeting a few weeks before King's assassination. Chicano farmworkers, Native Americans from the Plains and white coal miners from Appalachia sat with King to explore the revolutionary idea that their peoples might have causes and grievances in common.

Then King went to Memphis. And the idea has not been meaningfully explored since.

Neglect has made it no less tantalizing.

Yes, race matters. Most of us know this. But the genius of Martin Luther King in his final days was to understand that there are paradigms beyond race and that they matter, too.

So on Monday, as we are exhorted to seek paths of racial amity, one hopes we will also be exhorted to understand, as King did, that conscience has no color, that race is not destiny, that injustice anywhere threatens justice everywhere.

There are among us children who sleep in hunger, rise in cold, live in ignorance and they are of every color and every tribe. We ought not find their suffering easier to accept because they are not like us. Ought to realize that the dignity of all is the concern of all.

That, too, was Martin's dream.

TRAYVON MARTIN

Sunday, May 6, 2012

KILLED BY A STEREOTYPE

I don't care about George Zimmerman's MySpace page.

Granted, it was gratifying to read recently in The Miami Herald about his crude animus toward Mexicans ("soft ass wanna be thugs") and his reference to a former girlfriend as an "ex-hoe." Given the way white supremacists and other Zimmerman supporters have exaggerated and manufactured evidence to paint Zimmerman's unarmed 17-year-old victim, Trayvon Martin, as a thug who somehow deserved shooting, this unflattering portrait offers the same satisfaction one feels any time the goose is basted with sauce that was prepared for the gander.

But ultimately, Zimmerman's online profile is as irrelevant as Trayvon's to any real understanding of the social dynamics that were at play the night the boy was shot to death. Worse, our fixation on this ephemera, the need on the one hand to make Trayvon some dark gangsta straight from Central Casting and on the other to find a Klan hood in the back of Zimmerman's closet, suggests a shallow, even naïve, understanding of the role race seems to have played in this tragedy.

The pertinent fact is that Zimmerman found Trayvon suspicious because, as he told the 911 dispatcher, the boy was walking slowly and looking around. That might be the behavior of a boy who was turned around in an unfamiliar neighborhood. Or of a boy enjoying a cell phone conversation with a girl and not overly eager to return to where his sweet nothings might be overheard by his dad.

That no such alternate possibilities seem to have occurred to Zimmerman for even an instant suggests the degree to which we as a people have grown comfortable with the belief that black is crime and crime is black. Nor are African Americans immune to the effects of that invidious formulation.

Indeed, the dirty little secret of the Martin killing is that Zimmerman could easily have been black. True, a black Zimmerman probably would not have been sent home by prosecutors who declined to press charges – whiteness still has its privileges – but otherwise, yes. It is entirely possible.

Why not? Blacks watch the same TV news as anyone else. We internalize the same message. We drink the same poison.

Why else do you think black folk flinch when the mug shot goes up on television, hoping the face will not be brown – as if we bore some communal responsibility for the suspect's misdeeds? Why else do you think so much of our music is a song of violence and crime? Why else, when I ask an auditorium full of black kids how frequently the individual who murders a white person is black, do they figure it at 75 percent? Why else are they shocked to hear it's only 13?

At some subterranean level, we – African Americans – still believe the garbage of innate criminality we have so assiduously been fed, and struggle with hating ourselves, as America long ago taught us to do. We struggle with it, yet we know better from firsthand, man-in-the-mirror experience. So how much harder is the struggle for white folks?

This is why I grow impatient with those – black, white and otherwise – who think the salient social issue here is George Zimmerman's character. It is not. Nor is it Trayvon's.

It is, rather, that ours is a nation so obscenely comfortable in conflating black with crime that a civilian carrying no badge of authority nevertheless feels it his right to require that an American boy walking lawfully upon a public street justify his presence there. And it is the knowledge that at least some black men would have done the same.

To make this about Zimmerman is to absolve the rest of us for maintaining a society that, in ways both overt and covert, still makes criminality a function of skin. Trayvon Martin was killed by a stereotype. George Zimmerman is just the guy who fired the gun.

Sunday, March 25, 2012

GEORGE ZIMMERMAN IS WHITE

I'm here to explain why George Zimmerman is white.

This seems necessary given the confusion and anger with which some readers responded to my use of that word last week in this space to describe the man who shot an unarmed black teenager named Trayvon Martin to death last month in Sanford, Florida. One person wrote: "Mr. Zimmerman was Hispanic not White plez do your homework before writing your column!!!!"

But it is they who are wrong. There are two reasons. The short one is this:

"Hispanic" is not a race, but an ethnicity. As the U.S. Census Bureau puts it in its 2010 Overview of Race and Hispanic Origin, "People who identify their origin as Hispanic, Latino, or Spanish may be any race."

The long reason begins with an understanding that the word in question – race – is a term both meaningful and yet, profoundly meaningless. It is meaningful in the sense that it provides a tool for tribalism and a means by which to organize our biases, fears, observations, social challenges and sundry cultural products. It is meaningless in the sense that, well ... it has no meaning, that there exists no definition of "black" or "white" that carries any degree of scientific precision.

We are taught to believe the opposite, that "black" and "white" are self-evident and immutable. But I invite you to look up Walter White, the blond, blue-eyed "Negro" who once led the NAACP, or Gregory Howard Williams, the university president who didn't even know he was black until he was 10 years old. Dig up the old Jet magazine story about a woman who gave birth to twins – one "black," one "white." And then think again. Race is a fraud, a cruel and stupid fraud.

The people who came here from Europe did not automatically consider themselves "white." They identified as Irish, Hungarian, Italian, Jewish, Armenian. As David R. Roediger observes in his book, "Working Toward Whiteness: How America's Immigrants Became White," they were emphatically taught that "white" was the identity that conferred status and privilege and that it was defined by distance from, and antipathy toward, black. They were advised to avoid being friendly with blacks or else put their whiteness at risk.

Nor did Africans kidnapped into slavery think of themselves as "black." They were Mandinkan, Fulani, Mende, Songhay, Wolof. "Black" was something imposed upon them as justification for slavery and other means of exploitation. As one historian puts it: Africans did not become slaves because they were black. They became black because they were enslaved.

Well into the 20th century, America recognized dozens of "races." In that America, people we now regard as white – the Irishman, Conan O'Brien; the Armenian, Andre Agassi; the Jew, Jerry Seinfeld – could not have taken for granted that they would be seen that way. People like this had to become white, had to earn whiteness, a feat African Americans have found impossible to duplicate, no matter how many harsh chemicals they use on their hair and skin.

White, then, is not simply color, but privilege – not necessarily in the sense of wealth, but rather in the sense of having one's personhood and individuality respected, a privilege so basic I doubt it registers with many whites as privilege at all. We're talking about the privilege of being seen, of having your worth presumed, of receiving the benefit of the doubt and some human compassion, of being treated as if you matter.

Consider that, then consider the fair-skinned Hispanic man, George Zimmerman, who evidently stalked and killed an unarmed kid he wrongly thought was up to no good, yet was not arrested, nor even initially investigated. He said it was self-defense. Police took him at his word and sent him on his way.

Folks, that's not just white. It's blinding.

Wednesday, April 4, 2012

LET US NOT RUSH TO JUDGMENT

Once upon a time in the late '90s, a certain black newswoman was awarded her own column. She wrote 12 pieces, three of them about race. That was too many for her boss, who told her to tone it down. Confused, she went to a white colleague for advice. He explained that, being black, she lacked the judgment to decide if a given racial matter merited a column. In the future, he suggested, if she saw some racial issue she thought worth writing about, she should bring it to him and let him decide.

That paternalistic offer is brought to mind by a recent on air statement from Tamara Holder, a contributor to Fox "News, " about the killing of Trayvon Martin. "The blacks," she told Sean Hannity, "are making this more of a racial issue than it should be."

One is reminded that the more things change, the more they don't. One wonders how much of a racial issue Trayvon's death should be, in Ms. Holder's esteemed opinion.

There is a storyline coalescing here among conservative pundits. From Holder to Hannity to William Bennett to my colleague, Glenn Garvin, it says there's been a "rush to judgment" against George Zimmerman, the man who stalked and killed an unarmed 17-year-old black kid he found suspicious.

Candidly, there is good reason to fear such a rush. Anyone who remembers the Tawana Brawley hoax and the Duke lacrosse case, among others, knows many African Americans have proven prone to jumping to conclusions of racism even when the evidence thereof is dubious. Some black folks see racial mistreatment everywhere, always.

But some white folks see it nowhere – ever. That's a corollary truth that seems apropos to this moment. Indeed, when a black man named Abner Louima was maimed in an act of broomstick sodomy by New York Police, Holder's friend Hannity accused Lou-ima of lying. Don't rush to judgment, he warned.

For some people, that is less sage advice than default re-sponse. The Rodney King beating, said former Los Angeles Police Chief Daryl Gates, "did look like racism," but wasn't. "This is not a racial issue," said a school official in Louisiana after six black kids were charged with attempted murder for a schoolyard fight with a white classmate.

And so on.

There is a line – subjective, but there just the same – between avoiding a rush to judgment and avoiding judgment itself. If rush-ing to judgment suggests a reflexiveness that ill serves the cause of justice, refusing to judge suggests a moral cowardice that does the same.

Where this case is concerned, it is telling that judgments made weeks after the fact are being called rushed. The rapid re-sponse nature of media being what it is, we make judgments everyday based on much less than five weeks of reflection. We do this on matters of economics, war, politics, scandal.

But, of course, race is different. It scares some of us, particu-larly when it requires them to concede the continued existence of injustices they would rather deny. They are aided in this denial by a naïve belief that a thing can't truly be racist unless it is wearing a pointed hood or spouting epithets.

But racial bias is seldom so conveniently obvious. More often, it lurks behind smiles and handshakes, unknown sometimes even to its host. More often it is deduced, not declared, seen in excuses that don't add up, justifications that make no sense, logic that is not.

As in Zimmerman's decision to stalk Trayvon. Five weeks lat-er, for all the back and forth, push and pull, no one has yet explained what the boy did that made him suspicious. Five weeks later, the initial conclusion still feels like the right one: Trayvon did not seem suspicious because of what he did but because of what he was.

So fine, let us not rush to judgment. But let's not rush from it, either.

WAKE THE HELL UP AMERICA

Four words of advice for African-Americans in the wake of George Zimmerman's acquittal:

Wake the hell up.

The Sunday after Zimmerman went free was a day of protest for many of us. From Biscayne Boulevard in Miami to Leimert Park in Los Angeles, to the Daley Center in Chicago to Times Square in New York City, African-Americans – and others who believe in racial justice – carried out angry, but mostly peaceful demonstrations.

Good. This is as it should have been.

But if that's the end, if you just get it out of your system, then move ahead with business as usual, then all you did Sunday was waste your time. You might as well have stayed home.

We are living in a perilous era for African-American freedom. The parallels to other eras have become too stark to ignore.

Every period of African-American advance has always been met by a crushing period of push back, the crafting of laws and the use of violence with the intent of eroding the new freedoms. Look it up:

The 13th Amendment ended slavery. So the white South created a convict leasing system that was actually harsher.

The 14th Amendment guaranteed citizenship. So the white South rendered that citizenship meaningless with the imposition of Jim Crow laws.

The 15th Amendment gave us the right to vote; it was taken away by the so-called "grandfather clause." The Supreme Court struck that down, so the white South relied on literacy tests and poll taxes to snatch our ballots all over again.

Our history is a litany: two steps forward, one step back.

The Civil Rights Movement was the greatest step forward since emancipation. So we ought not be surprised to see voting rights eroded again, the Civil Rights Act attacked, the so-called "War on Drugs" used for the mass incarceration of black men. Or to see the killing of an unarmed child deliver a message as old as the Constitution itself: black life is worth less.

We are in another period of push back. And worse, we don't even seem to know.

It feels as if we have taken the great advances of the last half century – the protective laws, the rise of the black middle class, the winning of the ballot, the flowering of options once considered unthinkable – for granted. It feels as if we have come to regard progress as somehow inevitable, preordained, carved in stone, and irrevocable as a birthright.

So yes, we need to wake the hell up.

While we were celebrating, others were calculating.

While we were writing nasty rap lyrics, they were writing senators.

While we were organizing Obama victory parties, they were organizing tea parties.

While we were buying DVDs, they were buying candidates.

While we were sending texts, they were building propaganda machinery.

While we were resting on the past, they were seizing the future.

Granted, the preceding casts a wide net. Yes, there are many of us, African-Americans and others, who don't need the admonition, who are already awake, who have always been awake. More power to them.

But there are also many of us still sleeping. So let Trayvon Martin's death and the acquittal of his killer be a wake-up call. Let it be a spur to stop reacting and start pro-acting. Let it be a goad to become better informed. Let it be a reminder to organize.

Let it be a reason to send a check to the NAACP. Let it be an incentive to join the social justice ministry at church. Let it be cause to write your congressperson. Let it be an impetus to teach and nurture your kids.

Most of all, let it be an alarm clock, ringing in the darkness of a new morning, calling conscience to account. Do not waste this moment. The time for sleeping is done.

A VICTORY LAP OVER TRAYVON MARTIN'S GRAVE

It was not enough just to kill Sam Hose. No, they had to make souvenirs out of him.

Hose was an African-American man lynched by a mob of some 2,000 white women and men in 1899 near the town of Newnan, Georgia. They did all the usual things. They stabbed him, castrated him, skinned his face, mutilated him, burned him alive.

Then they parceled out pieces of his body.

You could buy a small fragment of his bones for a quarter. A piece of his liver, "crisply cooked," would set you back a dime. The great African-American scholar, W.E.B. DuBois, reported that Hose's knuckles were for sale in a grocer's window in Atlanta.

No, it wasn't enough just to kill Sam Hose. People needed mementos of the act.

Apparently, it wasn't enough just to kill Trayvon Martin, either.

Granted, it is not a piece of the child's body that was recently put up for auction online by the man who killed him. George Zimmerman is offering "only" the gun that did the deed. But there is a historical resonance here as sickening as it is unmistakable.

Once again, a black life is destroyed. Once again, "justice" gives the killer a pass. Once again, there is a barter in keepsakes of the killing.

Sam Hose was not unique. People claimed hundreds, thousands, of trophies from the murders of African Americans. They kept bones. They kept sexual organs. They kept photographs of themselves, posed with mutilated corpses. It happened with the killings of Thomas Shipp, Abram Smith, Rubin Stacy, Laura Nelson, Claude Neal and too many more to count. So perhaps we shouldn't be surprised to see it happen with Trayvon.

And someone will say, yes, but isn't there a lively trade in all sorts of murder memorabilia? One website alone offers a signed postcard from Charles Manson, a letter from Jeffrey Dahmer, pictures of Ted Bundy. So how is this different.?

Funny thing, though: All those men went to prison for what they did. Zimmerman did not. Initially, authorities couldn't even bring themselves to arrest this self-deputized neighborhood watchman who stalked and shot an unarmed boy four years ago near Orlando.

Not that it mattered much when they did. Zimmerman went to court, but it was 17-year-old Trayvon who was on trial. A nation founded, rooted and deeply invested in the canard of native black criminality very much needed to believe Zimmerman's improbable tale of self-defense, very much needed to find a way for the boy to be guilty of his own murder.

And so he was.

And the marketing of the gun that killed him by the man who pulled the trigger does not feel like simply another example of flagrantly bad taste. No, it feels like a victory lap on a dead boy's grave. It feels like America once again caught in its own lies.

"We hold these truths to be self evident, that all men are created equal?" No we don't.

"... with liberty and justice for all?" No there is not.

One is left breathless, not just with anger, not only with frustration, not simply with a sense of betrayal but also with a grinding fatigue at the need to, once again, ride out an assault on the basic humanness of African-American people.

Like Sam Hose, Trayvon Martin was "thing-ified," made into something not his singular and individual self, made into an all-purpose metaphor, the brooding black beast glaring through the night-darkened window of American conscience. And like Sam Hose his murder is now commodified, made into a trophy for display in someone's den.

African-American life is thereby – again – debased, and the nation, shamed. So when this thing is sold it really won't matter who writes the check.

We all will pay the price.

KATRINA

Sunday, September 4, 2005

THE SHAFT IS COLOR BLIND

Maybe if Terri Schiavo had been caught in the hurricane.

You think that would have done it?

Think maybe that would have moved federal officials off, to paraphrase the frustrated mayor of New Orleans, their posteriors a little faster?

After all, the feds moved heaven and Earth and every ZIP Code in between while imposing themselves in the medical care of that brain-ravaged woman. Congress passed legislation on behalf of her parents with lightning speed, and the president even made a dramatic dash from his beloved ranch to the White House to sign it. They said they did this out of respect for the sanctity of life.

Do you think if someone told them Schiavo was among those waiting for days on end at the Superdome or the convention center the government's response to this crisis would have been so slow-footed and confused? Do you think if it had been Schiavo waiting among filth and feces they'd have kept her waiting for days on end for help that was not coming?

Do you think Schiavo would have been left there to die, not from the storm, but from neglect, and have her wheelchair pushed ignominiously against a wall?

Do you think maybe somebody failed to see sanctity in these lives?

It has been suggested that had Hurricane Katrina struck Beverly Hills, Martha's Vineyard or Palm Beach, there's no way the response would have been so laggard. I think that's obvious beyond argument. It has also been suggested that race was the cause of this mistreatment. I think that's close to the truth, but ultimately wide of the mark.

Yes, New Orleans is a city that is almost 70 percent black and most of those left stranded by the government's ineptness were African American. But the city is also one of the most impoverished in the country. Those people were treated as they were not because they were black but because they suffered arguably the worst double whammy in American life: They were black and they were poor.

That this was not simply an issue of race alone seems evident from the fact that a number of the victims of after-storm neglect were white. Indeed, when TV cameras zoomed in on the body of the poor woman who expired in her wheelchair – an iconic image, I think – the arm that was sticking out from under the covering was unmistakably pale.

The wealthier and more powerful in this country have historically played a cruel con job on impoverished whites. It sold them on the notion that they might be poor but they were, by God, white and thus, members albeit junior ones, of that exclusive club of prerogative and privilege. You can see for yourself what that membership is worth.

When the going got tough, the privileged got going. And the poor were left where they always are. Behind.

Happens a lot when you're poor. Other people barely even know you're there. They have stereotypes of you, but no real concept of who you are and how you live. I'm reminded of an old Doonesbury cartoon which I reconstruct here from memory. It seems Congresswoman Lacey Davenport is explaining to a group of wealthy Palm Beach matrons how misfortune sometimes leaves the poor homeless. Appalled, one woman asks, "Why don't they just use their summer homes?"

So for the record: When you're poor, you don't have a summer home. Maybe not a winter, spring or fall one, either. When you're poor, you don't get decent medical care. When you're poor, you pay more for basic services. When you're poor, the cops and the courts abuse you. When you're poor, you have fewer options for escaping a killer storm and they don't send a fleet of school buses to get you.

When you're poor, you get the shaft. And the shaft is color blind. The government – their government – failed these people. It must be held to account.

As President Bush said, what happened here is "not acceptable."

For once, the president and I agree.

SYSTEMIC INEQUITY

Sunday, September 29, 2013

THE TWO GROVES

It was the suddenness that shocked me.

This is one night 22 years ago. I had just moved to Miami and was visiting Coconut Grove for the first time. I remember being charmed. The side streets were lined with cozy bungalows. On the main streets there was light and music and an air of bohemia going upscale that made you want to linger and people-watch as women who looked as if they just stepped from the pages of Vogue were squired to and from nightclubs, restaurants and boutiques by handsome men in guayaberas.

Leaving, I drove west on Grand Avenue and ... bang. Just like that, I was in another place. Here, there was less light and no music, nor flocks of date night couples, nor really anybody except a few guys standing around, silently marking my passage. The buildings rose shadowy and quiet in meager pools of illumination cast by street lights. These were not streets for lingering. These were streets for passing quickly through.

I didn't know it then, but I was in West Grove, the hardscrabble, historically black area that abuts Coconut Grove. I had driven less than a mile – and ended up on the other side of the world.

Ever since that night, the two Groves have struck me as a vivid illustration of the stark dualities of race and class in a nation which likes to tell itself it has overcome the former and made immaterial the latter. If you're one of those who still believes that fiction, consider this scenario: Dangerous levels of contaminants have been found in the soil of a residential neighborhood. What happens next?

Turns out – though not to the surprise of anyone who understood the fiction to be just that – that it depends very much upon race and class. Just days after the discovery of toxins in the soil of a park in Coconut Grove, residents were alerted, the park closed, the soil capped. All within the last few weeks.

Down the street on the other side of the world, it was a different story. There, in 2011, soil was found to be contaminated on the site of an incinerator – Old Smokey – that had belched ash into the air from the 1930s until it was closed in 1970.

County environmental officials ordered the city to find out if the contaminants posed a risk and draft a plan for dealing with it. They gave the city a 60-day deadline. The city missed it. They gave the city another deadline. It missed that, too.

Residents were told none of this, knew nothing about it, until the initial finding was unearthed this year – two years later – by a University of Miami researcher. Now we learn that city tests have found this land, which sits next to a park and a community center, to be chock full of poisons, among them arsenic, lead and benzo(a)pyrene, a carcinogen.

Just days ago, officials declared the site is not a health risk. West Grove residents can perhaps be forgiven if they are skeptical.

People often profess to be confused when I write about systemic inequity. Absent the caricature of some guy in a pointy white hood, they can see no racism. Absent the cliché of some society lady with nose elevated and pinky extended, they have no conception of classism. They can understand these as individual failings, yes. But what in the world is systemic oppression?

Well, it is this, right here.

It is a child whose health is zealously safeguarded at one end of the street and a child who is allowed to play on soil saturated with carcinogens and heavy metals on the other. It is the city making a determination, albeit de facto, that the latter child's life has less worth.

Shame on Miami for that.

Shame on us all. These inequities exist because we allow them, because we condone by our silence the two-tiered treatment and second-class citizenship of those who are not us. Well, in this country, people have the right to expect they will be treated as if they matter.

Even if they live along shadowed streets on the other side of the world.

Sunday, April 24, 2016

FLINT

Dear white people:

As you no doubt know, the water crisis in Flint, Michigan, returned to the headlines last week with news that the state attorney general is charging three government officials for their alleged roles in the debacle. It makes this a convenient moment to deal with something that has irked me about the way this disaster is framed.

Namely, the fact that people who look like you often get left out of it.

Consider some of the headlines:

"The Racist Roots of Flint's Water Crisis" – Huffington Post

"How A Racist System Has Poisoned The Water in Flint" – The Root

"A Question of Environmental Racism" – The New York Times

As has been reported repeatedly, Flint is a majority black city with a 41 percent poverty rate. So critics ask if the water would have been so blithely poisoned, and if it would have taken media so long to notice, had the victims been mostly white.

It's a sensible question, but whenever I hear it, I engage in a little thought experiment. I try to imagine what happened in Flint happening in Bowie, a city in Maryland where blacks outnumber whites, but the median household income is more than $100,000 a year and the poverty rate is about 3 percent. I can't.

Then I try to imagine it happening in Morgantown, West Virginia, where whites outnumber blacks, the median household income is about $32,000 a year, and the poverty rate approaches 40 percent – and I find that I easily can. It helps that Bowie is a few minutes from Washington, D.C., while Morgantown is over an hour from the nearest city of any size.

My point is neither that race carries no weight nor that it had no impact on what happened in Flint. No, my point is only that sometimes, race is more distraction than explanation. Indeed, that's the story of our lives.

To be white in America is to have been sold a bill of goods that there exists between you and people of color a gap of morality, behavior, intelligence and fundamental humanity. Forces of money and power have often used that perceived gap to con people like you into acting against their own self-interest.

In the Civil War, white men too poor to own slaves died in grotesque numbers to protect the "right" of a few plutocrats to continue that despicable practice. In the Industrial Revolution, white workers agitating for a living wage were kept in line by the threat that their jobs would be given to "Negroes." In the Depression, white families mired in poverty were mollified by signs reading "Whites Only."

You have to wonder what would happen if white people – particularly, those of modest means – ever saw that gap for the fiction it is? What if they ever realized you don't need common color to reach common ground? What if all of us were less reflexive in using race as our prism, just because it's handy?

You see, for as much as Flint is a story about how we treat people of color, it is also – I would say more so – a story about how we treat the poor, the way we render them invisible. That was also the story of Hurricane Katrina. Remember news media's shock at discovering there were Americans too poor to escape a killer storm?

Granted, there is a discussion to be had about how poverty is constructed in this country; the black poverty rate is higher than any other, with the exception of Native Americans, and that's no coincidence.

But it's equally true that, once you are poor, the array of slights and indignities to which you are subjected is remarkably consistent across that racial gap.

That fact should induce you – and all of us – to reconsider the de facto primacy we assign this arbitrary marker of identity. After all, 37 percent of the people in Flint are white.

But that's done nothing to make their water clean.

Chapter 10

AMERICA'S FUTURE

Friday, December 1, 2006

A GLIMPSE AT OUR FUTURE

There's a joke I tell behind Miami's back.

I'll be elsewhere in the country and someone will ask how race and diversity are viewed from a South Florida perspective. I reply that, according to the Census Bureau, Miami's polyglot population represents what America will look like in about 40 years. And if America really understood that, it would be worried. Rim shot.

My point is that, for most of the years of the American experiment, our dialogue about race and diversity has been strictly bipolar: black and white, minority and majority. But by 2050, the conversation will be three-way – black, white and brown – and none will have dominant numbers. We will all be minorities.

Given that America has never mastered the bipolar debate, the challenge of a three-way debate should give us pause. Especially when you factor in the racial and cultural stresses that periodically rattle and rend Miami.

Consider the young woman who told me once how her newlywed sister went to their mother with marital problems only to be told that such problems were what she deserved for being in a "mixed marriage." The upshot: Both newlyweds were black, one born in the U.S.A., the other in Haiti. Take it as proof that in South Florida, even black, white and brown is more complicated than you'd expect.

Similar complications are coming soon to the nation as a whole, as evidenced by the growing Hmong population in Minnesota and an influx of Africans in Maine. So the country ought to watch Miami with interest because it has a stake in the city getting it right.

Or, it could take the Tom Tancredo approach: write Miami off altogether. In a recent interview with a conservative website, Tancredo, an anti-illegal immigration hawk who has championed the building of a fence along the U.S. border with Mexico, said Miami "has become a Third World country. You just pick it up and take it and move it someplace. You would never know you're in the United States of America."

For this, Tancredo has been publicly and properly rebuked by two prominent fellow Republicans: Representative Ileana Ros-Lehtinen and Governor Jeb Bush.

Me, I think the fact that Tancredo calls Miami not just another country but a "Third World" country is rather telling. Apparently for him, Spanish accents and the smell of jerk chicken automatically equal poverty. It may surprise him to learn one seldom sees donkey carts on Miami streets, and electricity is available almost 24 hours a day.

It is worth noting that Tancredo represents Colorado's Sixth District, which is centered on the town of Littleton. Littleton, according to the last census, has a population of about 40,000. Just 1.2 percent of its people are black, 8.4 percent Hispanic – both significantly below the nation as a whole.

Not to dump on Littleton, but it represents precisely the sort of stark homogeneity that will become obsolete in the nation, the Census Bureau predicts. So it's not hard to understand why Miami scares the congressman.

For the record, Miami scares Miami sometimes. Like when Cubans are in a snit or American blacks up in arms or Haitians feeling put upon or whites feeling left out. You look around and ask yourself if, from this cacophony, it is possible to make harmony.

But really, what choice do we have but to try? What else have we ever done? Change is coming, but then, change is always coming. You cannot fence it off, cannot legislate it away. You can only face it and confront its challenges as best you can.

That's what we did when whites went West, when slaves became free, when Europeans streamed through Ellis Island. It's what's we are doing now. Miami is just the noise you get when a mix of peoples jockey for opportunity and shout to be heard.

Tancredo says that's not America. I say, when has America been anything else?

Sunday, March 13, 2011

WE'RE ALL VICTIMS NOW

There is a scholarship for students who wear outfits made of duct tape to their proms.

David Letterman offers a scholarship for kids with average grades. There are scholarships for students who vote Democrat – or Republican – scholarships for students who have cancer, diabetes, sickle cell, autism or Tourette's, students named Zolp, students who are blind, deaf, vegan, Arizonan, left handed, low income, African-, Hispanic-, Native-, Asian- or woman-American.

So it's hard to get worked up over a new scholarship for students who are white men.

It is offered by the Texas-based Former Majority Association for Equality, which would want you to know that it is not motivated by racism. Indeed, its mission statement reads in part: "We do not advocate white supremacy, nor do we enable any individual that does. We do not accept donations from organizations affiliated with any sort of white supremacy or hate group. We have no hidden agenda to promote racial bigotry or segregation."

I take them at their word and wish them Godspeed. But though I have no ax to grind against them, the FMAE's modest ($500 each for five needy students) scholarship does serve as a fascinating sign of our times.

Leaving aside those motivated by whimsy (a duct tape prom dress?), one of the reasons scholarships exist is to help those who, by dint of faith, gender, ethnicity or race, find themselves over-matched when competing against the mainstream. Mainstream being defined as white and male.

The FMAE scholarship suggests the mainstream itself is beginning to feel a little overmatched.

Indeed, one need not travel far these days to encounter signs of acute anxiety emanating from the nation's white majority, a visceral sense of dislocation and lost privilege.

You see it in the hysterical (in both senses of the word) reaction to the election of the first black president. You see it in the spike in the number of hate groups. You see it in the screeching that passes for debate on illegal immigration and in the clangor that seems to confront any Muslim who seeks to build a mosque anywhere. You see it in the apocalyptic rantings of Glenn Beck and in the peevish mutterings of Rush Limbaugh.

You see it also in a 2010 survey by the Washington, D.C.-based Public Religion Research Institute, which found that 44 percent of us believe bigotry against whites is a significant problem. Among tea party followers, the number rises to 61 percent.

If you didn't know better, you'd think white kids were being funneled into the criminal justice system in obscenely dispropor-tionate numbers (as black ones are) or that the unemployment rate among white workers stood at 15.3 percent (as it does nation-ally among blacks). But if the perceptions of 4 in 10 Americans and 6 in 10 tea partiers suggest estrangement from objective reality, they also suggest a certain ability to read the writing on the demo-graphic wall.

The Census Bureau says that within 40 years, there will no longer be such a thing as a racial majority. All of us will be minori-ties.

While such fundamental change will challenge every American, it seems to have already panicked some of those Americans for whom being a minority will be a new experience. Sympathy is in order. It cannot be easy to go from being lead actor to a member of the ensemble – from Gladys Knight to a Pip, as it were.

Thus we find ourselves in this odd new paradigm. Those who have felt marginalized by the color of their skin, the name of their God, the double-x of their chromosomes, find themselves joined in their choirs of the put upon by newcomers who feel marginalized by the loss of their primacy.

Nobody knows the trouble they've seen. And, Lord have mercy, we're all victims now.

EPILOGUE

WILL AMERICA EVER HONOR ITS PROMISE?

The greatest words any American ever said were spoken by a gaunt, war-haunted man in a tiny Pennsylvania college town 150 years ago Tuesday.

The celebrated orator Edward Everett had spoken first, a gusty address that began with a nod toward "this serene sky, overlooking these broad fields now reposing from the labors of the waning year," and wheezed to a close two hours later with a reference to "the glorious annals of our common country." One imagines a sonorous baritone, the "r's" rolling like carriage wheels.

When it was his turn, Abraham Lincoln stood in that cemetery in Gettysburg, a town whose walls were still pitted with bullet holes from the great battle four months before and whose heart was still scarred with the memory of bodies lying twisted, bloated and mangled in the rain.

"Four score and seven years ago," he said in that high, piping twang, "our fathers brought forth upon this continent, a new nation, conceived in liberty and dedicated to the proposition that all men are created equal. Now we are engaged in a great civil war, testing whether that nation or any nation so conceived and so dedicated, can long endure."

In a speech lasting just two minutes, he grappled with the challenge of defining America.

It is noteworthy that the second greatest thing any American ever said echoed the first. Standing at Lincoln's shrine a century later, Martin Luther King noted his "symbolic shadow" and his signing of the Emancipation Proclamation "five score years ago." And when he said, "I have a dream," the first dream King articulated was that "one day this nation will rise up and live out the true meaning of its creed: we hold these truths to be self-evident, that all men are created equal."

Of course, the need to define America outlived Lincoln. And for that matter, King.

That need assumes fresh urgency and new poignancy in a nation where secession is bruited about like some dirty joke, mosques are burned, mass incarceration is practiced, "hatred" is not too strong a word to describe the political atmosphere, and a black boy walking with candy and iced tea in his pockets is deemed worthy of the death penalty.

Obviously, we have work to do. And yet ...

Last month, after exhausting the usual "where are you folks from" patter, the driver of a tour bus in Gettysburg offered this view of the battle that happened there: "Neither side was wrong," he said. "Both fought for their beliefs." He seemed not to consider that the Nazis did, too.

It was an attempt at moral equivalence, a pretense that both sides are equally valid, and it is not uncommon. When offered a chance to define what America means, some of us rush from judgment.

But Gettysburg and the larger war of which it was a turning point, were fought to bring together a broken country and end the abominable practice of slavery. No American patriot can countenance moral equivalence on the first cause, no moral man or woman can accept it on the latter. And Lincoln, who had always instinctively embraced the one, was coming, by the time he spoke, to also embrace the other.

Because defining America was never really the challenge: The founders erected their new country upon a clear, albeit revolutionary promise – equality and freedom. No, the challenge was whether America would ever choose to honor that promise – a question that still awaits an answer. The "honored dead" of Gettysburg, said Lincoln, gave "the last full measure of devotion" fighting to answer it in the affirmative. This was an act of faith.

Now, he said, the work of validating that faith was left for the rest of us. A century and a half ago, Abraham Lincoln handed this country a trust. It was heavy. And burdensome. And sacred.

It still is.

PHOTO COPYRIGHTS